Inner Peace
Simplified

*Everything You Always Wanted to Know
About Your Timeless Identity of Love*

(But Were too Fear-based to Ask)

Cynthia Sholtis

BALBOA.
PRESS
A DIVISION OF HAY HOUSE

"Beyond the Clouds" by DeWitt Clinton.
The poem is in memory of Robert Koller.

Scriptures taken from the Macarthur Study Bible, New King James Version.

Balboa Press books may be ordered through booksellers or by contacting:

Balboa Press
A Division of Hay House
1663 Liberty Drive
Bloomington, IN 47403
www.balboapress.com
1 (877) 407-4847

Because of the dynamic nature of the Internet, any web addresses or links contained in this book may have changed since publication and may no longer be valid. The views expressed in this work are solely those of the author and do not necessarily reflect the views of the publisher, and the publisher hereby disclaims any responsibility for them.

The author of this book does not dispense medical advice or prescribe the use of any technique as a form of treatment for physical, emotional, or medical problems without the advice of a physician, either directly or indirectly. The intent of the author is only to offer information of a general nature to help you in your quest for emotional and spiritual well-being. In the event you use any of the information in this book for yourself, which is your constitutional right, the author and the publisher assume no responsibility for your actions.

Printed in the United States of America.

ISBN: 978-1-4525-1754-4 (sc)
ISBN: 978-1-4525-1756-8 (hc)
ISBN: 978-1-4525-1755-1 (e)

Library of Congress Control Number: 2014911535

Balboa Press rev. date: 09/04/2014

Contents

Dedication

This book is dedicated to my precious mother,
who always was and forever is pure love.

Acknowledgements

I would like to thank Jean Cappella. Her gentle spirit and wise counsel sowed the seeds for my growth from anxious to peaceful.

A very special thank you goes to my nephew, David Halajko. As my unofficial editor, he has been with me since the beginning when I thought my book was finished and has continued to offer insights as the months turned into years—even though he must have thought it would never end! I will always be grateful for his faith in my vision, his amazing grasp of structure, and ... his endurance.

I am deeply indebted to Liza Jane Brown for her invaluable clarity during the final editing stages. From being the catalyst that dispelled the vestiges of my childhood misconceptions, to providing the exact resource material I had been unknowingly missing, Liza has truly been a Godsend. It was no coincidence that she entered my life at the precise time I needed her support and candor.

Last, but by no means least, I extend my heartfelt appreciation to Bob Koller. His loving encouragement and meticulous technical assistance inspired me in the early stages. But I was completely unprepared for his most profound contribution at the very end. He influenced my writing in a way that I had never dared to imagine was possible.

Prologue

Do you suffer from an identity crisis? One sure way to tell is how you react to unexpected events. Are you even-tempered, or are you more likely to overreact or underreact? Do you usually handle life's challenges in stride, or do you tend to be anxious?

If you view yourself as a temporary physical being, you perceive a limited reality. If you define yourself as mind, body, *and* spirit, your eternity vantage point convinces you of your unlimited potential. When you recognize you are much more than meets the eye, love empowers you to live on a higher, spiritual level of consciousness that transcends the chaos of the world.

The foundation for this revelation has been germinating within me ever since I read *A Course in Miracles* in the early 1990s. This amazing book painstakingly details how generational misconceptions cause us to lose sight of eternal values. My ongoing evolution from fear to love has been my most important accomplishment. Without this vital transformation, I would still be unknowingly ruled by my childhood insecurities.

Discovering the necessity of a holistic approach to life has enabled me to simplify the complexities of *A Course in Miracles*. Most people view miracles as rare, supernatural events. They actually occur on a regular basis when we become attuned to our timeless identity. You can achieve emotional balance in a fraction of the time it took for me to learn how to stay centered during stressful times.

Peace of mind occurs when love governs one's behavior. This premise presents a twofold problem: 1) The vast majority identify with fear. 2) Misplaced trust results in mistaking conditional love for true love.

Most would agree that self-respect is an essential component of well-being. Unfortunately, few felt respected during their formative years. Typically, parents tell children they are loved but also regularly criticize their offspring and argue with each other. Religions teach people they are one with God but also portray humanity as sinful.

Love is ever present. Fear only seems real because self-deception is the prevailing mind-set on our planet. A mixed-message belief system creates an imaginary barrier between the spiritual and earthly realms. A mind designed to love that has been conditioned to process fear-based ideations is naturally out of balance. The destructive outcome is the development of mental and physical illnesses throughout the course of one's lifetime. Aggression, anxiety, depression, guilt, and somatic disorders are some of the most familiar consequences of denial of love.

A universal fear-minded construct is equating time on earth with suffering. This perspective produces feelings of powerlessness. Our fearful focus on the unpredictable nature of life prevents us from discovering our true power lies within. We can't sense our eternity connection to our Creator if we weren't taught to identify with the love of our perfect spirit-to-Spirit union.

Empty rhetoric passes for God's will. Humanity's oneness is reduced to judging individual flaws that don't conform to arbitrary standards. We seek relief in remedies that exacerbate our misery in the long run.

When my life was on the upswing and a steady stream of clients sought my counseling services, I felt content most of the time. Three months before I resigned from my job, I experienced one ordeal after another. Since I considered myself a Christian, I believed my distress would be alleviated by going to church on Sundays, praying regularly, and attending a weekly Bible study. After nearly two years with no relief in sight, my mounting despair led me to my former counselor. She explained that I was unable to find comfort in external solutions, because the problem was my fear-bound perceptions. She pointed out that I had to resolve my failure mentality to function from a power position of love.

Considering the way I had felt during most of my life, it made sense that I was controlled by fear. The simple solution—to love who I am—had eluded me. Even my cooperative nature and my degree in psychology couldn't lessen the overall negative impact of the fear-driven messages that I had internalized.

The lessons gleaned from my latter-day inner healing reveal it's never too late to change your life. Trading turmoil for tranquility is explained in an uncomplicated three-step plan. If you're tired of feeling your best efforts always fall short, you'll learn how to attract positive outcomes.

The key to success lies in developing your insight to see yourself without fear clouding your judgment. Love isn't something you have to be good enough to earn. It's who you are! Even though these ideas may seem inconceivable to you right now, the truth is you've always been one with God.

You reclaim your birthright of wholeness by resolving the emotional disconnect between your fleeting physical identity and your infinite spirit. 1 John 4:18 states: "There is no fear in love; but perfect love casts out fear, because fear involves torment." My journey from self-deception to becoming attuned to my spiritual perfection was instrumental in freeing me from the false grip of fear. The mental health turnaround that occurred in my life can become your reality when you actualize your inner power.

Most people can't comprehend that peace of mind is their natural state of being. The dissonance associated with a love and fear belief system deceives us into believing anxiety is normal. Our oppositional attitudes prevent our actions from consistently lining up with our words. As a direct result, our composed appearances frequently mask our inner turmoil.

If the public image you portray doesn't match the way you act in the privacy of your home, you're not being true to yourself.

When you don't learn to identify with love as an adult, your entrenched childhood fears keep triggering unhealthy response patterns.

As you discover how to align your thoughts with the Spirit of truth, your behavior will finally mirror your calm state of mind, regardless of how life unfolds. No relationship or amount of material gain comes even close to the priceless value of inner peace.

Gaining mastery over your untrustworthy feelings replaces faultfinding with compassion. Recognizing you've always been complete breaks the cycle of living a crucifiction life of judgment.

I deliberately misspelled crucifixion in the previous sentence to emphasize how important it is to be completely honest with yourself. If you didn't grow up believing your true worth is beyond measure, you've been leading a needless, fictional life. Developing spiritual insight restores stability to a mind that has been torn between contradictory messages since childhood.

This book is presented to inspire you to stop feeling victimized by circumstances beyond your control so you can start living your real life of love.

Chapter 1

Love Thyself

Familiar things happen, and mankind does not
bother about them. It requires a very unusual
mind to undertake the analysis of the obvious.
—Alfred North Whitehead

No war is as pervasive or has as much potential for mass
destruction as the imaginary mental conflict waged daily
between love and fear. God's will represents true love
that is eternal. It ensures peaceful, productive lives. Self-will
demonstrates the false fear that one either will cease to exist
or will be cast into hell after physical death. It leads to varying
degrees of anxiety that compromise the overall quality of life.

A time-bound thinker functions on lower levels of consciousness
that only allow him to perceive a material reality. His misery stems
from subconsciously believing he is a separate entity. He identifies
with fear. He suffers from a poverty mentality of loneliness and lack
due to his learned allegiance to self-centered goals for fulfillment.
Humanity is viewed from a judgmental standpoint of winners and
losers.

A timeless thinker functions on higher levels of consciousness
that encompass his spiritual component. His contentment
originates from knowledge of his oneness with God. He identifies
with love. He has insight to discern eternity encompasses now and
forever. He enjoys an abundance mind-set because he senses he
has everything he needs inside himself to succeed. Everyone wins
because he responds in the best interests of the whole.

Truth can't be wholly known by a divided mind. When we're not raised to believe *only love is real,* a delusional schism forms in our mind that prevents us from being consistently honest. We yearn for stable relationships, and then bristle at the first sign our own interests aren't being served. We don't practice what we preach to our children and then become angry when they misbehave. We attend church on Sundays and then spend the rest of the week being judgmental. Our claims that we value longevity are refuted by our lifetime indulgences in unhealthy habits.

The problems that arise from these mixed-messages invariably lead to trips to doctors, mental health practitioners, the clergy, and bookstores. These solutions are often tantamount to putting a Band-Aid on a gaping wound. Once the crisis is over, we tend to resume our habitual ways.

Anxiety abounds because love and fear can't coexist without turmoil. The most basic truth that God's will *is* humanity's will doesn't even occur to us if oneness of love isn't emphasized during our formative years. Perceived feelings of inadequacy inevitably develop when reality is defined by role models who learned to identify with fear.

Without an eternity perspective, we can't fathom the incomparable joy we would regularly experience from learning to actualize humanity's spirit-to-Spirit bond. Instead, our short-sighted, flesh-driven outlook forces us to settle for solutions that can only provide temporary relief from our unintentional denial of love.

Egocentric behaviors that define childish actions still claim undue attention for most adults. We typically exude an appearance of maturity that belies our unresolved resentments. We're highly sensitive to behaviors that trigger memories of childhood trauma. Self-deception forces us to deny our wholeness through verbal and physical assaults.

A spiritual person doesn't become angered by fear-based conduct. His mind isn't vulnerable to attacks of any kind, because he understands his true nature is eternal. He consistently manifests love from within in thought, word, and deed.

Healing our childhood misconceptions enables us to be authentic. We counter self-deprecating thoughts with love-centered affirmations. This spiritual recovery process ultimately results in depending on our inner power instead of the powerless self.

A fear-controlled mentality isn't attentive to promptings from the Holy Spirit. We allow the excitement of the world to drown out the "still small voice" (1 Kings 19:12) inside us. Restoring balance through an inner-directed approach to life isn't an option.

Peace of mind requires developing your sixth sense to discern spiritual truths humanity was designed to live by. All that is necessary is a heartfelt desire to be the person God created you to be instead of who your mistaken identity of fear has convinced you to be.

The Root of All "Bad" Fruit

Developing confidence in one's wholeness begins by understanding the origin of a subconscious attachment to self. The root cause—fear—develops in response to secular and religious training that doesn't focus on humanity's everlasting spiritual connection to God's Spirit. A false belief in fear forms the basis for all of the chaos in our universe. Like plants that don't thrive if they aren't properly nourished from within, a mind that believes it can be separated from its Source spreads apprehension throughout one's entire being. The bitter fruit of ongoing strife is the natural outcome.

We can't freely give and receive love if we weren't taught to feel secure in our inherent divine nature. Self-deception compels us to associate our mind solely with our physical beings. When we're inundated from childhood with threats of eternal damnation, we don't feel empowered to demonstrate our wholeness in thought, word, and deed.

Without inner healing, the uplifting speeches we hear about God's unconditional love are in constant conflict with the fear-bound input we receive. Our mixed-message mind-set experiences unnecessary angst. We automatically develop an unhealthy dependence on ego gratification to escape the ongoing inconsistencies of believing we're both sinful and saved.

A Course in Miracles describes the misery of a narrow mind-body viewpoint: "You who identify with your ego cannot believe God loves you. You do not love what you made, and what you made does not love you. You cannot conceive of the real relationship that exists between God and His creations because of your hatred for the self you made."[1]

An egotistical mentality is contradictory by nature. Its survival depends on maintaining the illusion of separation. At the same time, this self-serving thought pattern is responsible for perpetuating false feelings of emptiness that lead to premature physical deaths.

If children were universally trained to identify with their calm spirit through respectful behaviors, worldwide wars and personal battles wouldn't be the dominant response pattern. Global peace (the fruit) would prevail because humanity's focus would be on common goals. As a direct result, love (the true root) would be the conventional wisdom on our planet.

Your spiritual DNA contains every quality necessary to help you transition from anxiety to your birthright of peace. Galatians 5:22–23 describes the essential character traits that constitute a balanced mind, body, and spirit: "But the fruit of the Spirit is love, joy, peace, longsuffering, kindness, goodness, faithfulness, gentleness, self-control." Depending on whether you reject or accept yourself as a changeless spirit who briefly occupies an ever-changing body, you either feel victimized or empowered.

Adults who become upset by unexpected events never outgrew their childhood identification with self. A purely flesh-driven outlook keeps us stuck in personal perceptions of right and wrong.

An untenable love and fear belief system prevents you from comprehending your innate oneness with God. Viewing yourself as a solitary entity makes you feel insignificant. You're unconsciously ruled by untrustworthy feelings that reinforce your low opinion of yourself. Without developing faith in your timeless identity of love, you'll keep experiencing the uncertainty you felt as a child whenever differences of opinion arise.

When our parents are ruled by fear, we normally internalize their feelings of powerlessness. We aren't able to relate to our righteous spirit. We become susceptible to self-righteous swagger. We mask our underlying inferiority complex by passing judgment based on appearances.

Emotional balance is achieved when we reconcile our human imperfections with our spiritual perfection. Tempering self-will desires with a spiritual mind-set equips us to view character defects with compassion. We instinctively sense we're the embodiment of God's Spirit—despite the ongoing examples that seem to deny the never ending reality of love. Simply stated, love focuses on who we all are eternally. Fear judges every minor, as well as major, offense from a fleeting human nature standpoint.

Original Identity Crisis

From the very moment fear factored into the equation of life, humankind's inheritance of bliss has been denied. A fear-minded person doesn't understand that he already possesses every quality he needs to achieve his highest potential.

Those who identify with love aren't shaken by fear-rooted pronouncements, by how others behave, or by what transpires.

They don't waste their time harboring guilt and making disparaging comments. In Philippians 4:11, Paul describes the disposition of the mature adult: "for I have learned in whatever state I am to be content."

Following self-will is a surefire recipe for chaos. We become like the little child who desires the total love of a pet, without the drudgery of having to clean up the messes. We can only hope for brief periods of satisfaction as long as happiness is viewed as an attainable external goal.

The biblical story of Adam and Eve losing (in)sight of love through self-deception represents a universal problem. Genesis 2:17 reveals the warning the first couple received about the dangers of a an oppositional belief system: "But of the tree of the knowledge of good and evil you shall not eat, for in the day that you eat of it you shall surely die."

This scripture refers to Adam and Eve being blindsided by clashing forces that left them feeling spiritually dead. *Good* represents the true love within us that engenders harmonious interactions. *Evil* denotes a false belief in fear that promotes conflicted relationships.

The Garden of Eden symbolized humanity's rejection of heaven on earth. People ever since have been deceived into accepting fear as real. Our righteous spirit represents eternal life. A flesh-driven viewpoint deadens our mind to our true power within. We variously think in terms of superficial goals, judgments based on personal opinions, and external spirituality.

We can't be at peace because our contradictory reality prevents us from recognizing the whole(ness) truth: love can't reign where fear-rooted perceptions persist. A self-centered reality convinces us our happiness depends on controlling our environment and gaining approval from others.

The opposite is true. Contentment originates from within us. Searching outside ourselves for love keeps us off balance. Our external focus creates seemingly unending complications that wouldn't exist if we had been taught to rely on our inner power.

Becoming Spirit-minded enables us to rise above contrary thought patterns. We intuitively sense the oneness of God's will and humanity's will. Troubling events lose their ability to control us through false emotions.

Every time we consciously or unconsciously differentiate ourselves from God, we lose touch with reality. We aren't able to manifest the love of our eternal spiritual kingdom within us. Our attention is diverted to playing God by building our temporary earthly "kingdoms." We count on our own strengths. When we inevitably fall short, we compound our pain by seeking the false comfort of worldly idols.

Lack of insight prevents us from realizing human knowledge is a poor substitute for spiritual wisdom. "Trust in the Lord with all your heart, and lean not on your own understanding; In all your ways acknowledge Him, and He shall direct your paths" (Proverbs 3:5–6). Those who are familiar with this scripture may not recognize the glaring contradiction between professing faith in God while trying to achieve success on their own terms. Believing one's true power lies within has superficial meaning, at best.

We can't function with wholeness of purpose if our thoughts are divided between love and fear. Our misidentification with self makes us feel alone. On a subconscious level, we don't believe we deserve the good life.

When we realize God's Mind and Spirit is humanity's reality—now and forever—it becomes natural to express the love that flows from within us. This attitude transformation from feeling broken to discovering we've always been whole is what spiritual recovery is all about.

Without healing our faulty core beliefs, incongruent tenets promote defeatist thought patterns. When we aren't raised to emotionally reside in paradise on earth through love-centered beliefs, self-deception forces us to proffer judgments that constrain us to a mental hell.

In hindsight, I realized my parochial school training fueled my feelings of anxiety and inadequacy. I was unable to reconcile the teaching that God is both loving and condemning. I trace my former deep-seated fear of retribution to being taught I would go to hell if I didn't faithfully attend church. I also feared my father would be condemned because he didn't observe our religion's holy days.

The worst part of growing up afraid is the tendency to remain deceived by childhood misconceptions throughout our lifetimes. We act out the pain of our fear-addicted reality through worldly means or by hoping to appease God through external expressions of spirituality. Simply stated, instability is a natural consequence of learning to believe fear is real.

If we factor in the noise of everyday life, it's easy to understand why most people aren't attracted to a Creator who is portrayed to be loved and feared. We aren't able to fathom the blessings that result from heeding God's will until we make every effort to eradicate our double-minded thought patterns.

When the way we view ourselves doesn't include our spiritual perfection, it seems completely logical to judge humanity's imperfections. Unresolved feelings of victimization from childhood continue to blindside us as adults. The false grip of fear that enslaves us to the past reinforces our dismal views of life.

Irreconcilable ideations make it nearly impossible to comprehend the power that lies within us. When we grow up defining success according to worldly standards and allowing our circumstances to upset us, we certainly don't feel powerful.

Life becomes our tormenter instead of our teacher. We don't understand that difficulties are an indispensable part of the maturation process. We buy into the unreliable dictates of our temperaments and learned behaviors. The attendant dramas of our inherently flawed belief system make our anxiety, depression, animosity, etc., seem normal.

Even though we say we understand a balanced life is crucial to our well-being, we deceive ourselves into going for the gusto, regardless of the cost. Our compulsive need for quick fixes is intensified by the underlying fear that it could all be over forever at any moment.

Without an eternity perspective, we equate fulfillment with performance. But even if we succeed beyond our wildest dreams, we still won't be convinced we've accomplished enough for one simple reason: until we heal our childhood spiritual imbalance, we'll always feel something is missing.

If our mind isn't attuned to the peace of the Holy Spirit through our spirit (conscience), we incorrectly assume our hectic lives prove we were meant to exist in turmoil on earth. When we're controlled by fear, we don't realize the extent of the psychic damage that ensues from negative energy patterns. We jeopardize our health by routinely becoming angered by inconsequential matters.

Just like self-absorbed children, Adam and Eve didn't comprehend that their actions were akin to rejecting a life of harmony. The first couple's abrupt transition from being God-conscious to self-conscious overwhelmed them. Their worldly seduction catapulted them from mental, physical, and spiritual paradise into a stark reality of perceived powerlessness.

They immediately lost awareness of the present moment. Fear appeared to rule. Untrustworthy feelings prevented them from remembering that God's will and their will was identical. Their mind was besieged by separation anxiety, which has no meaning from a love-centered standpoint. They were spiritually blinded to the wholeness that still defined them.

When true love is muddied with false fear, we aren't empowered by the Holy Spirit to honestly process painful events. Instead, we unconsciously play God through false judgments. Egotistical impulses always demand a scapegoat.

Self-serving posturing was evident when Eve tried to fault the serpent, and Adam attempted to blame Eve and even God Himself. Their failure to grasp one simple fact kept them in bondage to self-hate: it's impossible to consistently follow God's will to love while identifying with fear.

Are you still holding yourself hostage to your childhood feelings of failure? Do temporary, everyday problems and trying situations have more power over you than your undying connection to an omnipotent God?

When compared to the lasting peace of trusting in God's perfect plan for our lives, trying to be the masters of our fates can only satisfy us short-term. It all boils down to whether or not you join the few eternity thinkers who mentally reside in heaven on earth through spiritual recovery. Believing it's possible to choose between opposing forces when *only love is real* characterizes the delusional mental battle of the vast majority—who unknowingly pick the hell of a fear-based reality. As Plato aptly stated: "The worst of all deceptions is self-deception."

Self-Deception Mentality

When we grow up with fear-driven ideations, we're unable to relate to the spiritual principle of prosperity. In our upside-down thinking, fulfillment is equated with material gain. Even though people generally agree money can't buy happiness, peace of mind isn't usually considered to be the standard for success.

Matthew 6:24 clearly states, "No one can serve two masters." Most people have no idea that their emotional pain stems from their incompatible love and fear belief system. Many are convinced they are following God's will through external displays of spirituality. In reality, their inconsistent behavioral patterns reveal their loyalty is to self-will.

Misidentifying with self automatically causes us to perceive lack. Even those who are well off financially never feel satisfied for very long. Compulsively amassing possessions is fueled by false separation anxiety. Being out of touch with our intangible power within can create an unquenchable need for tangible objects.

The greater the number of earthly attachments we have, the more complicated our lives become. Focusing on objectives that don't have eternal value ends up making us think life has no meaning. The most common indicators of self-deception include praying only after personal efforts fail; denying one's identity of love through relationships characterized by strife; and being overburdened by debt.

Our attempts to feel complete through flesh-driven pursuits ultimately fall short. There are numerous, undeniable examples of external power not equaling satisfaction. US presidents and other politicians have disgraced their offices and high profile celebrities and athletes, who engaged in excesses, have died prematurely.

Parents who suffer from self-deception never learned the correlation between lasting inner peace and modeling a healthy appreciation of mind, body, and spirit for their children. A stressful existence is accepted as normal when fear is perceived to be real.

Both financially secure and economically deprived parents tend to encourage a worldly route to a meaningful life. They seek to provide their children with all the latest status symbols, whether or not they can afford to do so. The apparent motivation is to instill in their offspring the desire to afford the adult version status symbols.

The necessity of strengthening a child's character is lost when we subconsciously learn to count on our circumstances for happiness. Without self-respect, children can't even begin to comprehend their eternity connection to God. When we observe material goals taking top priority in our role models' lives, we normally seek fulfillment in the same way.

You may protest that you've taught your children spiritual values by talking about God, donating to the less fortunate, etc. But unless children are assured they are loved and negative comments are kept to a bare minimum, they tend to relate to eternal truths on a superficial level. Simply stated, God's unending love has no real (heart level) meaning for those who don't realize their true value is incalculable.

Marilyn shared the success she has had teaching her six-year-old daughter and five-year-old son to identify with love. Her daughter had injured herself when she fell from her bicycle. An angry neighbor immediately berated her for leaving her bike in the street. Ignoring her bleeding knee, she ran sobbing into her mother's arms. Marilyn led her to the mirror and gently instructed her to repeat the following affirmations: "It's okay to make mistakes. I love myself." She was amazed at the calming effect those simple phrases had on her daughter.

Later, when Marilyn was having a bad day, her little boy reminded her, "You better go to the mirror, mommy." She responded as directed, but not before showering her son with praise and hugs.

True Power

Capitalizing on the love within us replaces overreacting and underreacting with self-control. When we transform our thoughts from self-serving to Spirit-led, we discover assertive language represents the only true power position.

Assertive personality types understand the necessity of adopting a spiritual perspective. They aren't riled by trying circumstances. They quietly trust adverse situations to turn around in due time. Their innate ability to look past deceiving outward appearances equips them to mimic their divine nature.

Think how different your life would be if you had observed your role models accepting situations that didn't work out according to their plans, instead of continually witnessing fear-minded reactions. You would have learned contentment ensues from staying faithful, regardless of how impossible it may feel at the time.

Consider how much calmer you would act if you had been corrected with assertive discipline. You would have discovered that consistent, love-grounded conduct is indispensable to fulfillment.

You wouldn't be caught up in the delusion of equating free will with choosing between God's will and self-will. Your choice would be clear. There is no deprived, anxiety-ridden self when one functions from an eternity standpoint; only wholeness of love.

In spite of his extreme suffering, Jesus never lost (in)sight of his eternal identity. Just as he endured the agony of the cross with dignity, we must be willing to view life's crosses as exactly what we need to develop a resurrection mentality.

Our only other choice is a crucifixion mind-set of guilt. For most of my life, I had no idea how imperative it was to love who I am. My temperament, learned behavior, and religious training had caused me to feel inadequate. I used to unconsciously imitate my passive mother or my aggressive father. I would either disrespect myself by repressing my true feelings or disrespect others by being argumentative.

Believing you're defined by your flaws and developing a fear-rooted attitude go hand in hand. Learning to view yourself as being spiritually one with God, despite your very worst human nature errors, largely dissolves negative energy patterns. Acquiring confidence in your holistic identity equips you to mentally transcend your personality deficits and your fear-controlled conditioning.

The second element necessary to be true to yourself involves becoming attentive to the present. A loved-based person values attributes that are timeless more than possessions that deteriorate

Cynthia Sholtis

over time. Love is ever present. It can only be accessed by staying focused in the moment.

When we consciously or unconsciously believe we're finite beings, we can't help but be judgmental. Our limited viewpoint to judge by sight prevents us from intuitively discerning humanity's spiritual perfection. Preoccupation with the past and future is commonplace. Instead of maintaining upbeat attitudes, we tend to dwell on perceived offenses or discouraging prospects.

Assertive communication denotes honest adult behaviors. Aggressive, passive, and passive-aggressive response patterns are indicative of self-deception. You can't prosper in the present if you keep responding the same way you did as a child.

Assertive individuals' actions don't normally contradict their words. The love they express lines up with how they subconsciously feel about themselves. Their overall positive demeanors demonstrate the abundant life really does emanate from the inside out.

The third crucial aspect of a centered person is persistence. A mixed-message belief system is extremely addictive. Old ways die hard when we're used to associating love with becoming defensive or denying how we really feel.

It was very difficult for me to accept situations that were beyond my ability to change. It often felt like an uphill battle to develop the self-control part of the "fruit of the Spirit" described previously from Galatians 5:22–23. I had unconsciously allowed myself to be governed by the short-term gain, long-term pain principle that typifies the response patterns of undisciplined children and adults.

Egocentric behaviors are governed by unresolved childhood fears. Underlying feelings that our Creator will condemn us fuel a victim mind-set of anxiety. A fundamental sense of failure hinders one's ability to consistently think logically. Life gets reduced to a false need to prove *I matter.* Self-centered and self-sacrificing behaviors pass for love.

As an adult, it's vital to alter response patterns that have kept you trapped in unhealthy behaviors. No matter how many times you regress to familiar, angry reactions, a fulfilling life requires you to change to love-grounded conduct; even though your ego will keep insisting on "my way."

Adults who don't grow beyond their false attachments to self base most of their decisions on untrustworthy feelings instead of facts. They suffer in the long run because the negative energy that is expended to sustain self-will ends up causing irreparable damage. Grown-ups who learn to be Spirit-minded tend to be more prudent. They understand inner peace isn't possible without paying attention to long-term consequences.

I had believed my book was ready for publication after three months of writing. My nephew, David, who is wise beyond his years, informed me I had only completed my first draft. Even though I now know I wasn't on a true spiritual path at that time, I sensed he was right. Had I given in to my initial impulse to market my book too soon, I would have been promoting information that was more ego-driven than truthful.

Spiritual recovery enables you to trust that God has your best interests at heart. Healing your mind from being continually torn between love and fear-based choices is well worth the temporary growing pains that change requires. Feeling calm in a world that is perceived to be ruled by fear is the long-term gain. Simply stated, be very wary of anyone who tries to entice you with the promise of quick solutions to lifelong emotional problems.

Adult/Child Split

Love Story was a hit movie released in 1970 that popularized the expression "Love means never having to say you're sorry." In real life, love means never having to be aggressive or passive. Relationships that are based on compulsive control and approval bear little resemblance to true love.

Parenting styles that fail to model assertive communication are rooted in fear. A child's reality is characterized by behaviors that deny humanity's wholeness. As children mature, the cumulative effect of affectionate language alternating with predominately angry messages, takes its toll from the inside out. Instead of feeling self-assured and well-equipped to face life's challenges as an adult, an oppositional belief system keeps one languishing in childhood insecurities and resentments.

To understand this concept, close your eyes and visualize your "stuck child" (who never learned to feel worthy of love) "living" inside you, dictating most of your behaviors. The one big difference is, as a child, you had no power; while now, as an adult with a childish inner self, you only know how to depend on the false power of defensive or repressed coping mechanisms. You aren't able to enjoy life to its fullest, governed by reasonable thinking. Unmet subconscious childhood needs continue to generate irrational response patterns.

When assertive language isn't taught as the norm, we grow up without knowing how to love. The seemingly stable adult personas we display are in stark contrast to the needy children lurking just beneath the surface. This disconnect from reality results in people generally displaying self-control in public and being argumentative or feeling depressed in private.

Offenses are regularly perceived when we lack awareness of humanity's spiritual perfection. The ability to handle problems from a wholeness viewpoint is lost when fear is in charge. The widespread contradiction to criticize others while largely ignoring our own weaknesses seems as natural as breathing. Everyday blessings are taken for granted. Aggression and depression characterize daily interactions when expectations are dashed. Simply stated, parental response patterns that aren't consistently assertive translate into generational disrespect.

Using the aggressive father/passive mother dynamic, a male child who identifies with his father would be inclined to treat his mother in much the same rude way he witnessed his father treating her.

Similarly, another son whose temperament was passive more than likely would be mistreated by his aggressive sibling and father. Since neither parent demonstrated the wholeness of love, their nonassertive children won't be empowered to identify with their divine nature.

Another common occurrence is a parent and child who alternate between aggressive and passive language. Children can learn to play the passive role in response to aggression from a parent. Likewise, parents can revert to a passive attitude when their child assumes the dominant stance.

An assertive person may become upset during difficult times but quickly recovers. His heartfelt understanding of spiritual love prevails. An aggressor automatically blames others when he doesn't get his way. The real reason he becomes irritated by outcomes beyond his control is because he can't trust the God he grew up loving *and* fearing to be in charge of his life. Likewise, a passive-aggressive individual's mistrust of God predisposes him to deal with anger by engaging in avoidance behaviors and other indirect, compulsive patterns. A passive personality tends to repress his feelings and misplace his trust in others.

Understanding that you're eternally complete and assertive conduct is one and the same. You'll no longer solely depend on the perceptions of your five senses. You'll recognize the necessity of honing your sixth sense. Worldly accomplishments pale in comparison to the blessings that flow from developing confidence in your timeless identity.

When you make a sincere commitment to identify with the perfect love of your spirit-to-Spirit connection, you'll finally be free from your personal hell of inner torment. You'll acclimate to life's ups and downs without feeling like you're trapped on an emotional roller coaster. As a result, you'll become more accepting of upsetting events without acting on your learned need to pass judgment on yourself and others.

The following chart demonstrates the striking differences between the assertive conduct of love and the passive and aggressive expressions of fear.

Passive	Assertive	Aggressive
Lives in the past	Focuses on the present	Out of touch with reality
Allows others to disregard your rights	Stands up for self without denying others' rights	Violates others' rights to get your way
Avoids problems	Addresses problems	Attacks people
Talks with respect for other people	Talks with respect for self and others	Talks without respect for self or others
Represses true feelings	Expresses true feelings	Denies true feelings
Builds anger and resentment	Deals with anger rationally	Acts out anger verbally or physically
Establishes a pattern of others taking advantage of you	Establishes a pattern of respect for future dealings with you	Establishes a pattern of others being in fear of you
Lets the other person guess how you feel	Lets the other person know how you honestly feel	Lets the other person know you only care about how you feel
Lacks self-worth	Confident, centered	Self-hatred, unstable
Assumes responsibility for others' mistakes	Assumes responsibility for own mistakes	Avoids responsibility for own mistakes

Passive	Assertive	Aggressive
Boundaries are rigid for self and loose for others	Boundaries are appropriate for self and others	Boundaries are loose for self and rigid for others
Accepts blame for events beyond your control	Accepts events that are beyond your control	Blames others for events beyond your control
Judges self	Nonjudgmental	Judges others
False need for approval denies spiritual wholeness	Balanced state of mind knows true power emanates from within	Compulsive need for control demonstrates powerlessness of self

Passive/Aggressive

It's safe to say most people have displayed this fear-bound response pattern. During an assertiveness training I conducted, the employees were asked which style was prevalent. With the notable exception of the executive director, every staff member—in unison—said passive-aggressive behaviors characterized the workplace. Office morale was low. Afraid of retaliation, the employees didn't voice their concerns openly.

People who have passive-aggressive temperaments act out their feelings of powerlessness in indirectly hostile ways. Instead of honestly discussing the reasons for their differing opinions, these individuals have been conditioned to gossip, complain, or make thinly veiled sarcastic comments or threats. This behavior can also take the form of forgetting on purpose, procrastinating, lying, or feigning illness to avoid fulfilling an obligation. Passive-aggressive conduct results from resentment over perceived unreasonable requests. This maladaptive coping method usually occurs when the following conditions exist: 1) A person feels a loss of personal control. 2) He believes a more obvious aggressive response wouldn't be effective.

An individual is most likely to react passive-aggressively when present day events trigger the same lack of validation he felt growing up. If your parents were domineering and you were unable to disagree out of fear of punishment, you're prone to substitute passive resistance for transparent communication. This self-serving behavior becomes ingrained as the normal way to respond throughout adulthood. A classic example is a parent who won't take no for an answer. If you pretended to be sick to avoid being obedient, you'll tend to repeat this same response pattern as an adult whenever you feel pressured by your parent, spouse, etc.

Victim Mentality

A person who remains in an abusive relationship is characterized as having a victim mentality. The overlooked truth is the definition is much more pervasive. A crucifixion mind-set develops from a love and fear belief system.

Children who are raised with conditional love identify with fear. The importance of being inner-directed isn't recognized. The natural consequence is focusing on the never ending appetites of our five senses, while remaining spiritually blind to the unmined treasure of our sixth sense.

Passive people manifest their victim mentalities by allowing others to take advantage of them. Aggressive and passive-aggressive individuals deceive themselves into believing they are the real victims. All three personality types are addicted to counterfeit self-esteem fixes from external sources. Remedies of this nature ultimately leave us feeling empty, because enduring change can only occur on a mind level.

Misidentification with fear and self-rejection are synonymous. When we don't grow up believing we're whole, despite individual aberrations, we can't even begin to relate to our spiritual perfection. Our flesh-driven orientation makes it seem appropriate to focus on human imperfections.

Judgmental behavior creates an unending power play free for all in which no one ever truly wins an argument. Love is denied in the name of self-preservation. We keep allowing conflicting viewpoints to energize our childhood pain. The ability to humbly admit "I need to change my own attitude" is all but quenched in a world where people unknowingly allow themselves to be ruled by their stuck children.

Misidentifying with self convinces us that becoming upset is normal when circumstances don't work out in our favor. We're too preoccupied with what *I* want to believe God's will represents our highest good.

Kathy learned to react aggressively from her mother, whose mood was often resentful, no matter how hard her daughter tried to please her. Kathy married Don, who exhibits the same personality traits as her mother. Deep down, Kathy feels responsible for Don's negative outlook because she was blamed for her mother's unhappiness. She automatically questions the reason for Don's attitude in a defensive manner. He perceives he is being attacked and responds with sarcasm. Predictably, this couple's behavior escalates into all-out hostility. Kathy and Don are unaware of the pivotal role fear-minded feelings play in setting the tone for relationships. Both of them are convinced they are each other's victims. The truth is they are their own worst enemies for failing to recognize happiness emanates from within.

Life's stumbling blocks are designed to maximize humanity's potential. True spiritual growth isn't possible without learning self-control to handle hardships with dignity. As long as you resist the lessons you must learn from your trials by complaining and blaming, you'll keep attracting far more trying encounters than gratifying experiences.

Excluding criminal actions, there are no adult victims, and there is no blame; there are only those who never emotionally move beyond their childhood victimization identity.

Faultfinding allows us to enjoy being right to counter feeling wrong deep down inside. If more people understood the short-term satisfaction derived from this ingrained practice *always* results in long-term pain, spiritual recovery would be a worldwide phenomenon.

Our fear-bound attitudes reinforce our sense of powerlessness. When we trade our feelings of inferiority for genuine acceptance of our divine nature, demonstrating love through assertive behavior becomes our top priority. We understand others' weaknesses originate from self-deception.

Authentic adults don't count on having their expectations met to be happy. They depend on their inner power for peace of mind, despite how others act. Viewing arguments as an inescapable part of life will keep feeling natural until we collectively make a conscious effort to stop being judgmental.

If you weren't born centered or grew up without consistent positive reinforcement—including observing disrespectful behavior between your parents—you regard a heightened state of stress as acceptable. Even though it's unhealthy to overreact and underreact on a regular basis, you've grown accustomed to feeling anxious or having a flat affect. Dissension is the only lifestyle you've known.

When we develop a victim mentality, we unconsciously find reasons to sabotage periods of tranquility. A person can't get sympathy when things are going smoothly. Without confidence to believe in our incomparable value, we either take out our underlying childhood insecurities on others or we allow others to victimize us.

Our faulty dispositions and learned behaviors prevent us from seeing the folly of insisting on getting our way or giving in. *When we don't grow up with a healthy image of ourselves, fear-based messages have a far greater psychological impact than love-grounded language.*

Over time, we accept the discomfort of our dual belief system as normal. Feeling disconnected from our Source of strength produces unstable thought patterns. We unconsciously regard quarreling or putting up with disrespect as a necessary evil to receive our temporary control or approval fix.

Throughout her childhood, Paula witnessed her mother's verbally abusive treatment of her overly accommodating father. In her own marriage, Paula was similarly disrespected. The second time around, the roles were reversed. Paula's demands could never be satisfied, no matter how often her spouse did her bidding. Currently on her third marriage, Paula has resumed allowing herself to be put down by her domineering husband. By anyone's objective standard, spouse number two treated Paula like a queen.

Witnessing her mother's need for control during her childhood caused Paula to sabotage this relationship with aggression.

Paula alternately allows herself to be mistreated and to behave disrespectfully. Her mixed-message reality forces her to either tolerate or incite conflicts, because she subconsciously believes she doesn't deserve to be loved. Self-deception prevents Paula from recognizing she is addicted to the chaotic lifestyle she grew up despising.

Despite claims to the contrary, people who believe in love and fear never felt truly loved as children. They reveal their lack of self-esteem by focusing on everything that is wrong and needing external validation. Love-centered people don't suffer from a compulsive need for outside reassurance. They have spiritual discernment to understand their completion comes from within.

> We're deadened by the ideals of how we think we should be and the way we think everybody else should be. It's a disaster. And the reason we don't understand that it's a disaster is because the dream can be very comfortable, very seductive. But when we are lost in our ideals and our fantasies, pleasurable as they may be, this is a disaster. We die.[2]

We can become so enslaved by the demanding *I* that we become volatile when our crucifixion mind-set is challenged. One young woman kept trying to convince me the husband who had divorced her was responsible for her distress. She eventually became so indignant by my attempts to get her to examine her own behavior that she started swearing at me. I quietly observed as she unconsciously displayed the abusive behavior that originally caused her to feel traumatized as a child. She stormed out with a parting shot: "I *am* a victim! Even my psychiatrist agrees with me!" The pleasurable effects of the adrenaline rush she experienced from the intensity of her reaction don't even come close to the mental and physical damage her attitude will eventually exact from her.

At the opposite extreme are those who have no awareness they are behaving like victims. They have learned to view the payoffs of being the center of attention and garnering sympathetic input as irresistible. God's all-encompassing love has no real meaning for those who lack spiritual insight to function righteously in a world where evil is falsely perceived to be more powerful than good.

Nonassertive adults tend to view their routine aggressive and passive conduct as justifiable, as opposed to defining themselves as angry. Fear-based thinking forces them to deny responsibility for the disrespect they regularly instigate or endure.

One of the most difficult beliefs to eradicate is the idea that people cause us to behave in a certain way. No one has that power without our permission. A Spirit-minded person is able to experience negative energy without responding inappropriately.

Thinking that it's acceptable to react any other way than assertively keeps you emotionally bound to the past. If your typical response pattern isn't assertive, you subconsciously believe the opposite of what is true: fear-controlled thoughts are real and love is an illusion.

There are no lifetime achievement awards for re-enacting childhood pain through adult dramas. When God's will doesn't play the starring role in our lives, our overall actions bear little resemblance to love.

Harboring a victim mentality leads to bitterness or depression, as was true in my case. While I still feel down at times, the big difference between then and now is I'm no longer ruled by fear-driven feelings. I'm too blessed to stay depressed.

Being inner-directed equips you to handle the inevitable bad times without regressing to childhood coping strategies. Learning to identify with your spiritual perfection dramatically decreases your inclination to dwell on human imperfections. You're no longer ruled by an inconsistent belief system that has prevented you from living your real life. You don't allow daily irritations or adverse circumstances to ruin your day. Even though you don't feel God's Presence, you still sense He's "in there" because you live by faith in humanity's oneness.

A love-based belief system requires humility to regard people from an eternal standpoint. Growing up with relentless messages about the failings of human nature results in judgments based on fleeting appearances. For example, people who abuse drugs tend to be judged more harshly than those who indulge in widely accepted addictive behaviors. Disdainful comments represent attempts to distance ourselves from those we deem socially unacceptable. The misunderstood truth is the clean-cut businessman who temporarily solves his problems by creating a long-term financial hardship is just as trapped in his own personal hell as the disheveled person who is controlled by drugs.

Most people are just better at covering up their instability. They may act out their fear-rooted childhoods in completely different ways, but the common denominator—a lack of self-respect—is still the same.

A related example is the individual who gets clean by surrendering self-will. Even though he has achieved a major victory in this specific area, his unresolved inferiority complex keeps him feeling detached from his Source. Freedom from drug abuse can result in him seeking ego gratification in relationships and material attachments. He finally looks respectable, but he is still riddled with anxiety. He doesn't realize that counting on people and possessions to feel good is just another version of being addicted to external solutions to solve a fundamental spiritual identity problem.

The Alcoholics and Narcotics Anonymous expression "self-will run riot," denotes the frantic search for the next fix to avoid the temporary misery of physical withdrawal. In much the same way, all fear-minded people rely on worldly fixes to evade the short-term pain of inner healing.

When we learn to identify with our shortcomings, we're unable to honestly express our feelings due to fear of further rejection. The emotional pain we've bottled up inside since childhood keeps surfacing in the form of nonassertive behaviors.

If you're only in a good mood when things are going well, you're not being true to yourself. You're being governed by a lack of self-acceptance that prevents you from actualizing your divine nature. Feelings of inadequacy need to be resolved on a subconscious level for peace of mind to prevail.

Another reason for not changing how we think is our "comfort" zones are defined by turmoil when we aren't raised to believe *only love is real*. Once we become accustomed to feeling anxious because we perceive we don't measure up, experiencing inner peace on a regular basis seems highly implausible.

A crucifixion complex is so insidious that we can end up succumbing to a downward spiral of self-rejection if we aren't vigilant. People illogically cling to a lifestyle characterized by self-deception, because a fear-controlled reality convinces us it's necessary to be judgmental.

The longer we wait to change our unsustainable core beliefs, the more difficult it becomes to stop relying on counterfeit self-esteem remedies whenever we start to feel anxious, depressed, etc. Like the person addicted to drugs, we can become trapped in a losing battle to maintain a tolerable level of comfort in a world viewed to be volatile.

I wasn't able to comprehend oneness of love until I developed insight to understand God's will is my will. I didn't experience true peace of mind until inner healing freed me from my childhood misconceptions.

My past involvement with Jim reveals how easy it is to succumb to a distorted reality. He would respond to situations beyond his control by verbally projecting his anger onto me. I responded with equal rancor and Jim would storm off, only to return later and apologize profusely. This cycle of abuse continued for nearly two and a half years until he agreed to go to counseling. Jim even took an antidepressant to curb his mood swings. I was initially encouraged by his improvement, but it turned out to be short-lived. When his agitation resurfaced, Jim admitted he had stopped taking his medication. He also confessed that he had spent his counseling sessions criticizing me instead of addressing his own issues.

Angry words ensued, and we broke up. His parting shot came back to haunt me years later when I decided to seek counseling myself. Jim had asked point blank, "When are you going to get help to deal with *your* anger?" At the time, that notion was inconceivable. I sincerely believed my only problem was Jim's antagonistic behavior, which reminded me of my father. I had convinced myself everything would be fine if he resolved his childhood issues. I justified my own heated responses because Jim had been the instigator. Self-righteous anger was so ingrained in me that I had no idea my own conduct was just as out of touch with reality as his actions.

Back then, I had never considered that being right is no justification for verbal aggression. Overreacting is a classic fear-minded response that makes fulfilling relationships impossible. Being set free by the truth didn't occur until I identified my failure mentality as the culprit for my argumentative attitude.

Striving to emulate your divinity by learning to love who you are enables you to rely on logical solutions to problems that used to send you into emotional tailspins. Learning to realistically decrease your dependence on your five senses paves the way for your intuitive sense to flourish. Those who regularly spend time being reflective are less likely to render snap judgments based on how others respond. Gaining awareness of your everlasting spirit-to-Spirit bond equips you to mentally rise above fear-rooted conduct.

Discovering Your Beautiful Mind

One of the first assignments I would give to new clients was to watch the movie *A Beautiful Mind*. I requested that they envision themselves as John Nash, the movie's central character. This true life account chronicles one man's courageous battle to recover the sanity he lost to schizophrenia. Far more than just another film about mental illness, Nash's predicament, in a very real sense, is everyone's story.

We all grow up with disordered thinking in one way or another. In the case of someone diagnosed with schizophrenia, the difference lies in the degree of delusional thoughts that hinder the ability to discern truth. The bizarre manifestations of Nash's illness actually worked in his favor. He retrained his mind, which significantly improved the quality of his life.

By contrast, resistance to inner healing is so strong that most people will remain unhappy rather than change the way they respond. I refer to this phenomenon as "learned schizophrenia." Feeling separated from the ever present reality of love by whatever form fear-based conduct takes—be it genetic illness or lack of self-worth—leads to an existence that is characterized by delusional thought patterns.

To further clarify how a fear-minded belief system perpetuates self-deception, think about the times you lost control of your temper; pouted until you got your way; didn't stand up for yourself against your better judgment; or got even by ignoring someone who had slighted you.

Although these actions are immature, adults regularly engage in these faulty expressions of their childhoods. Therefore, if we respond contrary to the way we know to be right, as though some unseen force is controlling us from within, this lie, in effect, becomes our reality. Living in subjection to fear is the end result.

Learning to identify with the love inside you breaks the vicious cycle of re-living the trauma from your childhood through disrespectful interactions. You'll no longer feel compelled to personalize conduct that isn't real from an eternity perspective.

Believing in your oneness with God dramatically decreases the false power of your childish inner self, "who" forces you to repeat behaviors to get it right so you can temporarily feel good enough to be loved.

A Spirit-led reality heightens awareness of countless opportunities that confirm love really does rule. We become receptive to what's happening in the moment. Being governed by inner truth—instead of our inner children—frees us to respond as mature adults who are in sync with our divine nature.

The primary goal becomes countering the false fear of the world by honestly demonstrating love. We live according to the law of governing dynamics, which garnered Nash the Nobel Prize in Economics: "The best result will come from everyone in the group doing what's best for himself and the group."

If this cooperative existence sounds more appealing than the turbulent lifestyle you've grown all too accustomed to, enlightenment begins with admitting your need to love yourself. After all, this challenge can't be nearly as daunting as the one from which Nash emerged victorious. As graphically depicted in the movie, his tortured reality included multiple taunting, illusory characters.

Have you been unconsciously suffering from the bondage of learned schizophrenia? The good news is discovering how to disengage from fear will empower you to reclaim your beautiful mind.

CHAPTER 2

Dynamics of Fear-Based Behavior

The evil that is in the world almost always comes
of ignorance, and good intentions may do as much
harm as malevolence if they lack understanding.
—Albert Camus

ommunication is often subject to interpretation. Your
viewpoint may differ completely from mine. If I expend
negative energy trying to convince you to agree with me,
I'm blocking the supernatural flow of love from within. My need
to be right originates from my underlying fear that I'm separate
from my Creator. I subconsciously try to overcompensate for my
feelings of powerlessness by playing God.

A person who doesn't identify with his whole mind, body,
and spirit tries to manipulate circumstances to conform to his
personal expectations. Depending on a spirit-to-Spirit connection
one can't see doesn't make sense from a temporal orientation.
Those who don't learn to value a holistic approach to life struggle
on their own terms in a world marred by half-truths.

Preserving the illusion of self is debilitating over the course
of a lifetime. The unreal world is transitory. It's accessed through
one's five senses. It consists of human bodies and everything
else tangible that perishes over time. It's ruled by fear that defies
logic. Millions are spent in vain attempts to achieve physical
perfection of false shells that eventually decay. The primary focus

is on worldly gain that ceases to have any meaning at the point of physical death.

The real world is never ending. It's accessed through one's sixth sense. It consists of humanity's mind and spirit centered in God's Mind and Spirit. It's ruled by love that defines logic. Millions are spent in noble efforts to alleviate the suffering of the masses. Those who are in touch with their spiritual perfection wisely balance their material desires with altruistic goals.

Fear-addicted conduct persists because most people have been trained to live by sight. Without spiritual insight, we automatically dwell on the deficiencies of human nature. Following self-will prevents us from comprehending the steep price we pay for our narrow frames of reference over time.

We can't intuitively discern the best in everyone if we're trapped in false feelings of inadequacy. Our relationships are characterized by conflicting viewpoints. The resulting anxiety creates an ongoing need for superficial remedies. Simply stated, we tend to view the world as Goliath and ourselves as David— minus the confidence and slingshot.

History is replete with stories of people like David, who overcame all odds to triumph over seemingly insurmountable obstacles. One such present day heroine involves a kidnap survivor who was freed after eleven grueling years. Michelle Knight is beyond resilient. This amazing young woman gives a whole new meaning to the word "courage." Michelle suffered unspeakable horrors at the hands of a mad man during her excruciatingly long captivity. To make matters even worse, she is estranged from her family. Although she lives alone, she hasn't allowed herself to indulge in self-pity. In the year since her rescue in 2013, Michele has built a new support network, written a book about her incomprehensible ordeal, and has enthusiastically entered culinary school.

It's reasonable to assume Michelle wasn't inner-directed when she was kidnapped in 2002. But if her mind had remained exclusively on her circumstances (flesh-driven), she never would have survived her lengthy torture. During a television appearance, she related she kept singing Celine Dion's hit song, *My Heart Will Go On,* to keep from killing herself. It's no coincidence Michelle chose that particular song. She had every reason to feel bereft as each agonizing year passed. And yet, she must have instinctively sensed in her spirit that she would survive her hellish nightmare.

Michelle's incredible story drives home the point that there is only one choice to make if you're serious about living your real life of love: Align your thoughts with your all-powerful heart-to-Heart connection to mentally triumph over even the very worst of hardships.

Separating Fact from Addiction

A false belief in fear evolves in the following manner: behaviors that don't personify love are based on self-deception. When we aren't taught to believe *only love is real*, we grow up unaware of humanity's oneness. A delusional love-fear division in our mind causes us to exclusively identify with our physical beings. We fixate on egocentric goals. This limited orientation compels us to contradict ourselves through two subconscious ideations: 1) I can have the abundant life on my own terms. 2) I don't deserve the abundant life.

Our bodies become the idols we serve when we aren't raised to be mindful of our innate wholeness. A false attachment to self creates mental and physical imbalances because the body symbolizes death. A spiritual perspective promotes healthy living because God's Spirit represents eternal life. As Ephesians 4:23–24 states: "and be renewed in the spirit of your mind, and that you put on the new man which was created according to God, in true righteousness and holiness."

Parenting styles that aren't spiritual convey mostly critical comments and negligible expressions of affection. When we aren't raised to respect our mind, bodies, and spirit, we don't realize that our routine judgmental response patterns deny our timeless identity. Nonassertive communication is deemed acceptable when individual performances don't conform to personal perceptions. The problem is we can't trust our feelings to tell us the truth if we're unconsciously suffering from an identity crisis. Simply stated, believing in love and fear produces an unstable, fear-controlled mind-set.

An assertive youngster, who has fear-driven parents, has a distinct advantage over children who weren't born with even tempers. His natural maturity can mitigate the adverse effects of his learned behavior.

Someone born with a fear-based temperament, who has assertive role models, is emotionally immature. But he still fares far better than children who don't have the benefit of love-centered parenting.

Children who have both nonassertive personalities and learn fear-minded messages have the most difficult time identifying with love. Nature and nurture are both critical factors in determining whether one feels alienated or empowered as an adult.

Speaking as one who fell into the least optimal third category, I can unequivocally state that fulfillment emanates from having a sincere desire to live on a higher, spiritual level of consciousness. From this vantage point, you don't jeopardize your health with ongoing overreactions or underreactions that indicate lack of self-respect. Your consistent assertive responses ensure everyone's best interests will be served

Confusing teachings of love and fear are difficult to eradicate. Childhood feelings of victimization tend to be reinforced throughout adulthood. By the time a person acknowledges life hasn't turned out as planned, many years have gone by. Without confidence to respond instinctively according to our divine nature, we become all too comfortable criticizing human nature.

Shifting the blame from ourselves when problems arise seems logical if that was the way we grew up. Adults who suffer from a crucifixion mentality generally have difficulty accepting accountability for their contributions to fear-bound dramas. This is why even being aware that attitude is more important than circumstances doesn't usually motivate people to change how they think. The vast majority maintains the status quo of judgmental commentary rather than admit that living from a self-will orientation just isn't working.

Self-deception is like an iceberg. The tip represents the full range of love and fear-based behaviors you consciously and unconsciously exhibit. If you close your eyes and envision the submerged portion beneath the surface, this formidable mass represents the power you've allowed your underlying feelings of unworthiness to have over you.

If you grew up feeling devalued, your reality is based primarily on personal perceptions that have nothing to do with your true identity. You never learned your happiness is dependent on discovering the love within you. Your flesh-driven attitude deceives you into believing your happiness depends on favorable circumstances.

The pain generated by giving false power to fear-rooted beliefs manifests in the form of worrying, complaining, depression, and an irritable disposition, to name just a few of the most familiar consequences.

Spiritual recovery bridges the gap between our conflicted mind and peaceful spirit that prevents us from discriminating fact from fiction. The more eternity minded we become, the less affected we are by what temporarily transpires in the false name of fear. Forsaking the blame habit to mentally transcend an earthly realm steeped in misconceptions is a small price to pay for experiencing the satisfaction of being authentic.

Lost Innocence

Left to our own devices in the form of faulty temperaments and learned behaviors, kingdom living in the present is the furthest thought from our mind. Fear-driven thinking always diverts our attention to the physical realm. Proof of this statement can be easily found by considering how most of us were raised.

Whenever parents are physically or emotionally unavailable to calm real or imagined anxieties, little children feel they have nowhere to turn. They take comfort in tangible objects and self-stimulation.

It would feel natural to love if we had been trained to pay attention to our spirit-to-Spirit unity through assertive behavior. Sensing God's still small voice would be commonplace. When self-will is modeled, our conditioning to expect fear-based outcomes is what convinces us feeling uncertain is normal.

The average child in America learns to pay far more attention to food and material possessions than to love and respect. Fear-controlled parents become angry when their acts of generosity don't result in obedience. They don't understand their contradictory communication styles foster lack of gratitude in their offspring.

When we're trained to regard negative energy displays as normal, we can't even begin to imagine the harmful side effects. If left unchecked throughout adulthood, devastating consequences can ensue. Sacrifices you make and material objects you provide are all secondary to how you talk to your children, how you allow them to address you, and how they observe you and your partner relating to each other, as well as to your own parents.

When the emphasis is on criticism, children define themselves in terms of their mistakes. Their true identity of love is never really developed. Instead of a resurrection mentality of self-acceptance to honestly demonstrate wholeness in thought, word, and deed, a crucifixion mind-set of self-doubt prevails.

Flawed response patterns are so prevalent that few people truly comprehend just how destructive clashing love and fear language can be to a child. Inconsistent messages only seem acceptable because that's how most of us were raised. Nonassertive language results in arrested emotional development that is typified by egotistical behaviors.

Fear-minded training that takes root during our formative years is considered real on a subconscious level. Youngsters who don't have assertive personalities and don't learn self-respect tend to identify with a childhood victim mentality throughout their lifetimes.

Feelings of mistrust abound when we don't recognize our true power emanates from within us. Errors are magnified. We settle for giving and receiving nominal positive feedback, because that's all we unconsciously believe we and others deserve.

Lack of insight sabotages a parent's best efforts to demonstrate love. While exercising proper authority is a necessity in a healthy parent–child relationship, there is a world of difference between love-grounded and fear-driven control.

Parents who scream in response to misbehavior underestimate the psychological impact of their tones of voice, especially if they were disciplined in a similar harsh fashion when they were young. Aggressive and even passive language is damaging. The message you're sending is that it's acceptable to act rudely or to be mistreated when one is in a position of external power.

Nonassertive children don't have the maturity to interpret an overreaction strictly as disapproval of their conduct. They subconsciously register adults' abrasive behavior as personal rejection.

"But no man can tame the tongue. It is an unruly evil, full of deadly poison. With it we bless our God and Father, and with it we curse men, who have been made in the similitude of God" (James 3:8–9). This classic mixed-message explains why berating children for their misdeeds is acceptable from a purely human nature standpoint. If we aren't raised with assertive messages to feel complete in God's love, we're controlled by fear-bound responses. Countering negative energy patterns with affirmations strengthens us to identify with our righteous spirit.

Moderating unhealthy reactions through willpower only works in the short-term, because misidentifying with self is deep-seated in our subconscious. Without spiritual discernment, we're unable to comprehend the depth of feelings of unworthiness that imprint on a youngster's mind.

More often than not, intimidating tactics are justified with familiar excuses, such as "Yelling is the only way I can get his attention" and "I survived my parents' anger." If more parents realized how illogical it is to respond aggressively, then act offended when their children imitate their behavior, self-respect would become a top priority.

Unless children are taught that heartfelt expressions of love are vital to emotional stability, they normally follow in the footsteps of their angry role models. Comfort is automatically sought in counterfeit self-esteem. Pleasurable feelings derived from external sources are a poor substitute for true self-love that can only come from within.

A good way to encourage young children to relate to their eternal spirit-to-Spirit bond is to regularly play a game called heart-to-Heart. Begin when the child is age five. Draw the outlines of two intertwined hearts. Ask your child to color them red so they appear more indistinguishable. Place the drawing in his hands, and instruct him to close his eyes without making a sound. Set a timer for one minute. Then ask if he can "see" the hearts without opening his eyes.

This concept acquaints a child with sensing God's Presence. It's important to follow up with praise for however long he keeps his eyes closed. When the goal time is achieved, you can both do a victory dance or engage in some other form of positive reinforcement. The time is increased in one minute increments, according to age.

The sooner a youngster can adjust to being silent, the greater chance he has to develop viscerally at an early age. Children who are accustomed to engaging in one activity after another will be resistant initially to keeping quiet. Learning to feel comfortable by simply "being" instead of always "doing" introduces kids to an introspective approach to life.

When anger overrides reason, apologizing without qualifying statements that put the blame back on the child is essential to honest communication. This act of humility teaches a child to take responsibility for mistakes. Most parents underestimate the importance of providing ongoing reassurance that disapproval of a child's actions will never change how much he is loved.

Children who are regularly exposed to negative feedback usually don't develop insight about their true value. They identify with a failure mind-set. They perceive the world as a hostile, threatening place.

Besides reminding children that parents are fallible after tempers have flared, this is also a good opportunity to teach them about the necessity of seeking divine solace. Mothers and fathers can use the analogy of pregnancy to explain how two entities can occupy one space. Instilling the idea that a supreme comforter, who loves forever, is always as close as one's heart will facilitate understanding of a spiritual approach to life.

The more opportunities little ones have to equate contentment with their inner power, the more reassured they will feel. They will be much less likely to believe they are disappointments to their parents when they are subjected to inappropriate anger and broken promises. An overall sense of security will replace feelings of rejection that normally takes root in children who internalize nonassertive response patterns.

Little children who aren't spiritually grounded perceive their parents as angry all-powerful gods and relate to God's everlasting love on a superficial level, if at all. When we're not centered, it never occurs to us that aggressive and passive behaviors keep reinforcing a victim mind-set. If you continue to define yourself by your past through arguments, indirect anger, or by suppressing your true feelings, your unconscious legacy to your children will be lack of self-worth.

Assertive parenting that emanates from self-respect is paramount to raising children who feel empowered to fulfill their divine destinies. Awakening from the nightmare you've mistaken for your real life requires accepting a fundamental spiritual truth: you're not your core belief system that expresses unresolved childhood pain through fear-minded conduct.

Being raised with a crucifixion complex can result in exaggerations of even the most minor problems. You automatically feel like someone or something is always working against you. Even though I had God's power to conquer my false anxiety as an adult, my childish persona was subconsciously in control. Until I developed confidence in my timeless identity, my victim mentality predisposed me to become judgmental whenever situations didn't work out the way I had anticipated.

Fear-driven patterns typically range from receiving support that validates our position of being wronged to a whole host of ego gratification outlets that placate us only until we need our next self-pity fix.

Parents who grow tired of the whining they can never satisfy grudgingly concede they may have enabled their offspring to take advantage of them. The number of adults in America who never leave home or return home is at an all-time high. And the primary reason has less to do with finances than it does with codependency. People who live intuitively by faith aren't typically shaken by economic downturns. Their eternity orientation generally prevents them from making emotional purchases that only provide short-lived satisfaction. They understand the fleeting value of earthly attachments.

Well-intentioned parents who are governed by guilt can end up providing financial bailouts they can't afford throughout their child's life. Repeated acts of generosity never work because they don't address the root problem: misidentification with the fear-based self that results in feelings of powerlessness.

Beth was shaken when her fiancé broke off their engagement. She described Paul as loving and generous. Their disagreements mainly revolved around Beth's grown children. Whenever they needed a babysitter, transportation, money, etc., Beth always catered to them. Paul finally decided five years of taking a backseat to her family was long enough.

Initially, Beth thought Paul was being unreasonable. As weeks went by and Beth really started missing him, she was forced to admit she had taken her fiancé for granted. Beth was also unaware her behavior demonstrated lack of self-value. Between trying to accommodate her children's egotistical requests and meeting Paul's needs, Beth was ignoring her own health. In addition to elevated stress and developing rashes on her face and chest, Beth was having trouble concentrating at work and suffered from insomnia.

Parents who don't identify with their divine nature aren't able to relate to the absolute necessity of maintaining assertive boundaries. Alternating love and fear communication creates the subconscious thought in a child's mind that his emotional survival depends on manipulating others or on obtaining excessive approval.

An oppositional belief system produces populations of single-minded thinkers who largely function without wholeness of purpose. Self-centered and self-sacrificing behaviors become the norm, while love-centered conduct in the true sense of the word is rarely demonstrated.

Parents who have a compulsive need for approval give in to their children's demands. They go against their better judgment because they fear losing their kids' love (which, ironically, they have never had, because they failed to model self-esteem). The opposite extreme of controlling behaviors causes parents to fault their children and other family members, and even blame societal influences to avoid relinquishing their martyr role.

Developing a healthy appreciation of your mind, body, and spirit addresses your spiritual imbalance. When you heal your faulty personal perceptions, you'll no longer be confounded by fear to repeat the mistakes of your childhood. No harm comes from admitting you've been out of touch with reality. The tragedy lies in dying without discovering how to truly love.

Parental Responsibility

These conclusions aren't intended to blame parents, who could just as easily pass the blame onto their own mothers and fathers. They are meant to demonstrate how self-deception prevails, despite each generation's disclaimer that there's "no way" their own children will grow up feeling as inferior as they did.

You may provide your children with better lifestyles and more attention than your parents gave you. And yet, if your decisions are based on self-will, your children still won't grow up feeling safe to express their needs and opinions honestly. Without faith in our eternal connection to God, we have no other choice than to play God by living according to our own rules.

If your spiritual perfection wasn't modeled through consistent assertive behaviors during your childhood, you never understood that valuing who you are is crucial to your well-being. Without a foundational belief that *only love is real*, it's nearly impossible to stay centered when situations don't turn out as planned.

Learning to depend on our circumstances for fulfillment cancels out genuinely trusting God. When we aren't raised to believe in our inner power, we simply don't comprehend we're doing the opposite of what we need to do to encourage children to fulfill their true purpose.

It's critically important to recognize the futility of continuing to blame yourself for your children's problems. However, if you agree it's time to be delivered from your false guilt, it's important to understand the necessity of embarking on your own spiritual journey posthaste.

Of all the gifts you can give your children, modeling self-worth and teaching God's unending love are the only offerings that have lasting value. Note: this isn't to be confused with verbal expressions of affection. If you tell your children you love them, then scream at them for their misdeeds, this contradictory message will make them feel devalued. Similarly, if you allow your children to scream at you or each other, you haven't taught them the meaning of love. Assertive behaviors and respect go hand in hand. You'll know you're being true to yourself when you respond firmly, but calmly, to your children during most trying situations.

A parent who blames his children for his outbursts becomes dependent on the short-lived satisfaction of gaining obedience through guilt. One age old theme among parents who instill guilt in their children is they proclaim their kids will finally see things their way when they have families of their own. What this anticipation of self-satisfaction fails to take into account is that an egocentric viewpoint always leaves us with the same deceptive thoughts that have plagued us since the Garden of Eden: mistrust, blame, and denial.

If you have a nonassertive personality and were never taught self-control to deal with difficult situations, you grew up feeling anxious. The chaos of your home life overshadowed any positive messages you may have been taught about God's everlasting love. Now as an adult who lacks spiritual discernment, you unconsciously keep your childhood feelings of victimization alive in the present.

Adults who either got what they demanded during their childhoods or grew up observing manipulative response patterns suffer from a false need for control. Reality dictates every time we overreact or react indirectly to regain control, we end up with the same feelings of powerlessness we experienced as children. Even if we derive pleasure from winning an argument, it's a hollow victory. The illusion of being in charge lasts only until the very next time we give someone or something the power to cause us to become angry when we don't get our way.

A popular talk show featured spouses who agreed to have their marital battles videotaped. While embroiled in successive scenes of trading vicious insults, one couple was oblivious that their two-year-old son was clearly distraught. He even screamed "Stop!" but his frantic pleas were drowned out by his parents' raging self-hate. This far too frequent behavior is a perfect example of people being out of touch with reality on both a conscious and a subconscious level. During one part of the segment, the wife became indignant when her husband implied she wasn't a good mother. Yet, the video provided ample evidence that their displays were inflicting emotional trauma on their child.

Their ongoing tirades represented futile attempts to master their own childhood feelings of inferiority by trying to control each other. Predictably, unless their child has an assertive or passive temperament, history will repeat itself. He too will dramatically act out his learned identification with fear in front of his own children, without understanding the deep-seated damage he will be causing them in the process.

High Cost of Denial

A closer look at this common practice of becoming angry when others don't conform to our viewpoints demonstrates how a false attachment to self causes untold misery. Until you develop insight to see yourself from God's perspective of your spiritual perfection, you'll never be content—no matter how many times people comply with your wishes.

Fear-rooted conditioning forces you to see in others the lie you believe deep down inside about yourself, namely, *I just can't do anything right.* This is the reason you often hear the lament, *No matter how hard I try, it's never enough to please him/her.*

Whether or not we were intentionally victimized as children doesn't absolve us from victimizing others through nonassertive conduct. Restoring our divided mind to demonstrate wholeness of love is essential to a balanced, productive life.

I won't be able to experience my legacy of peace if I continue to judge others the way I was criticized as a child. Changing my attitude to accept full responsibility for my happiness frees me from becoming upset when others don't accommodate my desires.

Learning to love who I am equips me to stop obsessing over trivial concerns that have no eternal value. I finally recognize what will bring me lasting contentment: identifying with the kingdom of God within me.

Unfortunately, the choice, more often than not, is for the overly emotional or underreacting adult to justify his misidentification with self to the bitter end. Failure to emulate the Mind of God through assertive behaviors predisposes us to a whole host of emotional and physical illnesses that lead to premature physical deaths.

Those who do get real—by discovering God's will is their will—usually only do so when the pain of resistance makes life unbearable. At this point, the irrational "my way" stance is humbly exchanged for spiritual recovery.

Aggressive Angst

The passive-aggressive nature I was born with was exacerbated by the aggressive behavior I observed in my father and the passive reactions I learned from my mother. As a result, I lived most of my life alternating between passive-aggressive behaviors and aggressive and passive extremes. I didn't discover the necessity of changing my attitude until I sought counseling in 1997.

A notable regression was a particularly long visit to my former fear-controlled ways. Shortly after my marriage to Bob in 1998, my hostility resurfaced with a vengeance. Bob's temperament is aggressive like his mother. For the first year of our marriage, self-will manifested through control. I kept responding in kind whenever Bob overreacted. Although I knew this behavior always led to escalation, I was subconsciously driven to repeat this pattern.

The need to prove I was right reared its ugly head after I had been in counseling for more than a year. This gives you some idea how easily egotistical behaviors can blindside you if you let your guard down. The "clash of the titans" continued until I finally remembered to start responding assertively, so we could stop re-living our parents' drama-filled marriages. On the surface, the minor conflicts that erupted into major combat were between adult Bob and Cindy. But deep down, childish Bob and Cindy were really running the show. We were loaded with all the ammunition we had been storing away ever since we had first witnessed our parents' angry behaviors.

In effect, the illusory battleground involved four children. It regressed from Bob and Cindy in the present to Bob acting like his unstable mother and me acting like my childish father. I was convinced the intensity of my reaction was justified, because Bob's behavior reminded me of my father's verbal mistreatment of my mother. While this was true enough, it only told half the story.

The admonition that we reap what we sow was in full force. When our feelings of powerlessness aren't resolved, the way we judged our parents during childhood is destined to come back to haunt us in adulthood. Whether our parents were right or wrong is immaterial, because fear-driven behaviors aren't real. When we heal our thought patterns on a subconscious level, we develop discernment to understand that demonstrating respect takes precedence over our conditioning to act self-righteously.

As a little child, I couldn't tell my dad how his behavior was causing my anxiety level to soar. But as an adult, my inner child had the perfect cover to release her pent up resentment. When I "became" my father, I was really subconsciously shouting at my dad through Bob. Likewise, he was unconsciously telling off his mother through me.

If we aren't taught to honestly express ourselves as youngsters through assertive behaviors, we develop anxious feelings that overshadow our naturally peaceful states of mind. When we're blocked from expressing the love of our spirit-to-Spirit union, our only other option is to respond with the fear-rooted conduct of our stuck children. Without spiritual recovery to heal from the inside out, we keep attracting the disheartening outcomes that we learned to believe we deserve.

Aggression is a prime example of a false emotion that keeps being triggered when present day events remind us of our childhood insecurities. The familiar adage, "You act out what you don't work out" characterizes our delusional mind-set when we learn to misidentify with fear. Simply stated, when humanity's eternity connection to God isn't emphasized from birth, self-deception prevents us from fulfilling our true purpose to love.

Passive Pitfalls

Many people mistakenly believe it's preferable to be passive than aggressive. Even though passive behavior is more socially acceptable than aggressive conduct, this personality type is just as stuck in the past.

Those born with submissive temperaments seek to feel good about themselves by deferring to others. Passive individuals unconsciously sacrifice their self-respect to gain approval.

Repressing your real feelings takes its toll and can even be more detrimental than overreacting in the long run. This is true from an emotional, as well as a physical standpoint. Depression is anger turned inward. While those who underreact are more skilled at hiding their feelings, they still experience inner turmoil from being dishonest.

Carl gave his opinion to his wife, Janice, regarding a joint purchase he really didn't want to make. She disagreed. Carl attempted to end the discussion by reminding her that the whole idea of the shopping trip was to buy something they both liked. Janice's terse retort—"Okay, fine"—was followed by her storming out of the store. Carl caught up to Janice in their car. He took one look at her sullen demeanor and capitulated. Janice was suddenly all smiles. She wasted no time heading back to the store, leaving Carl shaking his head.

Carl functions under the delusion that his sacrificial stance will result in Janice mending her self-centered ways. The opposite is true. Carl's inability to hold firm to his convictions reinforces Janice's subconscious belief that childish antics guarantee she'll get her way. Like most people, Carl doesn't understand the pivotal role core beliefs play in determining whether we live out our lives as martyrs or victors. Not only do his acts of self-denial fail to change his wife's behavior, his lack of self-value fuels his false feelings of victimization.

Passive-Aggressive Avoidance

Passive-aggressive people represent a subtle combination of their histrionic aggressive and repressed passive counterparts. They express their need for control without overt hostility. What all three behavioral patterns have in common are feelings of unworthiness from identifying with their shortcomings.

Arlene grew up observing her mother and father act out their failure mentality through aggressive and passive-aggressive behaviors. Now in her mid-forties, Arlene's similar conduct has resulted in the disrespect of her coworkers. During a staff meeting, she was offended by a comment made by one of her supervisors. Afterward, Arlene vented to Donna, the secretary. She pretended to be sympathetic, then gossiped to Sharon, another coworker, about Arlene's pettiness. Arlene then tried to enlist support from Lisa, a different supervisor. Lisa concluded that Arlene had overreacted and decided to let the matter drop. When Arlene followed up later, Lisa lied and said she had spoken to the supervisor in question on her behalf.

What Arlene, Donna, Sharon, and Lisa all have in common are judgmental behaviors and the false satisfaction of believing their personal perceptions are all accurate. What they don't recognize is the long-term emotional and physical damage they will suffer from not being honest. Instead of responding assertively in agreement with their wholeness, they each relied on passive-aggressive behaviors to individually feel a fleeting sense of power.

A brief disclaimer must be added that none of these nonassertive communication styles is absolute. People who are ruled by fear mainly identify with one particular temperament, while alternating between the other two, depending on the circumstances.

False Power of Fear-based Conditioning

It's essential to understand humanity's false perception of fear generates turmoil from the inside out. The vast majority are unaware that the key to reversing this destructive dynamic lies within themselves.

When our belief system is founded on love and fear, we tend to remain emotionally torn between an adult/child mind-set as grown-ups. This disconnect from reality occurs because the inner children who govern our thoughts are incapable of logic; in much the same way we were unable to think sensibly as youngsters.

The guiding principles governing self-will are a nonassertive personality and a learned need for superficial remedies. To describe this combination as highly addictive is a huge understatement. This subconscious pain-pleasure pairing is responsible for humanity's premature earthly demise.

Blindly seeking endless external fixes in the absence of never obtaining the desired result of lasting contentment is completely illogical. And yet, that's exactly how adults who don't identify with love are forced to act.

The evolution of humanity's learned schizophrenia dissociation from reality starts at infancy. Most newborns become accustomed to getting their basic needs met quickly. As toddlers acquire language skills, healthy maturation requires learning the value of delayed gratification to develop patience. Without this vital developmental skill, a child learns to respond to disappointments and demands with frustration and anger.

Just as children who aren't trained to think in terms of long-term benefits are referred to as spoiled, adults who never outgrow their need for immediate ego gratification are labeled childish. When dependence on a dual belief system isn't resolved before parenthood, fear-bound behaviors persist on a generational scale.

Doctor Pavlov's Nobel Prize winning work on conditioned response patterns revealed the power false connections in one's mind have to create addictive behaviors. Initially, Pavlov trained dogs to relate the ringing of a bell to receiving food. The bell eventually became such a potent stimulus that the dogs would salivate at the sound even when they weren't rewarded with a morsel. It didn't matter that the bell itself had nothing to do with food. The dogs learned to pair a false prompt with a positive outcome, evidenced by drooling.

In much the same way, most people learn to associate mixed-message communication with love, even in the glaring absence of respectful behaviors. Love is ever present. The various manifestations of fear only seem real if we cling to our lifelong misconceptions. Simply stated, self-deception addicts us to re-enact childhood trauma through unhealthy response patterns.

Believing fear can coexist with love creates the subconscious delusion that controlling and needy conduct is part and parcel of fulfilling relationships. Learning to connect pleasure with painful stimuli keeps your hurtful childhood memories alive. Becoming an adult translates into exchanging the physical and emotional "prison" of your family of origin for continued mental bondage to a fear-driven reality. You won't be empowered to live your real life of love as long as you keep reinforcing your victim mentality through judgmental behaviors.

Bev's story is typical of the way a false belief in fear perpetuates a chaotic lifestyle. Throughout Bev's childhood, whenever she was scolded by her aggressive mother, her passive live-in grandmother would privately console her. The grandmother didn't know how to raise Bev's mom to be assertive. All three generations didn't understand the value of honest communication.

Over time, Bev unconsciously linked the pain of her mother's hostility with the sympathy she subsequently received from her grandmother. Her mother's aggression soon became *inseparable* from her grandmother's nurturing follow-up attention. Bev's grandmother had inadvertently set her up to mentally pair being victimized with a positive outcome. As a direct result, Bev's mind formed a fear-rooted neural connection that had nothing to do with love. Simply stated, fear-driven messages combined with love-based messages equal a fear-minded reality.

This false correlation taught Bev that love is synonymous with controlling and approval based behaviors. Completely unrelated messages implanted two fundamental fallacies in Bev's mind: 1) She doesn't deserve unconditional love. 2) Self-worth originates from external sources. Simply stated, the addictive pain-pleasure cycle of self-deception undermines our ability to discern our eternity connection to God.

The adult version of Bev's fear and love pairing was accepting abusive treatment from men, alternating with sporadic displays of affection. This all too familiar role play was followed by the sympathy she received from close friends.

Since Bev had been trained to associate feeling good about herself with how she was treated, the mixed-messages she received from her mother and grandmother prevented her from discovering her immeasurable value. Her moods varied with her circumstances. Like most people, Bev never learned that it's impossible to be authentic without recognizing that love originates from within oneself.

By accepting aggressive conduct from her partners after the novelty phase ended, Bev was reaffirming her childhood victimization pattern. She became addicted to settling for counterfeit self-esteem from her support system. Bev's fear-rooted mentality kept her emotionally bound to her childhood, languishing in powerlessness. Had she been raised to have confidence in her true identity, she would have attracted men who were love-centered.

Just as Bev associated aggression with a subsequent reward, children who grow up flesh-driven learn to equate painful actions with pleasurable payoffs. They subconsciously incite others to devalue them so they can justify pursuing the enjoyable fixes that follow. This is why consistently overreacting has the opposite of the desired effect to produce positive change.

Without insight to live by faith in God's will, we place greater value on personal opinions that can cause us to function from a position of weakness. We illogically expect fear-based people to do for us what we all must do for ourselves: stop misidentifying with feelings of helplessness from our past so we can start living our real life of love.

As a child, you had no other choice than to personalize hurtful experiences that led to feelings of unworthiness. As an adult, you're fully capable of changing the way you view your circumstances. A wholeness perspective frees you to live the abundant life by counting on your inner power to sustain you.

When you learn to love who you are—warts and all—you won't be dependent on your conditioned coping strategies. You'll happily recognize you've always been complete, with or without positive reinforcement from others. The end result is responding from a position of strength.

It can't be stressed often or strongly enough that we automatically revert to our childhood feelings of insecurity when we allow our comfort zones to be defined by fear-addicted behaviors. We can't grow up emotionally until we're willing to hold ourselves accountable for the nonassertive way we demean others, as well as for the disrespectful way we permit others to treat us.

A victim mentality wreaks havoc. It doesn't matter if you're a public figure toppled from power by scandal or the average person seeking relief from fear through ego gratification. Whether rich or poor, you sabotage your peace of mind to line up with your subconscious belief that you don't deserve love.

My Story

My perception of both of my parents is that they did their best to demonstrate love, and were generous to their three children. However, due to our differing temperaments, each of us was affected by our parents' lack of self-esteem in very different ways.

I was overly sensitive and prone to depression for most of my life. I would dwell on a comment I regarded as hurtful for days on end, or even longer. I believe this was the primary reason my father's verbal aggression toward my mother caused me to make an unconscious vow never to marry. I also believe it was no coincidence that I married Bob in 1998 after I began spiritual counseling in 1997.

A particularly vivid demonstration of my sensitivity occurred when my father attempted to help me study math. He quickly became impatient with my lack of progress. He slammed down the pencil and left the room. I can still remember sitting frozen in my chair until my older sister eased my anxieties by patiently reviewing the lesson.

As a child, I wasn't able to reason that my dad's behavior was governed by his feelings of inadequacy. I carried the stigma of that memory into adulthood, even though I was generally well treated by my dad. Neither of my parents had ever made disparaging comments about my intelligence. In fact, my dad frequently bragged about my good grades.

I didn't fully understand why my father's loss of self-control had impacted me so profoundly until I was well into spiritual recovery. Nonassertive children who are raised to believe in opposing realities automatically process negative energy displays from a fear-based viewpoint.

When we aren't taught our mind and spirit is centered in our Creator's Mind and Spirit of everlasting love, we attribute more importance to what is said and done in the false name of fear. Self-condemnation and judging others is the destructive end result. Simply stated, learning to identify with a holistic perspective ultimately frees us to deal with offenses without personalization.

My temperament and learned behavior predisposed me to subscribe to a poverty mentality. I unknowingly internalized my father's poor self-image. His lack of self-respect manifested in his constant struggle to adequately support our family.

Likewise, although I have a college degree, I settled for being underemployed and scrambling to make ends meet. Even though both of my parents encouraged me to succeed, I still followed in the footsteps of my father as an underachiever. This is just one of countless ways that self-deception keeps us in bondage to fear.

Bob's Story

Bob's story offers a stark portrayal of the dire consequences of self-hatred that is far too prevalent in today's society. He grew up in a Christian family with a loving mother and father. Like me, Bob was the middle child. His intelligence was obvious at an early age. He possesses two college degrees and graduated with honors. Bob's mother suffered from schizophrenia. As in my case, the aggressive parent's rage was projected onto the passive parent, not the children. This is where the similarity ends.

As a young child, Bob didn't understand the ramifications of his mother's illness. He repressed his painful feelings regarding her bizarre behavior. He initially took out his underlying resentment on himself. By the time he had turned sixteen, Bob had begun his long descent into the cunning world of addiction. He first experimented with marijuana and various other drugs and then became a full-blown heroin addict at age nineteen.

Bob was being maintained on methadone when he married Regina. She rejected drug use. Their predictably tumultuous union produced a son, Steve. Bob was somehow able to maintain a semblance of normalcy until age thirty-eight. He went from owning a beautiful home with his family and being on the fast track to success with a Fortune 500 company to living in a homeless shelter in my hometown.

After a nearly twenty year heroin addiction, Bob drifted into a Narcotics Anonymous (NA) meeting. It didn't seem any different from all the other meetings he had considered a waste of time. At the end of the hour, he still felt hopeless. He attempted to slink out when a man tapped him on the shoulder. Bob felt an instant connection when he turned and saw Martin. Bob described his countenance as "ethereal." God used Martin's divine nature to create a sense of hope in Bob that he hadn't felt since his nightmare began. He surrendered to God's will and gradually started making his way back to sanity in 1994.

After reading these two accounts, the initial reaction may be to conclude Bob had a far more serious problem, but that would be missing the point. Although dramatically different, there is a common denominator in our stories. Our caring parents' unknowing legacies to their children included their lack of self-worth. It really doesn't matter that my inferiority complex assumed the more subtle forms of depression and anxiety, while Bob acted out his self-hate through drug addiction and aggression.

Reclaiming your legacy of peace begins with learning to love who you are so you can identify with your perfect spirit. The longer you discipline yourself to heal your fear-rooted perceptions, the less judgmental you will act and the calmer you'll feel.

The key to success lies in perseverance. I know many people who claim to have self-confidence, but whose actions clearly indicate otherwise. A good way to know if you're settling for counterfeit self-esteem is if you only rely on external sources of comfort to ease your anxiety when the unexpected happens. The only reason I understand the way this insidious dynamic operates is because I not only used to fall into this category, I also have to be vigilant on a daily basis not to relapse.

Most people are unaware that they haven't mentally moved beyond their childhoods. Whether denial of wholeness is expressed through primarily aggressive, passive, or passive aggressive conduct, the end result is still the same. Distorted thinking can be summed up by the following unconscious monologue:

> If I change course now, things could get even worse. It's better to stick with what I know. Besides, I'm not the problem. I keep proving I'm

right, but my family is too stubborn to agree with me. If only they thought the way I do, and I could find a way to make more money, I'd have it made. What I really need is to take my mind off my problems. I deserve to relax, have a beer or two, maybe buy myself that high definition TV I've been wanting. That will make me feel better.

Continuing to ignore the still small voice to settle for short-lived solutions guarantees you'll keep feeling dissatisfied.

Just how widespread the problem of self-deception is will now be expanded to include walks of life where love and healing are supposed to flourish.

CHAPTER 3

Roadblocks to Success

To live happily is an inward power of the soul.
—Marcus Aurelius

In the first two chapters, the insidious ramifications of believing fear is real were explained. This chapter explores the topics of counseling and religion. The fear-minded nature of a mixed-message belief system can be best demonstrated by examining fields where one would expect to find consistent love-centered solutions.

Before delving into these specific areas, it's necessary to fine tune your awareness of the way self-deception perpetuates childhood insecurities throughout adulthood.

Reality Check

I met Bob in 1997, three years into his healing from drug addiction. In addition to NA meetings, he attended a weekly spiritual progress group until the fall of 2004. Whenever problems developed between us, Bob was instructed by his sponsor to take ownership of his part in the disagreement, no matter how strongly he felt I was to blame. We can't grow emotionally strong if we deny our contribution to conflicts.

I believe Bob's attendance at spiritual progress meetings contributed to our marriage's stability for several years, after we made it through the first tumultuous test year. Nevertheless, we continued to be susceptible to depression. Predisposing genetic factors aside, I believe the main reason we felt down was our deep-rooted feelings of inadequacy.

It's possible to be assertive without loving yourself when things are going relatively well. However, it isn't possible to stay centered during prolonged stressful periods if you're not secure in your true identity.

A holistic lifestyle largely releases us from paying undue attention to humanity's temporary character defects. We either unconsciously view ourselves and others in terms of our perceived childhood failings, or we learn to function on the higher levels of consciousness by identifying with the Mind of God. Simply stated, depending on one's perspective, life is either agonizingly complicated or amazing in its simplicity.

Continuing the judgmental patterns we were steeped in during our formative years keeps reinforcing our false belief in fear. We ultimately feel defeated from allowing the unpredictable nature of life to determine our moods.

A divisive love-fear belief system forces us to function at a frenzied or mindless pace. Regularly becoming impatient with others—because you've learned to operate in crisis mode—is the flip side of vegging out in front of the television and spending unproductive hours on the Internet. As long as you stay stuck in these extremes or alternate between both, peace of mind will seem more like an impossible dream than your divine birthright.

Changing your viewpoint from your limited self to the unlimited potential of wholeness thoughts anchors you in the present. You'll no longer be ruled by fear-bound behaviors from childhood that promote conflicts. You won't be consumed with energy draining feelings from your past or worried about your future. A mind that has its spirit-to-Spirit connection restored has all the power it needs to demonstrate love, in spite of how others act.

An important point to remember is spiritual recovery only works for those who genuinely desire to respond in the best interests of the whole. Peace flows freely when we address the underlying cause of all instability: misidentification with the fear-rooted self.

Trying to remain calm through willpower won't work long-term. A self-will focus leads to the substitution of another fear-driven behavior that will continue to exacerbate your anxiety. Until you become inner-directed to trust in eventual positive outcomes, you'll keep feeling irritated or discouraged every time your expectations aren't satisfied.

In my case, the aggressive anger from my marriage turned into a general feeling of dissatisfaction. Anxiety and depression represented the bad fruit I originally reaped from my temperament and learned behavior. My decision to become an assertive adult only affected temporary improvement on a surface level. I still lacked insight to identify with my peaceful spirit.

My conditioning to be judgmental intensified my depression. Until I became serious about healing my failure mentality, I remained stuck interpreting life's events according to my childhood insecurities.

Tracking from Fruit to Root

I sought help for my depression through the interventions of counseling and medication in January 1997. Since November 2002, I've functioned independently of my counselor and antidepressant. As if on cue, I began experiencing a series of difficult challenges. During the latter part of 2004, my chronic depression resurfaced.

The big difference between 1997 and 2004 was my discovery of the reason for my melancholy mood. I was relieved when I realized identifying with my shortcomings was responsible for my lack of inner peace. I didn't have control over how life unfolded, but I was reasonably certain I could change my attitude to love who I am.

If you grew up with contradictory messages, fear's seemingly subtle influence keeps feeding into your preexisting victim mentality. If it's always seemed normal to blame your circumstances for your unhappiness, developing false feelings of powerlessness is an inevitable consequence.

The downward spiral to an ultimate sense of hopelessness can occur from failing to discover true power always emanates from within. One's mind must be trained to reframe negative energy events according to the ever present reality of love.

One of the greatest benefits of inner healing has been my freedom from clinical depression. Even though my situation continued to worsen over the past ten years, I've been able to prevent fear from regaining a foothold. Instead of depending on medication or bemoaning my problems to others, becoming Spirit-minded stabilized my mood.

A case in point is one two-week period when I provided total care for my mother and my dog. A car hit Buddy. He lost an eye and required drainage tubes and stitches. I was hand feeding both my mom and my dog. On the second day, my anxiety level began to intensify. I took a low dose of Xanax for the next two days to cope with the added stress. No further medication was necessary. (A cautionary note: I would have resumed taking an antidepressant if I had sensed in my heart that it was necessary).

A fear-based identity prevents us from seeking honest answers. Without faith to trust in our inner power, we naturally respond to life's stressors with the same maladaptive coping skills we learned as children: depending on external control and approval and temporary fixes. Our insistence on self-will solutions ends up taking its toll on our health. A wholeness vantage point frees us from the love-fear contradiction we demonstrate through the stability we appear to exude and our inner turmoil.

Five primary indicators of a fear-rooted mind-set include:

1. Identifying with conflicts through non-assertive conduct.
2. Choosing worldly pursuits or external expressions of spirituality over a heartfelt relationship with God.
3. Personalizing perceived mistreatment.
4. Avoiding responsibility for happiness through self-condemnation or faultfinding.
5. Withholding forgiveness consciously or unconsciously.

A sense of alienation ultimately occurs when the accepted definition of reality revolves around choosing between opposing forces. Peace of mind won't be the norm as long as we believe we're unworthy deep down inside. Regardless of our educational or income levels, we'll never be content if we don't recognize our happiness comes from within us.

The logical way to stop being controlled by unhealthy feelings is to alter our core beliefs. Self-deception convinces us it's normal to keep repressing how we really feel or to continue overreacting when confronted with situations that reopen old psychic wounds.

An eternity orientation provides insights into solving problems that our mixed-message mind can only complicate. Trusting that God's will is humanity's will dispels dependence on worldly and external spiritual solutions for long-term fulfillment.

When you align your thoughts with assertive behaviors that demonstrate oneness of love, you're led to discover answers that are simple, yet profound. Your challenge is to start regarding life's setbacks as opportunities to grow in wisdom by developing your sixth sense to discern the still small voice.

Functioning as an eternal spirit who temporarily inhabits a physical form replaces inconsistent emotional reactions with calm responses. When you identify with love, you aren't easily perturbed by an unpredictable world system that is only as real as humanity's fears.

Always keep in mind that negative energy patterns flow all too freely from a fear-bound subconscious. Steadfastly countering childhood conditioning with uplifting thoughts and actions enables you to walk in the light of God's truth. Simply stated, the way you think determines whether you're in heaven on earth at peace or in hell on earth in emotional torment.

Buyer Beware

There are many ways in which the counseling process can work against one's recovery. This statement isn't intended as an indictment of mental health professionals. They are generally motivated by a sincere desire to help others.

This roadblock involves lack of awareness. It isn't determined by one's level of academic achievement. It universally affects the perceptions of psychiatrists and psychologists, therapists, and counselors; as well as everyone else who isn't inner-directed. I'm referring to spiritual blindness: the inability to identify with humanity's wholeness due to a subconscious attachment to self.

The downside of believing we're fleeting, separate entities is the attendant drama. When we grow up identifying our mind exclusively with our bodies, we automatically dissociate from our peaceful spirit. Anxiety ensues because oppositional attitudes become the (dis)order of the day. We're spiritually blind to our inner power if we only live according to the perceptions of our five senses.

The most dramatic literal illustration of physical and spiritual blindness in the Bible involved the Apostle Paul, who murdered Christians. He didn't "see" the light until God temporarily blinded him. He wouldn't have been empowered to write most of the epistles in the New Testament if he hadn't been humbled to live by faith.

While we may shudder at the thought of such a rude awakening, we can also agree the end justified the means. Spiritual recovery rescues us from merely muddling through life feeling blindsided by circumstances beyond our control.

Changing how you see yourself improves the overall quality of your life. You finally recognize the futility of clinging to faulty thought patterns that force you to search for endless transitory remedies.

When a child isn't taught to identify with his divine nature by assertive parents, it's as though the combined effect of temperament and learned behavior imprints "reject" on his heart and soul. In the extreme sense, Hitler was maximally deceived by feelings of rejection, while Mother Teresa was minimally deceived.

The professional who can relate to humanity's wholeness is in the best position to help clients maximize their potential. I'm not suggesting all mental health professionals should be like Mother Teresa. Rather, this is a reminder that the effectiveness of counseling is determined by how well your teacher understands the true meaning of love.

Someone who unconsciously identifies with fear is less likely to emphasize the importance of self-acceptance due to his own lack of awareness. I used to be one of those counselors until I saw the dramatic difference it made in my own life. A good question for a client to ask a prospective therapist is how extensively he has worked through his self-esteem issues.

I'm familiar with three areas of counseling that don't serve the clients' best interests: legal addiction, rescue behavior, and codependent counseling.

Legal Addiction

As someone who has benefited from drug therapy in the past, I'm a firm believer in the prudent dispensation of medication, the operative word being prudent. For those who suffer from biochemical deficits, counseling would be largely ineffective without medicinal support.

This was true in my case. I was in denial that my identity included my mind, body, and spirit for so long that I believe I created a chemical imbalance. When I was finally motivated to seek treatment, I resisted my counselor's advice to take medication for several months.

Even though I implemented her other suggestions, I couldn't shake my melancholy feelings. Three weeks after I decided to try drug therapy, the shroud of darkness that had clouded my thinking disappeared. I was amazed at how much better I felt.

As in all areas of life, the problem is one of balance. On the one hand, there are people like me who avoid taking medication until they reach the point of "critical mass;" on the other hand, there are those who convince themselves (and their doctors) that the quick fix of a pill is preferable to doing the work to resolve childhood trauma on a cognitive level to effect a positive outcome.

Taking mood-altering drugs without dealing with your inferiority complex won't relieve your symptoms in the long run. Over time, you'll need to keep increasing the dosage and changing medicines to maintain your artificial level of comfort.

In the movie, *Starting Over*, the lead character was in a furniture store. He started to hyperventilate at the thought of being involved in yet another committed relationship. As he gasped the line, "Anybody got a valium?" several shoppers—in unison—nonchalantly offered him their pills.

When the movie was released, the audience (including me) got a good laugh out of that scene. Today, more than thirty years later, widespread pill popping is clearly no laughing matter. Millions of Americans are hooked on twenty-first century versions of this drug or narcotic painkillers. Fifty percent of preventable deaths in America are linked to drug overdoses.

Methadone clinics paved the way for alternative addiction management to be available in doctors' offices. Certified physicians can prescribe the narcotic suboxone in their offices to wean people off other addictive medications. They also may be contributing to our ever-burgeoning drug abuse epidemic.

This widespread practice of substituting a legal fix for an illegal one can lead to a false sense of security, especially in cases where a comprehensive outpatient treatment plan isn't required. I know people who claim to be drug free because suboxone or methadone was prescribed by their doctors.

Mental health therapists can also cross the line when it comes to drug therapy. A healthy counseling relationship never involves control. After I initially communicated that I didn't want to take medication, I wasn't pressured to comply. Bob's experience was the opposite.

Bob's drug counseling history occurred over a sixteen-year period. In the 1980s, drug therapy wasn't part of his treatment plan. In the 1990s, however, the push was on for him to take medication. When Bob was clean for a year in 1995, he was strongly advised to take advantage of antidepressants. The therapist touted the virtues of the newer, non-addictive drugs. She then espoused the theory that since he had been self-medicating through his addiction, this was an indication of his need for medication. This questionable tactic was followed by her less than subtle approach that she wouldn't be able to recommend continued visitations with his son unless he complied. After this bluff failed, both she and her supervisor double teamed him during one session.

Bob more than likely would have benefited from taking an antidepressant. Unfortunately, the therapist's fear-based approach clashed with Bob's false need for control. He was also convinced he would be more likely to relapse if he ingested any type of mood altering drug.

Note: I must reiterate these statements aren't intended to discourage anyone from legitimate drug usage. As I stated, taking an antidepressant was invaluable in stabilizing my mood. What I take strong exception to are physicians who present a mixed-message by purporting to offer help, when the underlying motivation is personal profit.

Rescue Behavior

Many people who are self-sacrificing naturally gravitate to the field of counseling. On the surface, they appear to have noble motives. I unconsciously started playing the savior role during my adolescence.

Due to my empathic nature, I was my mother's rescuer. While I never became directly involved during my father's verbal attacks, I was her sounding board in the aftermath. I was always more than willing to comfort my mom with assurances she wasn't to blame for my father's irrational anger. When we identify with self-deception, assuming the adult role of confidant to a parent seems normal.

I wasn't even aware of the extent to which rescue behavior surfaced in my work until I began to focus on acquiring self-esteem in 2004. Prior to that time, my job involved counseling crime victims of all ages. In hindsight, I understand why I was drawn to female victims of domestic violence. The contexts in which I displayed rescue behavior included giving out my phone number so clients could contact me during times of crisis and even helping them monetarily on rare occasions.

Intellectually, I knew this behavior could foster codependency, but I felt compelled to lead with my emotions. At the time, I was unable to connect this course of action to my adolescent response to my mother.

The unhealthy aspect came into play full force when this enabling pattern took the form of repeated phone calls that weren't crisis related. This often led to sleep deprivation and feelings of exhaustion. Since I had learned it was normal to be more concerned about others, I was in denial about the emotional toll my behavior was exacting on me.

I now understand that, deep down, I didn't feel I was important enough to set healthy boundaries for myself. A professional who possesses self-worth wouldn't fall into this trap.

Rescue behavior occurs any time people make unilateral decisions to help others by imposing their will on them. Anyone who is inclined to save someone from him or herself should stop to consider that external pressure often has the opposite of the desired effect. To be lasting, change normally must be a voluntary internal decision.

Codependent Counseling

The goal of counseling is emotional stability. Whether or not this will be achieved depends on two factors: 1) the teacher must identify with love. 2) the client must be willing to be completely honest.

If you're in denial that you need to change your definition of reality, counseling will be a waste of time. You'll either quickly decide against the process, or you'll unconsciously sabotage a healthy outcome. These extremes occur because your misidentification with self-will prevents you from seeking heartfelt truth.

Codependent personalities who do follow through with treatment use the experience as a means of validating their position of being the injured party. The counseling process turns into a forum for stroking one's ego. These sessions primarily involve the client deflecting attention from inner healing to external events. They point the finger at others to avoid examining the central role their own lack of self-value plays in undermining their happiness.

This addictive relationship evolves from the emotional high a client experiences from his therapist affirming his behaviors. He returns for his reassurance fix whenever he perceives his circumstances to be too stressful. A centered professional would avoid becoming enmeshed in his client's pain-pleasure cycle. Eradicating faulty thought patterns would be emphasized.

The natural appeal of this addiction is understandable. It's certainly much easier to depend on the temporary comfort from your therapist than it is to discipline yourself to respond according to the reality of love. The downside is the longer you delay seeking a permanent spiritual solution, the more likely you are to deteriorate mentally and physically as you age.

I understand all too well how easy it is to unwittingly reinforce false feelings of victimization. That was the course I followed with one of my clients. I now know the value of accepting that most individuals remain trapped in their irreconcilable love and fear mind-set: they claim to want to change the way they think but are too afraid to let go of the status quo.

Carol blamed her faithful husband for her learned need to seek ego gratification from other men. When her paramours' controlling natures eventually surfaced, she redoubled her efforts to gain their approval. When the hostility became intolerable, she played the "helpless victim due to my past" card. Her husband responded on cue by taking her back. She said she was finally ready to change her ways. Shortly after providing two years of counseling, I ran into Carol, with yet another male companion. We only exchanged glances, but her unmistakable look of guilt said it all.

I instinctively knew she had never really been serious about becoming inner-directed. Carol's need for her weekly spiritual fix to offset the pain of the worldly lifestyle she was unwilling to let go had run its course with me. Feel good counseling that affirms the client without subsequent evidence of self-respect—especially to gain repeat business—never works because it isn't based on truth.

In hindsight, the five years I spent in counseling were completely out of proportion to my temperament and learned behavior issues. My counseling experience would have been significantly shortened had I recognized the absolute necessity of resolving my failure mentality.

Familiarity Breeds Addiction

Do you tend to gravitate toward people who don't serve your best interests? Is your communication style keeping you tied to past conduct you grew up hating? Are you so accustomed to feeling mistreated or verbally assaulting others that you're willing to continue to settle for fleeting moments of pleasure until you die?

The reason behind the self-perpetuating nature of these occurrences is basic: a mixed-message belief system deceives us into believing a conflict-filled life is unavoidable. After all, there appears to be no shortage of evidence to confirm we live in a fallen world.

The problem with this viewpoint is it distracts our attention from the all-important question: do you unconsciously choose turmoil, or are you willing to make a conscious effort to be tranquil? The difference lies in reacting based on your conditioning to be judgmental or learning to respond based on instinctively sensing humanity's wholeness.

My religious training depicted the earth as a proving ground of suffering to merit being worthy of one's eternal reward in heaven.

Extolling an earthly reality of joy, peace, and the abundant life was never mentioned.

While it's true everyone experiences ordeals, we don't have to succumb to their false power. We can't fulfill our highest calling to manifest heaven on earth in thought, word, and deed if our reference point is limited to our physical dimension.

Spiritual recovery sensitizes us to the whole(ness) truth we've had inside us all along. The love of our spirit-to-Spirit bond is ever constant. The conditional love of a flesh-driven reality is in a continual state of flux, because it's based on love and fear.

When we're not raised to believe in our inner power, experiencing transcendent spiritual love seems like a lofty goal indeed. But if true love isn't attainable, the Lord's prayer wouldn't contain the instruction, "Thy will be done on earth as it is in heaven."

Perception determines whether life is viewed as awful or awesome. Having a Spirit-led orientation gives us insight to understand earthly trials are necessary to build character. When we're in touch with our divinity, we discover the ability to love in heaven and earth is one and the same. Being attentive to eternity now and forever enables us to accept events beyond our control without gossiping. We supernaturally attract abundance.

An egocentric viewpoint forces us to judge everything that is contrary to our personal expectations. Our fear-controlled reality erroneously convinces us heaven is the exact opposite of the earth. We dismiss the timeless reality of love through nonassertive behaviors we accepted as real during childhood. We naturally attract scarcity.

Lack of self-value prevents us from looking at ourselves too closely. We can't risk receiving confirmation of our own worst fears that we're unlovable. By focusing on everyone else's perceived offenses, we deflect attention from our own need for inner healing. We then compound our self-deception by convincing our support systems to agree with our fear-based opinions.

Gaining sympathy for behaviors that aren't founded on love can only restore short-term balance. No matter how many times we're comforted for being mistreated, our situation never changes for the better because our misery is self-imposed. Denial of our innate wholeness leaves us at the mercy of untrustworthy individual agendas. Seeking relief through external means is doomed to fail. We're literally looking for love in all the wrong places.

If you're not inner-directed, you depend on people for love they don't feel for themselves. When they inevitably disappoint you, you feel justified becoming angry. The very idea that you've been responsible for your happiness since you became an adult doesn't sit well at all with your ever demanding inner child!

An egotistical orientation doesn't allow us to even consider the possibility that we possess a divine nature on earth. When we don't grow up grounded in spiritual truths, who we are now and forever is nearly completely overshadowed by our learned feelings of powerlessness.

Living the abundant life requires a serious reality check. True fulfillment never ensues from controlling or approval based behaviors. Regularly becoming upset by unforeseen events or letting someone else dictate the terms of your life is like saying you want to remain stuck in your childhood, where you had limited or no ability to be honest.

Learning to identify with love, starting with yourself, enables you to evolve to higher levels of consciousness. A mind that is restored to its original state of wholeness isn't governed by conflicting emotions that keep refuting your true identity. Peace flows from discovering the power of God's kingdom within you to ultimately triumph over whatever befalls you in the material realm.

> All things exist simultaneously in the unmanifest
> [Spirit], enfolded, implicit universe, expressing
> itself as the manifest, unfolded, explicit perception
> of form. On the level of nonduality, there's

observing but no observer, as subject and object are one. You and me become the self who experiences all as divine. The "all is" state is one of being: all is consciousness (life, infinite, God), and there are no parts, beginning, or end. The physical body is a manifestation of the self who, in experiencing this dimension, had temporarily forgotten its reality, thus permitting the illusion of a three-dimensional world. The body is merely a means of communication; to identify one's self with the body as I is the fate of the unenlightened, who then erroneously deduce that they're mortal and subject to death. Death itself is an illusion, based on the false identification with the body as I. In nonduality, consciousness experiences itself as both manifest and unmanifest, yet there's no experiencer.[3]

As Dr. David Hawkins's description of spiritual unity suggests, *all pain stems from acting as though God and humanity can ever be separated.* There is no room for fear when you actualize the love that is enclosed within your physical being. Your transitory, conflicting flesh-driven perceptions are transformed into the infinite, unifying joy of your spiritual identity.

A holistic reality heals the lifelong contradiction between what you say and how you really feel. You no longer experience the misery of "laughing on the outside, crying on the inside," because your healed mind consciously *and* subconsciously confirms your completion in thought, word, and deed.

Healing our illusory attachments to self replace our crucifixion mentality with a resurrection mind-set that attracts fulfilling results. The struggle between love and fear-based actions dissolves into nothingness when we heal our misconceptions for one simple reason: love has no opposite in eternity now and forever.

If our bodies are only real in a fleeting earthly context and our spirit is everlasting, then it stands to reason that only our perfect spirit-to-Spirit bond is real. Our imaginary mental battlefield has always been God's will versus self-deception. God's will is real. Self-deception is based on half-truths that are widely considered to be real.

If you're finally tired of accepting the instability of an oppositional belief system, identifying with the love within you restores your peace of mind. Heaven and earth simultaneously become the same reality when needless **F**alse **E**vidence **A**ppearing **R**eal is exposed as the source of all torment. Simply stated, believing in the false power of fear prevents us from recognizing the oneness of love that surrounds us in the parallel universe of heaven *now.*

Mixed-Message Religion

Of all the roadblocks to inner peace, religious teachings are right at the top of the list. There are nearly as many doctrines about the correct way to be spiritual as there are religions. On the one hand are Christians who profess to have been set free to love by the blood of Christ. In reality, they live in bondage to self-condemnation. On the other hand of self-hatred, are Islamic radicals. They believe the way to salvation is through the bloodshed of others, as evidenced by the 9/11 catastrophe.

Growing up with arbitrary theologies is troubling, to say the least. Most religions preach the universal message of love. Joel Osteen is a humble, passionate minister. He stresses the importance of rising above fear-based thought patterns to experience the victorious life God intended. His televised, packed stadium broadcasts have aptly earned him the title "America's preacher."

Problems arise when the freedom of resurrection teachings are weakened with the bondage of crucifixion messages. I've heard evangelists consistently convey these themes: "No one deserves to go to heaven," "grace is more than we deserve," and "God loves you in spite of who you are." A child who heard his parents state that they loved him, despite who he is, would naturally feel discouraged. In much the same way, adults who didn't feel valued as children relate to these interpretations of how God views them as being "damned by faint praise."

When we don't comprehend the long-term damage of mixed-message communication, our best intentions to proclaim the salvation message can have the opposite effect. A person who grows up with an inferiority complex processes his faults from a fear-bound perspective.

Even when the shift from love to fear is visual, the impact on one's thinking is still the same. Instead of portraying a resurrected Christ, many churches feature a depiction of Jesus on a cross, not to mention the cross jewelry in general. I've never seen a necklace with Christ in resurrected form. A crucifixion fixation can result in one languishing in a guilt-ridden mind-set.

Until you learn to love who you are, you won't be able to think of yourself as being one with God. Even your unselfish actions won't ring true. Without self-worth, you subconsciously perform good deeds in the hope of gaining God's favor. A friend of mine represents how feelings of inadequacy can negate a resurrection mentality. Amanda and Paul were childhood sweethearts. Aside from the expected differences of opinion, their concern for each other is genuine. They are devout Christians who have played pivotal roles in their church's efforts to serve the poor for nearly twenty years. Their caring teenage daughters are actively involved as well. From all appearances, Amanda and Paul are living the American dream: stable marriage and family life, well-paying jobs, and savings for their retirement. And yet, Amanda suffers from recurring bouts of depression.

She had grown up believing fulfillment would ensue from attending to the needs of others. After a lifetime of pursuing this goal, Amanda confessed that she had to be doing something wrong to still be feeling so empty inside.

These stories are commonplace from people who thought making the right external moves would provide more than short-term satisfaction. They demonstrate the pressing need for inner healing to counter the lifelong damage caused by a mixed-message belief system. No matter how much time we spend helping others, we won't be empowered to identify with the peace of God's Spirit if childhood fears aren't eradicated.

The ability to impart wholeness thinking to a congregation depends on whether a minister's spiritual insight is superficial or subconscious, regardless of his command of the Bible. This conduct is evidenced by consistent assertive behaviors, commonly referred to as "walking the walk."

Freedom or Legalism?

Attending church services to be in compliance with religious training is the flip side of being controlled by worldly desires. It's easy enough to convince yourself you're doing the right thing based on appearances. But if your underlying motivation to express your piety is related in any way to feelings of guilt or fear of retribution, you're actually conforming to the constraints of legalism.

Our denial can be so strong that pastors and parishioners alike will claim to reject rigid rule thinking, even in the face of overwhelming evidence that this judgmental practice continues unchecked. Until you believe love defines who you are, you'll continue to feel disheartened. Humanity's only real dilemma is a conflicted mind that primarily finds expression through fear-driven behaviors. The following two experiences from my early twenties illustrate how easy it can be to confuse religious rules with an authentic spiritual lifestyle.

I was never encouraged to read the Bible. I grew up believing the interpretation of God's Word was best left up to the clergy. As an adult, I sought relief from my anxiety and depression by watching television evangelists. They stressed the importance of immersing oneself in the Word daily. I subsequently read through the Old and New Testaments in their entirety. This act of overcompensation didn't result in peace of mind, because I was still identifying with fear. Unaware of my true motivation, I turned to the opposite extreme and stopped reading the Bible altogether.

I didn't make any real progress eliminating my fears by reading the Bible, because I lacked spiritual discernment. I had to subconsciously resolve my failure mentality by changing how I viewed my relationship to God.

Today, I stay centered with love-affirming thoughts and scriptures that automatically come to mind. My top priority is to keep the lines of my spirit-to-Spirit communication open by paying close attention to my conscience. Throughout the day, I thank God for my blessings. Whenever stressful events try to command my attention, I silently repeat "spirit … love … peace" to concentrate on my true identity.

I also have Galatians 5:22–23 posted on my refrigerator. I use this convenient fruit of the Spirit reminder to counter my tendency to dwell on the negative energy of a misguided world. When you become transparent, you lose your conditioned fear of being judged unredeemable for not abiding by religious rules.

My second example involves a clerk in a health food store. She asked if I was willing to receive Jesus to live in my heart. After I responded affirmatively and she prayed, she jotted down the day's date. She excitedly pronounced me to be saved. She then handed me the paper as a reminder of the day I had been reborn to enter the kingdom of heaven.

I clearly remember not understanding why she was being so dramatic. My attitude was still the same. The clerk's enthusiasm didn't have the power to do what spiritual recovery demands of all of us: learn to identify with the love within us to genuinely heed the dictates of the Spirit of truth, instead of the duplicity of our egos.

John 3:3 states, in part: "Unless one is born again, he cannot see the kingdom of God." The intended meaning of this scripture is often diverted from restoring one's mind to wholeness thoughts to conforming to arbitrary criteria. Religions variously equate being born again with making a statement of faith, baptism, speaking in tongues, being attired in a particular way, etc. 1 Corinthians 2:16 addresses the necessity of an inward focus: "But we have the mind of Christ."

Many people find comfort in regular church attendance and reading the Bible. But external actions alone won't normally ease inner turmoil. Without healing our learned schizophrenic identification with love and fear, we unconsciously undermine our true identity through nonassertive behaviors.

Since the location of the kingdom of God is plainly stated to be "within you" (Luke 17:21), the "born again" reference cited in John 3:3 logically refers to spiritual rebirth—that is, a mental identification with one's spirit-to-Spirit union as opposed to viewing oneself solely as a physical being.

Spiritual discernment is essential to inner peace. When we're flesh-driven, we mainly pay attention to expanding our fleeting earthly "kingdoms." We associate happiness with what we personally consider to be favorable circumstances. Consequently, we criticize whatever doesn't line up with our subjective versions of reality.

When we identify with the love within us, we concentrate on expanding God's eternal kingdom. Our intuitive understanding of humanity's oneness fortifies us to endure offenses with dignity. From this transcendent level of consciousness, we refrain from judgmental attitudes.

A Christian who claims to be born again, while still mired in fear-driven conduct, has no awareness that he is contradicting himself. Mixed-messages are entrenched as his comfort zone.

Jen is largely responsible for the efficiency of her department at work. She is conscientious, well organized, and dedicated. Jen has always been openly critical of her supervisor, Bill, as well as many others. She frequently clashes with Bill over staffing issues. She reports that he brushes off her valid complaints. On several occasions, she has bypassed Bill by going to his supervisor.

Like many Christians, Jen's primary focus is on avoiding hell. She believes in the practice of informing people that getting saved gains them entry to heaven. Like the clerk I had encountered in my twenties, Jen eagerly witnesses to misguided followers of self-will. When Bill developed a serious illness, Jen immediately took the opportunity to convince him to accept Christ as his Savior. She also demonstrated many acts of kindness to express her concern for his well-being.

Jen's overall actions certainly don't match her claim to be saved. She doesn't comprehend the fear-rooted nature of her behavior. She grew up depending on the false power of aggressive and passive-aggressive communication for her survival.

It's natural to be sympathetic when someone like Bill is in a vulnerable physical and mental state. If Jen was a true follower of Christ, she would react assertively even when she isn't treated with respect.

An eternity perspective removes the blockade of anxiety that prevents you from recognizing our Creator has never been apart from His creations. You no longer take it personally when your legitimate concerns are ignored. You experience a paradigm shift from angrily judging the flaws of human nature to becoming calmly mindful of everyone's divine nature.

As well-meaning as Jen is, until she effects inner healing, there is no difference between her and the person who never makes a declaration of faith. Both are self-deceived. Being set free by the truth occurs when one's timeless identity of love isn't regularly opposed by behaviors that revolve around subconscious attempts to gain control and approval. Simply stated, a person who is spiritually reborn has died to the judgmental response patterns of his childhood.

Self-Esteem versus Self-Deception

After providing instruction that the greatest of all the commandments is to "love the Lord your God," Mark 12:31 states, "You shall love your neighbor as yourself. There is no other commandment greater than these."

This mandate to love God and others is logically impossible if you don't first love yourself. And yet, the vital role self-acceptance plays in determining one's emotional stability continues to be misunderstood. During my childhood, sermons that evoked guilt and shame were never in short supply. Messages about self-respect were nonexistent.

If I'm subjected to non-assertive language as a child, I automatically identify with my deficiencies. Since I don't feel loved by my parents, I won't be likely to trust God. The conflicting love and fear religious messages that are preached reinforce my underlying belief that I don't count. Renewing my mind with daily affirmations about my true essence helps counteract the misconceptions I internalized during my childhood.

Those who are trained in theology tend to equate any mention of self with sin. This characterization has more to do with semantics than truth. Self-will refers to conduct that denotes undisciplined actions. Self-esteem represents the healthy expression of one's ego.

When fear-rooted beliefs are perceived to be real, it feels completely natural to focus on good and evil. But the very fact that Adam and Eve were warned to steer clear "of the tree of the knowledge of good and evil" underscores the harm that ensues from a belief system founded on incompatible forces.

Fear darkens our thoughts. We aren't receptive to spiritual wisdom. If I'm unfamiliar with Mark 12:31, which tells me to love myself, and all too familiar with scriptures like Isaiah 64:6— "But we are all like an unclean thing, and all our righteousnesses are like filthy rags"—I'll more than likely identify with the disheartening verse. Likewise, gospel songs abound that alternate between resurrection and crucifixion messages. Their well-meaning themes illustrate how easily a love-fear correlation can keep us bound to guilt and shame.

In America, religions teach people from a young age that self-will represents the lust of the flesh. Combined with being conditioned to associate our mind solely with our bodies, we grow up completely unaware that we suffer from a serious spiritual deficit. We don't naturally demonstrate the wholeness of love that emanates from our perfect spirit-to-Spirit bond. Our misidentification with fear creates false separation anxiety. Deep-seated feelings of insecurity are mistaken for a façade of superiority. In reality, people who appear to be full of pride are self-deceived. They are unconsciously covering up for the scared, stuck children within they never outgrew.

In the imaginary battle we learned to wage between love and fear, our perceptions are based on superficial judgments. Flesh-driven viewpoints automatically perceive arrogance. When we hone our spiritual insight, we sadly see the seemingly impenetrable walls of self-hatred that govern fear-driven behaviors.

A popular television evangelist characterized the discrepancy between his public image and his personal angst. He grew up with childhood abandonment issues. He candidly recounted a revealing comment he made thirty years ago. From all appearances, he seemed to be the personification of love. He was blessed with a great wife and family, and large crowds flocked to his speaking engagements. When one of his followers asked when he found the time to pray, he replied, "You pray, I preach."

After realizing the condescending nature of this statement, he confessed to his wife that the confidence he displayed was a far cry from how he really felt. No matter how convincing our words may be, our underlying fears tell very different stories. When we aren't taught to believe we're whole by centered role models, self-deception convinces us that we're unworthy of love.

A more telling example can be found in the sexual abuse scandal involving the Catholic priesthood. Anyone—much less members of the clergy—who truly loves himself never would have been able to betray the trust of innocent children in such a shocking manner. This deviant behavior was clearly the result of self-rejection misdirected onto helpless victims.

Pastors who disagree about the necessity of advocating a healthy self-image reveal the deep-rooted nature of denial. I was also guilty of falling into this trap. Being a counselor didn't afford me the advantage of surrendering my faulty core beliefs in a timely fashion. As explained in the prologue, I had convinced myself I was a faithful Christian through external acts of spirituality. I went through a two-year period filled with ordeals, before I barely started to grasp that my inferiority complex was responsible for my depression. Simply stated, when you learn to love who you are, the spiritual insights that ensue over time transform your life.

People commonly confuse counterfeit self-esteem that is derived from ego gratification for lasting self-worth that can only come from within. It's routine for men and especially women who don't feel good about themselves to link their value to worldly standards of what constitutes an ideal body shape, facial appearance, lifestyle, etc. Some advertisers try to sell products by equating self-esteem with such diverse external factors as teeth whitening products and home ownership. Or people will talk about how their insecurities skyrocketed after they broke up with a loved one or suffered a job loss.

In reality, a person who is confident from the inside out remains secure, regardless of what transpires. The Apostle Paul is a prime example. Although he was shipwrecked, stoned, beaten multiple times, and imprisoned, Paul's faith was steadfast.

Regardless of how difficult you perceive your circumstances to be, a spiritual point of view instinctively draws your attention to your true power. As Luke 17:20–21 proclaims: "The kingdom of God does not come with observation; For indeed the kingdom of God is within you."

Fear or Faith?

Learning to view yourself as a timeless spirit who briefly functions as a physical being frees you from the debilitating nature of a purely flesh-driven existence. When you grow up self-deceived, you're unaware that routinely becoming agitated by unexpected events contradicts your true identity. What starts out as a minor hairline fracture in your thinking gradually evolves into a major rupture in your thought patterns over decades.

Eventually, a mind that is conditioned to believe love and fear can coexist can produce feelings of hopelessness. Destructive behaviors that lead to death through unnecessary illnesses, accidents, murder, and suicide regularly occur.

A good analogy is a commercial that aired years ago depicting the difference between a stable mind-set and a drug-abused mind. As a whole egg was revealed, the announcer intoned, "This is your brain." The next segment depicted an egg being fried in a skillet. The announcer tersely stated, "This is your brain on drugs."

The spiritual version of this commercial would feature the same visuals, but with two modified pronouncements. First, the whole egg display: "This is your brain heeding God's will."

Then, the fried egg presentation: "This is your brain deluded by self-will."

Like the vast majority, I wasn't raised to function on a higher, spiritual level of consciousness. As a young adult, I couldn't imagine how much needless pain my misidentification with self would generate throughout my life. The abundant life God intended humanity to enjoy normally isn't fulfilled on earth or is delayed for many years.

The biblical story of Joseph, who was destined for greatness, illustrates exactly how high a price we pay when we deny our oneness. When Joseph was seventeen, he had a dream about his amazing future. The problem was he just couldn't wait to boast about it to his jealous brothers. He told them he saw them one day bowing down to him.

Predictably, Joseph's vision was met with scorn. His ego blindsided him to the folly of bragging. Christians are familiar with the consequences Joseph suffered for his unbridled brashness. He did eventually rise to power as he had predicted. Joseph was appointed second-in-command to Pharaoh when he was thirty-years old.

But his rise to fame was anything but meteoric. In the time between his dreams and their actual fulfillment, Joseph had to endure severe hardships. His brothers initially threw him into a pit. He was eventually sold into slavery. He was falsely accused of attempted rape. He spent many hard years in prison.

Joseph easily could have railed against God during the thirteen years it took him to ascend from the pit to the palace. Most people don't suffer through experiences that are nearly as devastating. And yet, failing to comprehend humanity's eternity connection to God is a universal problem that has worsened throughout history.

Joseph's naïveté led him down a path he hadn't intended to take. But, more importantly, he didn't try to blame anyone for his mistakes. Instead of wallowing in his misery, he never gave up hope that God would deliver him. He even forgave his brothers for their treachery when they did indeed bow down before him after he rose to power.

We can't be genuine without faith in our true identity. Had Joseph succeeded without the benefit of his eye-opening trials, the outcome would have been entirely different. He wouldn't have developed the character that is necessary to sustain a leadership role long-term.

Likewise, the seemingly impossible hardships we must endure to mature are designed to produce our greatest victories—providing we don't succumb to self-pity. Habitually complaining is like saying we prefer to identify with our unfavorable circumstances.

A moth keeps drawing nearer and nearer to the flame that eventually kills it. In much the same way, believing in fear can turn into tragic endings unless we humble ourselves to draw closer and closer to God's Spirit within.

A spiritual orientation grounds us in the power of the present. We no longer become upset by events that have absolutely no meaning from a love-based standpoint. One of life's biggest illusions is thinking we must be in charge to be happy. Without insight to respond in agreement with our divinity, it's easy to conclude that trying to control life's outcomes is more important than developing self-control. We're mistakenly convinced that by living on our own terms we'll avoid the unhappiness we felt growing up.

On a subconscious level, we liken God's authority to the oppressive nature of aggressive parenting. The opposite is true. Children who are raised in an atmosphere of hostility identify with anxiety. Recognizing God's will is humanity's will produces peace.

Overreacting to conduct that triggers painful memories is a difficult habit to break. Telling someone off produces a heady sense of power. Due to its short-lived duration, we have to keep repeating this toxic behavior to obtain our control fix whenever we feel threatened.

In reality, losing control of our emotions is a sure sign of weakness. When we develop a compulsive need to exercise undue influence, we're really playing God with one huge difference: our actions aren't inspired by unconditional love.

Our misconstrued reality becomes thoughts and actions that defy logic. We don't view ourselves as controlling in a pejorative sense. Self-deception convinces us we're right. The ongoing stress of believing in both love and fear forces us to make mountains out of molehills, followed by seeking fleeting relief in external remedies.

Are you finally tired of feeling defeated by your dual belief system? If you're ready to trade in your fear-minded attitude for the whole(ness) truth, it's time to simplify the meaning of love.

CHAPTER 4

The Facts of Love

We live in a fantasy world, a world of illusion.
The great task in life is to find reality.
—Iris Murdoch

I f I said all negative energy such as anxiety, depression, hostility, guilt, etc., doesn't exist in the present, you would more than likely tell me I'm wrong or crazy. After all, you've undoubtedly experienced these emotions firsthand. The overlooked truth is these feelings are only real to you due to a learned belief in fear.

Most people are aware of the fight or flight response. Excess adrenaline and cortisol swarms into the bloodstream to enhance one's reaction to a perceived threat. When we grow up believing it's normal to overreact and underreact to fear-based stimuli, the chemicals these response patterns release have toxic effects over time that undermine our health.

Throughout my childhood, my father's lack of self-control never posed an actual physical threat; but to a little girl who was overly sensitive, his outbursts were destabilizing. When my father raged at my mother, my stress level increased in direct proportion to how dangerous I perceived the situation would become.

This dynamic, combined with my mother's fretful nature, predisposed me to anxiety. As an adult, I was capable of reacting rationally to stressors. Unfortunately, I had no idea my personality and learned behavior had ensnared me in the fear-minded reality of my childhood.

Like the vast majority, my well-meaning parents didn't identify with their inner power. Their moods were determined by their circumstances. I wanted to believe I'm a timeless spirit housed in a temporary body the few times I had heard variations of this eternity message. But living by faith seemed more like an unattainable ideal than a practical pathway to peace.

I would admit to being a Christian without realizing my actions confirmed my thinking was closer to an atheist's viewpoint. I knew I lacked self-worth, but I had no idea I was contradicting my belief in God by allowing fear-bound emotions to dictate my conduct.

My faulty behaviors were neither outrageous nor illegal. I tried at various times to gain some semblance of control and approval by becoming argumentative and perfectionistic, repressing my feelings, procrastinating, excelling in school, biting my nails and cuticles, picking at my scalp, financial mismanagement, and eating junk food. Nevertheless, I was just as out of touch with reality as those who commit crimes.

Life ends up having no real meaning for people who don't discover they are eternally complete. A fear-driven mind-set believes life ends at death or fixates on the devil and hell. Separation anxiety deceives those who are ruled by fear into viewing God as remote and condemning. The unconscious thought process is, *I'd rather depend on those I can see and material objects I can possess for fulfillment.*

This shortsighted premise sets us up for failure. Happiness becomes associated with unpredictable people, places, and things or on trying to fulfill others' insatiable egocentric wishes. When God's will to achieve the common good isn't our primary motivation, mental and physical diseases are rampant.

Serious health problems can develop when core beliefs aren't founded wholly on love. My feelings of failure resulted in a two-month hospitalization for a nervous breakdown when I was twenty-two years old.

Even though I appeared to be emotionally stable when I was discharged, fear was still in charge. My anxiety was smoldering beneath my calm exterior.

While I had mentally and physically recovered, my spiritual recovery was sorely lacking. Inner power was a foreign concept.

It wasn't until decades later, when I became serious about pursuing higher levels of consciousness, that I finally discovered my contentment isn't dependent on tangible factors. My transformation from misidentifying with self to a wholeness vantage point freed me to maintain a state of calmness, even during the most demanding period of my life. Simply stated, love grounds you in supernatural peace that defies mere human understanding.

Childlike or Childish?

Love that is childlike is expressed simply without pretense. Unlike self-centered and self-denial patterns that typify dishonest communication, a childlike quality denotes playful innocence. It mimics the response of little ones who have no compunction about running into the open arms of a cherished relative.

This trusting reaction is the way we would relate to each other if our belief system wasn't marred by feelings of unworthiness. We wouldn't be encumbered by thoughts of being separated from a distant God or condemned by a punishing God.

A fear-controlled reality results in being too trusting of others or acting generally mistrustful. Those who are passive are often referred to as pushovers due to their compulsive need for approval, while aggressive and passive-aggressive individuals are described as untrustworthy due to their unquenchable need for control.

We subconsciously cling to nonassertive response patterns in the false hope of avoiding the rejection we felt growing up. Unfortunately, the very thing we fear often ends up occurring.

Self-hate ultimately takes its toll on our health mentally, physically, and spiritually unless we make every effort to demonstrate childlike love.

We can't comprehend that the endless nature of God's grace opens up to us if we don't discover that love originates from within us. "Assuredly, I say to you, whoever does not receive the kingdom of God as a little child will by no means enter it" (Mark 10:15). Simply stated, you won't experience heaven on earth through peace of mind until you develop innocence to trust the promptings of the Spirit of truth.

A mature adult has endearing, childlike qualities. An immature adult behaves childishly. He never learned the value of modeling the fruit of the Spirit; particularly self-control. Without spiritual discernment, our perceived powerlessness causes us to become irritated or depressed by circumstances beyond our control.

Eliminating your inferiority complex is essential to your well-being. When you understand love has always defined you, the stranglehold of fear that has kept you from fulfilling your divine destiny will be broken. Lifelong disheartening actions will be replaced with adult or childlike expressions of heartfelt love.

Subduing the Whirlwind

When we aren't taught to develop our sixth sense to live by faith, we tend to mimic our role models' oppositional attitudes. Learning to rely on our true power within cues us to remain calm during most stressful situations. We either respond assertively or we ignore fear-minded conduct, while insulating ourselves with uplifting thoughts.

Learning to appreciate who you are dispels negative energy patterns that aren't real in the context of eternity now and forever. You intuitively understand that love defines humankind, despite worldly evidence that suggests most people remain stuck in their childhood pain. You regard everyone else's opinion of you as secondary to the serenity you gain from being attentive to the still small voice. Peace of mind will start to become familiar as you learn to detach from the chaos that had defined most of your interactions. You'll compassionately extend forgiveness that isn't based on how others act.

When our attention shifts from self-centered to wholeness thoughts, our attitudes undergo an extreme makeover. We no longer feel compelled to personalize behaviors that are indicative of lack of self-worth. I couldn't believe how much better I felt when spiritual recovery freed me from my defensive response patterns.

Searching for love in the world that has always been inside you in the formlessness of your perfect spirit reduces you to a false existence. John Nash's schizophrenia trapped him in a delusional world until he healed his divided mind; the same is true of everyone's learned schizophrenia.

Fear represents the denial of your eternal identity through nonassertive behaviors that can hasten your physical demise. If a genetic illness can be overcome, then surely there can be no greater motivation than reclaiming heaven on earth as an irresistible incentive to become led by the Spirit.

As the great, "I am," God's power can only be accessed in the present. When you don't communicate assertively, you contradict the only truth that has eternal value: you are love because His perfect love dwells within you. When you discipline yourself to heed the directives of your conscience, peaceful exchanges become more familiar than the conflicts you grew up mistakenly believing were inevitable.

The following illustration portrays the stark contrast between a divisive mentality and a wholeness mindset:

Adult/Child Persona

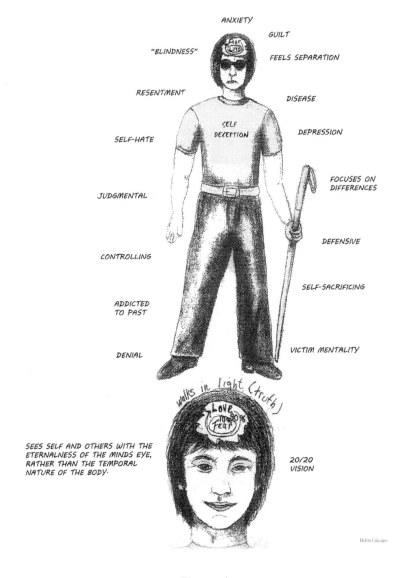

Figure 1

I had explained to the artist that I needed two depictions representing love and fear. I anticipated receiving two separate renderings. When she handed me a single page, I immediately knew her concept was exactly the way my message was intended to be conveyed.

The man represents spiritual blindness. We can't function at our peak performance when our mind, bodies, and spirit aren't in sync. The significance of the headshot becomes clear if you equate love with humanity's mind joined with God's Mind.

To increase your understanding of the deceptive nature of a mixed-message belief system, it's important to examine two of the most common manifestations of fear that most people grew up equating with love: guilt and sacrifice.

Guilt

There is no room for guilt in true love. But you likely can recall times when you have tried to make someone you professed to love feel guilty; as well as when you've been on the receiving end of this control tactic.

The degree of guilt a person experiences is based on a fear-driven temperament and learned behavior. Vulnerability to these feelings ranges from a complete absence, resulting in murder without remorse, to an overwhelming presence, leading to suicide. The common denominator for the vast majority who suffer from guilt is punishment. The variable factor is the amount of time that is spent chastising oneself or others. This fear-rooted pattern is so pervasive that most people are unaware their lives are governed by guilt.

You may protest guilt is necessary to convince those who engage in self-serving actions to change their ways. The opposite is true. Inducing guilt can intensify feelings of failure. An inferiority complex and guilt go hand in hand.

Let's assume you learned to take comfort in material objects after you were shamed during your formative years. As an adult, this pattern has escalated. Your partner becomes irate because you exceeded your credit limit again. Instead of being motivated by guilt to stop this compulsive behavior, you react the opposite way. Your partner's angry reaction (which reminds you of your childhood) cues you to temporarily alleviate your accompanying anxiety with yet another shopping fix. Guilt leaves us with one of three fear-based options:

1. denial, in order to maintain our false comfort zones
2. rationalization, in hopes of lessening the consequences
3. admission, with an attachment to self-loathing

If you were inner-directed, you wouldn't feel guilty; you would simply take corrective action. With an eternity mind-set, you instinctively know love defines who you are, whether or not you inadvertently engage in egocentric behaviors.

While you still must suffer the natural consequences of your actions, you don't feel condemned. There would be no need for guilt for two reasons: you accept full responsibility for your conduct, and you're free from the fear that you internalized during childhood.

A wholeness perspective not only releases you from guilt, it also enables you to set everyone else free. This is a supernatural outgrowth. To judge someone as guilty, you first had to be taught to perceive guilt in yourself. A closer look at relationships that revolve around one's performance reveals how this dynamic unfolds.

Guilt reigns when we grow up with critical comments being much more familiar than assertive response patterns. Feelings of inadequacy originate from trying to conform to subjective standards that can never be satisfied. A temporal mind-set forces us to judge practically everyone and everything—including ourselves—as being wrong. Love is sacrificed for self-righteous and self-abasing actions.

Most of us identify with our weaknesses. When we aren't taught our true power comes from within, we have no idea that our exclusive external focus is the real source of our misery. A worldly point of view creates an insatiable need for outside reassurance. Our egocentric perspective either causes us to be manipulated through guilt or we try to make others feel guilty when we don't get our way.

Judy's mother made repeated accusations that she never spent enough time with her. Three years after her mother died in her mid-eighties, Judy continued to express regret that she would still be alive if only she had been more attentive. Judy's denial was so entrenched she was unable to make the connection between her guilt and her learned behavior. This example illustrates the power fear-controlled emotions have to dominate us even from the grave.

In codependent marriages, spouses resort to guilt tactics that often involve periodic threats to leave. The fear of being alone usually prevents this outcome from materializing. What both parties don't realize is their misidentification with self already makes them feel more alone than any physical separation ever could.

Guilt thrives when you don't emulate your divine nature through respectful behaviors. You remain rooted in the past, where you learned to believe you're not good enough. Restoring your mind to wholeness thoughts keeps you attuned to your true power in the present. Your relationships aren't contaminated by guilt. When an internal script of love and peace guides your behavior, you don't personalize mistreatment.

Liz and I have been friends for more than thirty years. At the beginning of our friendship, I was ready to call it quits. Liz is a workaholic like her parents. She learned to feel guilty if she doesn't stay busy. Long before she was married and had five children, Liz barely found time for me. Aware of her conditioning, I was understanding until she missed my very first speaking engagement. I had really counted on having a familiar face in the room. Despite her promise to attend, Liz never showed up.

That was the final straw. My inner child refused to return her calls. I wrote her a letter detailing her lack of consideration for my feelings. The next thing I knew, Liz's sister was on my doorstep pleading her case. I agreed to meet with Liz. But I avoided telling her I was glad my guilt trip had worked. In my fear-minded past, I was convinced Liz deserved to be treated the same way she had treated me. I was basking in the false sense of satisfaction I felt over being the one in control.

I didn't realize back then that our behaviors demonstrated lack of self-respect. People who are centered don't get upset by fear-rooted actions that aren't real from a spiritual viewpoint. Cultivating a holistic approach to life dramatically changes your attitude. You understand the necessity of refusing to allow minor matters to steal your peace of mind.

After we resumed our friendship, there weren't any signs that anything was amiss until recently. The year 2012 was marred for me by excruciating losses. In addition to the Holy Spirit's comforting Presence, I had an amazing support system—minus Liz. Christmas and my birthday occurred within a few months of my most recent devastating loss. On both occasions, Liz was once again a no-show. Even though she now was juggling the needs of her grandchildren and ailing father, Liz had always been available on special occasions.

Liz set up dates for us to get together that never materialized. As if on cue, I stopped responding. But this time I was mindful of my spirituality. I didn't want to re-enact the drama that had transpired when we were young.

Liz has never resolved her feelings of inadequacy. She is performance oriented. She learned to associate her worthiness with how much she does for others. Despite developing serious health issues and being repeatedly taken advantage of, Liz's fear-controlled reality compels her to overextend herself.

I had planned to calmly inform her there was no point in making plans in the foreseeable future. The next time Liz called, I was going to cite her overloaded schedule as my reason for suggesting we go our separate ways. As time passed, I was unable to shake the gnawing feeling that I was kidding myself. I knew deep down that even my subdued reaction would make her feel guilty, because she isn't Spirit-minded. Like most people, Liz equates the need for spiritual recovery with those who abuse drugs.

When Liz did contact me, I accepted her latest invitation without any judgmental commentary. God had granted me an opportunity to right a thirty-year wrong. Even though I didn't want to let her off the hook so easily, I knew it was the only honest way to respond.

People who are in touch with their divine nature forgive even when they don't feel like it. An eternity perspective frees you from faulty personal perceptions. If you can behave assertively—even when everyone around you is entrenched in fear-driven conduct—then you understand the true meaning of love.

Self-acceptance is an effective antidote to guilt. You won't be able to comprehend your everlasting value to God without dispelling your feelings of failure. Your childhood victim mentality will keep resurfacing to cause you to experience guilt or blame your circumstances for your unhappiness until you're ready to surrender your untenable love and fear belief system.

When we make a committed effort to respond knowing *only love is real,* nonassertive behaviors no longer trigger painful memories from the past. When we capitalize on our internal power, our false need for control and approval dissipates.

To facilitate understanding of the spiritual recovery process, think of self-will as representing your childhood tendency to never be satisfied. Your adult desires flow from following direction from God's Spirit with your whole heart and soul.

Sacrifice

Sacrifice and the ultimate act of love it represents are inextricably linked in the minds of most Christians. As a natural extension, this concept has been taught as being necessary to leading a Godly life.

A closer examination reveals the fear-bound nature of this dogma for one important reason: sacrifice made from a human standpoint involves guilt. One needs to look no further than the Bible for confirmation. There are countless references to animal sacrifices offered as atonement for sins.

Sacrificial behaviors are normally fear-rooted. The underlying motivation is to gain counterfeit self-esteem through others' approval or by controlling others. The subconscious thought process is, *I did this to please you, and now I expect you to make me happy in return.* Focusing on what we do for others reveals lack of insight to appreciate who we all are from a wholeness orientation.

Marge never had children. She doted on her sister's son, Jason. Karen wasn't nearly as financially well off as Marge. When Karen ran short, she always counted on her sister to bail out her family. Marge had been conditioned to assume the mother role after their mom died. She would scold Karen for being irresponsible, just like their mother did. But she never adhered to appropriate boundaries. As Jason grew, so did his demands on his aunt. Finally, after Marge lost a substantial amount of money in the stock market, she was forced to significantly curtail her support. Both Karen and Jason became indignant. Marge was devastated. She couldn't believe her family would turn on her after how generous she had been.

Marge was unaware she had set herself up to feel victimized. The whole truth is her expectations were unrealistic. Karen and Jason were just naturally following their temperaments and learned behaviors. Marge unconsciously taught her sister and nephew to define love according to how much money she spent on them. If Marge had concentrated on overcoming her false feelings of inadequacy, she never would have felt the need to buy their love to feel good about herself.

When we learn to identify with intrinsic values like self-respect and self-control, we readily admit that doing favors with strings attached is more self-serving than sacrificial. Those who are love-based don't need others to comply with their personal desires to be happy. They freely give without expecting anything in return.

If your underlying motive in helping others is to get something in return or to stay in God's good graces, you'll never be happy. Your attention is on your personal performance instead of on humanity's oneness. True love is based on reacting assertively, regardless of how many people try your patience.

We can't stay focused on the present until we move beyond the contradictions we accepted as normal during our childhoods. Discovering that love originates from within frees us to understand there is nothing we can say or do that can ever alter our relationship with God.

No matter how many personal sacrifices you make for those who are controlled by fear, it will never be enough, because the ego can never be satisfied. You may feel good in the moment but you'll be doing more harm than good in the long-term.

When we unconsciously encourage others to depend on us instead of their inner power, we keep them emotionally stuck in childhood. We can't grow spiritually strong as long as we allow ourselves to be governed by feelings of powerlessness.

My former tendency to take calls from my clients on my personal time (to subconsciously confirm my value as a counselor) illustrates the no win nature of a false attachment to self. Not only did the codependency involved hinder their progress, my identification with fear caused me to feel guilty if I missed their calls in my off-work hours.

It's easy to go overboard when we grow up without recognizing how crucial a spiritual perspective is to maintaining good health. Even at age ninety, my mother was one of the most selfless people I've ever known. Her devotion to her family knew no bounds. In 2003, Mom fractured her ankle and was confined to a nursing home for two months. I felt compelled to spend nearly all of my free time by her side, in much the same way that she had always been attentive to me. This routine continued until I was able to make the connection between my mother's past sacrificial stance and my guilt ridden need to respond in kind, regardless of my own health considerations.

Needless sacrificing is often prevalent in marriages. The partner who continually gives in is taken advantage of by the mate who is never appreciative. Without self-esteem to connect with their innate oneness, couples quickly become disenchanted from expecting to find fulfillment through each other.

Eliminating conflicting love-fear ideations empowers you to be genuine. You don't view yourself as both saved and sinful. You recognize your deficiencies don't define you. Your confidence in your perfect spirit-to-Spirit union equips you to fulfill your purpose to love.

I believe the most compelling reason against performing sacrificial acts is found in Matthew 9:13. Jesus himself rebuked the Pharisees in this scripture for concentrating on outward ritualistic aspects that don't convey God's heartfelt intention: "But go and learn what this means: 'I desire mercy and *not* sacrifice'" (emphasis mine).

Fear-Rooted Christianity

The ultimate contradiction involves the crucifixion and resurrection. People who function with a corresponding fear and love reality identify with fear. Humanity's mind is designed to thrive on fruit of the Spirit thoughts of love, peace, joy, faithfulness, etc. A mixed-message mentality prevents us from discerning the whole(ness) truth. Proclaiming redemptive messages along with those that communicate dire consequences cancel out the uplifting language. Childhood guilt and shame are reinforced throughout adulthood. When we aren't born with assertive temperaments, we associate our value with the input we receive from fear-minded role models. The end result is that we live with a crucifixion mind-set, which ranges from the drama of self-righteous anger to the despair of self-condemnation.

The egocentric self becomes synonymous with a poverty mentality that leaves us feeling alone and lacking. Our limited reference point deceives us into thinking worldly or external spiritual solutions will restore balance.

Preoccupation with the past through painful relationships convinces me defensive or repressed measures are necessary whenever I feel threatened. Fear-bound conditioning prevents me from accessing the unlimited power of my spirit-to-Spirit bond.

A spiritual identity problem logically requires healing on a subconscious level for suffering to be alleviated. A self-will orientation keeps us from identifying with the source of our dissatisfaction: the denial of love that ensues from an inconsistent belief system. Life will always seem unfair if we keep focusing on wrongdoing. It can't be any other way, because we were created to act as righteous extensions of God's grace.

When we aren't raised to identify with our divine nature, we lose touch with reality. We automatically feel powerless, because our attention is on our ever changing circumstances instead of on our changeless God.

When we only associate our mind with our bodies, being led by the Spirit has superficial meaning at best. Without healing our childhood fears, we place our trust in personal perceptions that aren't based on unconditional love. Ego gratification patterns that are only significant in a fleeting worldly setting become our top priorities.

We can only be honest with ourselves and others when our mind, bodies, and spirit work together for the common good. People who are centered recognize the importance of paying attention to their sixth sense. Simply stated, the way we think determines whether we rise above the chaos of the world or succumb to it during our brief time on earth.

Identifying with your triune nature fortifies you to fulfill your true purpose. Your healed mind is attuned to abundance thoughts. Being attentive to the present enables you to trust that you possess God's power to triumph over your difficulties. As a direct result, you respond assertively during most stressful times.

Unresolved feelings of unworthiness make us extremely vulnerable to fear-based pronouncements. Statements that focus on humanity's sins, combined with salvation messages of grace, can't help but be unsettling.

An adult who identifies with his shortcomings responds to conflicting messages from a position of weakness. His ego overrides his inner wisdom. No two emotions are more diametrically opposed than love and fear. When we grow up feeling inferior, fear-driven statements have a far greater impact. In spite of professions to the contrary, most people subconsciously believe: crucifixion + resurrection = I'm unworthy of love.

Our heartbreaking world is overrun by torment caused by a false belief in fear. Just as a house divided against itself cannot stand, neither can a mind that falsely perceives it's not whole be stable. We unknowingly allow ourselves to be deceived by core beliefs that aren't real from an eternity standpoint of now and forever. If we remain too afraid of change to surrender self-will, we struggle to maintain a delusional reality that ultimately exacerbates our false feelings of emptiness.

As long as I continue to blame my circumstances for my unhappiness, my time-bound mind-set won't be receptive to the Spirit of truth. Self-deception only allows us to perceive the pressing need for change in others. We don't realize that being controlled by anger and creature comforts that can be withdrawn at any given moment is just as deadly to our well-being as substance abuse. People who are addicted to drugs may physically die sooner, but the common denominator is still the same: being out of touch with the ever present reality of love.

A flesh-driven orientation prevents us from relating to a Creator we can't experience with the same intensity of feeling as our sensual desires. The call of the still small voice within just doesn't seem that appealing when we're accustomed to the stimulating feelings of superficial remedies.

It doesn't matter if failure to identify with God's will compels us to disrespect ourselves or others. Without changing the way we think, we sadly never move beyond our lifelong misconceptions. The end result is regularly demonstrating the lie that we're damaged goods through nonassertive conduct.

A Course in Miracles provides an exclusively love-based interpretation of Christ's crucifixion. Humanity's infinity connection to God refers to one's heart and soul. Since one's body ceases to exist at death, the true purpose of Christ's life on earth is lost the moment we fixate on His crucified Body.

Reminders of His battered appearance promote a crucifixion mentality. The devastating separation anxiety thoughts of a purely flesh driven focus—Jesus's *physical* death for humanity's sins— automatically flood one's mind with guilt. The joyful resurrection mind-set of redemption doesn't fully register with most people: the worst life and death imaginable doesn't alter the everlasting nature of love.

Shifting the emphasis to the eternity message, *only love is real*, would teach people to stay focused on their oneness with God's Mind and Spirit, despite dastardly deeds perpetrated in the worldly realm. Without fear-controlled beliefs distorting one's perceptions, a true spiritual lifestyle would be the norm rather than the exception. A divisive love and fear reality that naturally produces aberrant behaviors would be practically nonexistent.

Christ didn't personalize his persecution for a very important reason we all need to remember. As the Physical manifestation of pure love, Jesus knew His perfect Spirit wasn't affected by His decimated Body. In spite of how long His suffering appeared to be from a temporal standpoint, it occurred in the blink of an eye when compared to being vibrantly alive forever!

When we aren't raised to intuitively sense our spirit is an integral part of God's Spirit, living by sight dictates we can't possibly be one with a perfect God. Our conditioning to feel separate and unworthy causes us to dwell on fear-driven outcomes of mortality, the devil, and hell. The deep-rooted nature of self-deception even causes the glorious resurrection message to be lost on most people.

A time-based orientation fixes our attention on verbal and physical assaults that aren't real from an immortality perspective: "For I consider that the sufferings of this present time are not worthy to be compared with the glory which shall be revealed in us" (Romans 8:18). Simply stated, a crucifixion complex compels us to subconsciously deny the undying nature of love.

A child who learns to misidentify with fear through nonassertive behavioral patterns becomes addicted to chaos. He grows up with painful feelings lodged in the recesses of his mind that have nothing to do with his true identity. When fear-rooted judgments aren't replaced with love-grounded neural connections through spiritual recovery, adults remain mentally stuck in their childhood pain.

Ongoing references that blame humanity for Christ's death make it doubly difficult not to feel unredeemable. Graphic images that portray a gruesome execution keep triggering underlying feelings of worthlessness: *I'm too despicable to be loved by anyone, much less God.*

If the goal is genuine unification in thought, word, and deed, eradicating mixed-message religion should be a top priority. Only the rebirth theme of never ending love should be demonstrated by the way we regard ourselves and others. A God of unconditional love, Who is portrayed as sanctioning the murder of His perfect Son to atone for humanity's sins, is a confusing teaching indeed.

When we substitute "self-deception" for "sins" we discover there is nothing to forgive, because humanity's misguided actions aren't based on willfulness. Starting with Adam and Eve, *everyone* who believes in love and fear has been deceived into feeling powerless to manifest heaven on earth from within.

We won't experience higher levels of consciousness as long as our contradictory beliefs remain intact. We're either free or we're undeserving. We can't be both without creating an emotional imbalance that significantly impairs our reasoning abilities. Just as Jesus conquered fear by rising from the dead, so we must crucify our half-truths by celebrating the whole(ness) truth: love can't be sacrificed because it's eternal.

"The crucifixion cannot be shared, because it is the symbol of projection. But the resurrection is the symbol of sharing. Only this is knowledge. The message of the crucifixion is perfectly clear: teach only love, for that is what you are."[4]

"Projection" refers to the self-hate of the mob that was translated into hatred for Christ. People who are out of touch with reality rebel when their comfort zones of fear-minded conduct are threatened. The subconscious rationale is that the victimizer deceives himself and others into believing he is the real victim. This tactic only temporarily relieves inner turmoil, because external sources aren't the root cause of one's misery. The way we feel about ourselves inside determines whether we experience life being generally content or dissatisfied.

Christ's detractors experienced extreme dissonance. They had never been in the company of anyone who was the Embodiment of perfect love. His peaceful demeanor was inconsistent with the judgmental way they had been conditioned to act. These feelings of discord can intensify to the point where preserving the status quo of fear becomes more important than the ultimate cost to aggressors and their victims—as was the scenario that played out to justify Christ's crucifixion.

Subtle and not so subtle variations of self-will dramas continue on a daily basis without any sign of abatement. If you grew up feeling less than lovable, you won't be able to relate to God's unconditional love without changing the way you think.

An exclusive flesh-driven focus attributes false power to circumstances that remind us of our hurtful childhoods. We either crucify others with our anger, or we allow others to crucify us with theirs.

Aggressors' equate love with control. Their mood swings can be like a volcano when they don't get their way. They can spew their fury on others one minute, act perfectly calm the next minute, and then seethe just beneath the surface a short time later.

Passive personalities deny the reality of love by depending on others for the approval they have always had from God. Passive-aggressive individuals demonstrate their lack of faith by seeking control through indirect means.

Assertive people have self-esteem. They don't live in bondage to a crucifixion mentality of judgment. Their resurrection mind-set of peace sustains them during good and trying times alike.

Spiritual recovery heals childhood trauma at its source. When you learn to appreciate your true value, extending love becomes far more important than focusing on differences that are only real in a fleeting earthly context. Identifying with humanity's oneness releases you from regularly engaging in self-condemnation and judging others.

The admonition from the aforementioned quotation to "teach only love, for that is what you are" can be understood only from a spiritual perspective. Viewed in terms of Christ's resurrection, this statement makes perfect sense, while a crucifixion orientation nullifies this concept as too radical to accept.

A friend of mine returned to church after several years' absence. The minister announced that anyone who backslid after being saved would be judged more harshly than someone who had never been saved. My friend spent a whole week worrying about whether she was going to hell.

Another example of mixed-messages was featured on a signboard outside a local church. The sermon was titled "We're all lepers." Another title, "Remember who you are," was in its place two weeks later. Are we supposed to remember that we're lepers or love?

Love and fear religious messages can only convey partial truth. Compliance to church doctrine is motivated by a desire to avoid punishment. A widespread consequence is turning away from God altogether.

These conclusions aren't intended to suggest members of the clergy deliberately mislead their followers. Many preachers who didn't grow up feeling valued simply don't understand that developing self-worth is a prerequisite to love-centered thinking.

Love Denied

The secular version of fear-driven conditioning can cause children to feel anxious, because they don't know what mood to expect. Children who internalize parental wrath and parental approval messages can grow up untrustworthy or depending on unreliable people for fulfillment. Conflicting teachings prevent us from being authentic. Actions speak louder than words when we learn to profess love, while regularly acting disrespectfully.

When we identify with fear, our pain stems from our flesh-driven orientation. False feelings of powerlessness deceive us into believing our circumstances dictate our moods. The opposite is true. A spiritual person has discernment to understand his internal state determines his fulfillment. Without a holistic approach to life, it's easy to convince ourselves being anxiety-ridden is normal. We don't realize that we'll never be satisfied until we actualize the love within us. Simply stated, we can't be happy if we don't learn to love who we are.

A fear-controlled reality mistakes infatuation for love. Infatuation is superficial. It's a temporary feeling of romantic attraction based on the subjective perceptions of one's five senses; hence the phrase, "love at first sight." These feelings are unpredictable. They vary according to one's personal opinions and mood swings.

Love is Spirit-minded. It's an everlasting feeling that isn't found in the initial attraction stage. Love isn't dependent on physical appearance, nor on anything of worldly value. It's based on trust and respect that develops slowly and deepens as the years go by. Love withstands the test of time. The attributes of love are personified in 1 Corinthians 13:4–8:

> Love suffers long and is kind; love does not envy; love does not parade itself, is not puffed up; does not behave rudely, does not seek its own, is not provoked, thinks no evil; does not rejoice in iniquity, but rejoices in the truth; bears all things, believes all things, hopes all things, endures all things. Love never fails.

If we don't possess the positive energy of self-acceptance, we aren't likely to attract someone who understands love flows from within. The false power of self-deception prevents us from recognizing we've always been complete, with or without a partner.

In the typical marital relationship, one or both partners act like the injured party. Denial of reality leads to one of two outcomes: 1) You leave your partner emotionally through judgmental behaviors, compulsive spending, workaholism, pornography, etc. 2) You leave your partner physically through divorce.

Fear-based unions are characterized by ego gratification. What *I* want overrides what is equitable for us. When we're raised to rely on feelings instead of faith, the pleasurable sensations that result from initial physical attraction represent counterfeit self-esteem because they are triggered by an external source. These emotions are so powerful at the outset that people routinely deceive themselves into believing they have found the person who will make them happy forever. Without insight to know happiness is a state of mind we either subconsciously refuse or consciously choose, it's easy to see how fickle feelings that are mistaken for love fade once the thrill of newness wears off.

Lack of self-value emerges full force through fear-rooted judgments. As tensions escalate from expecting others to make us feel complete, we illogically keep relying on superficial remedies to quell our disappointment. This is why hoping to escape the angst of your childhood through your adult relationships ends up compounding your pain instead.

Cheryl and Richard both grew up with controlling mothers. She had been married most of her adult life. Richard had wed briefly many years ago. He is used to coming and going as he pleases. Cheryl's need for more accountability triggers memories of his mother. He responded with hostility. Richard's forceful reactions denied his claim to be on a spiritual path. If he honestly believed his spirit is one with Cheryl's spirit, he would be attentive to the still small voice. There would be no need for verbal assaults.

Lack of insight prevents us from seeing through our partner's shortcomings to his or her spiritual perfection. If we're inner-directed, we don't attribute false power to external events. We don't become embroiled in pointless arguments that eventually cause our health to suffer. People are much more likely to be receptive to our points of view if we communicate calmly.

Richard didn't realize that Cheryl views her comments as necessary to point out the "error of his ways." He thought she knew full well she was trying to control him. Self-deception reigns when mixed-message communication is regarded as normal. Fear-based neural connections determine our primary response patterns.

As a child, Cheryl observed her mother in the dominant role in her parents' marriage. She identified with her mom's will. Cheryl was unaware she contradicts her assertion that she trusts Richard by regularly questioning his whereabouts.

Like most people, Cheryl subconsciously plays God. She believes it's reasonable to expect Richard to agree with her definition of right and wrong. In reality, people in love-based relationships gracefully accept each other's differences and focus on the commonalities.

When we meet strenuous resistance trying to change one's behavior, it's because we're triggering the pain he felt as a child when his opinions were routinely discounted.

If I don't feel good enough deep down inside, I can never get enough outside reassurances to allay my fears. I'm not empowered to demonstrate wholeness of love. Misidentification with self diverts my attention to how *I* believe your actions need to line up with *my* perceptions for *me* to be happy.

If I had been raised to demonstrate God's will in thought, word, and deed, I wouldn't need to prove I'm right to gain counterfeit self-esteem. My inner confidence would be evidenced through my consistent assertive behavior.

Without resolving our lifelong identity crisis between self (fear) and wholeness (love), we keep denying our spiritual perfection through faultfinding. The ego is endangered by anyone who doesn't comply with what the illusory I wants. The resulting anxiety compels us to garner allies to regain emotional balance. In this particular case, Cheryl based her sense of worth on having Richard conform to her expectations. Likewise, he expected me to validate his position. Simply stated, if we don't learn to identify with spiritual love, we become addicted to short-term fixes to alleviate the misery of our conflict-filled lifestyles.

Richard's breakthrough occurred when he recognized the need to moderate his attitude. He was well aware his aggression was making a bad situation worse. Even though he wasn't complying with Cheryl's version of how he should behave, he was still allowing her to control him through his emotional outbursts.

It's imperative to recognize there is nothing to be gained by becoming upset with those who cling to oppositional attitudes. Every time we personalize fear-minded conduct, we're actually nursing our childhood insecurities. The angry child-adult connection between our past and current relationships is broken when we learn to center our thoughts on the love within us.

When Love Rules

The following hypothesis explains the basis for believing *only love is real*:

1. A mixed-message belief system promotes false separation anxiety. (As discussed in chapter 1, the turmoil I felt about church as a little girl was the direct result of the teaching that strict attendance was necessary to escape eternal damnation).

2. Separation anxiety produces untrustworthy behaviors when core beliefs aren't founded on truth.
3. Truth is demonstrated when one's mind, body, and spirit resonate with the love of God's Spirit.
4. Spirit-minded love flows from within through the assertive communication of self-esteem.
5. Therefore, learning to love oneself eliminates the need for teaching and believing in anything other than love.

An easy way to remember this supposition is: Teaching love plus fear = a fear-based mentality. Teaching love = a love-grounded mind-set.

Here is another way to understand that love is the only reality that matters. If someone pulls a gun on me, reacting with panic is automatic only because I've learned to place too much value on my body. My self-preservation instinct will be intensified if I'm uncertain or unconvinced about life after death. If I had been raised to believe the real me is indestructible, because my eternal spirit is encased within my body, I would instinctively know my physical being is only significant in an earthly sense. I wouldn't react nearly as fearfully.

A female guest on a talk show discussed how making the transition from fear to faith saved her life. She woke up during the night to discover her estranged boyfriend standing beside her bed holding a knife. Her immediate reaction was to pull the covers over her head and cower in the fetal position. In the very next instant, she recovered and began silently praying to God. An ensuing sense of peace empowered her to throw off her covers, calmly lead her would-be assailant outside, and firmly announce, "You're leaving now." He left, and she called the police.

The more attuned you are to your eternal legacy of peace, the less fearful you'll be of physically dying, with or without your loved ones present. A God-centered existence eliminates our need to be in relationships to feel secure.

There is a fundamental reason why no human being can completely satisfy another long-term. By definition, humanity's oneness with God would be negated if it was possible to be totally fulfilled with one special person. True fulfillment emanates from recognizing the love that encompasses everyone.

Being raised without the knowledge of our innate wholeness is what causes us to seek meaningful relationships apart from God. When we're subsequently left with feelings of emptiness, self-deception compels us to keep repeating this exercise in futility.

A mind that wavers between love and fear automatically favors self-will desires. "For where your treasure is, there your heart will be also" (Matthew 6:21). We become slaves to people, jobs, possessions, and being ruled by angry response patterns; until tragedy strikes and we turn to God in desperation.

Living in denial that God's will is humanity's will slowly kills us mentally, spiritually, and, ultimately, physically. If I don't subconsciously believe in oneness of love, false feelings of powerlessness assail my mind with self-doubt and mistrust. It doesn't matter whether or not I profess to believe in God, have a strong support system, and am considered to be successful. I'll still tend to react to daily stressors with coping tactics that betray my inner turmoil.

By contrast, if I have confidence in who I am eternally, I'll be content, even when I'm physically alone and struggling to make ends meet. Identifying with God's Mind keeps me focused in the present during the lean times: "For I know the thoughts that I think toward you, says the Lord, thoughts of peace and not of evil, to give you a future and a hope" (Jeremiah 29:11). Years ago, Bob returned from a spiritual retreat with a variation of this Bible verse carved in stone. It's one of my most cherished possessions. I still have it on my nightstand as a daily reminder of the importance of staying faithful.

If you don't learn to love who you are so you can trust in God's boundless love, you won't be able to truly count on anybody, not even yourself. When you become attuned to your everlasting spirit-to-Spirit union, you finally recognize it makes no sense to judge others for not filling a void in your heart that never existed.

Reversing the imbalance between self-will and the Spirit of truth requires familiarity. Just as intimacy can't be cultivated through casual encounters, faith develops by regularly communing with God. A good way to reinforce this practice is to start each day with love-centered assurances to counter fear-based thoughts as soon as they come to mind. When we learn to react according to our divine nature, we admit our mistakes without experiencing the childhood dread of being judged unworthy.

Always remember, the greatest threat to your well-being doesn't involve material addictions, loved ones, enemies, serious accidents, or life-threatening illnesses. It's self-deception; the imaginary war you wage daily between false self-hate and true self-respect. You either continue to chart your own lonely course of fear by acting on untrustworthy feelings from childhood, or you respond with love by faith to function as an eternal spirit who temporarily occupies a physical body.

When we hold ourselves accountable for faulty reactions, ranging from self-pity to rage, the false need to blame ultimately vanishes. This is what is meant by the call in Romans 12:1 "that you present your bodies a living sacrifice, holy, acceptable to God." This scripture refers to symbolically dying to focusing on flesh-driven cravings that don't define who you are. The short-term pleasure you derive pales in comparison to the long-term pain that is depicted in Figure 1 in this chapter. The rendering of humanity's healed soul in this same illustration denotes replacement of spiritual blindness with insight. This transformation is referenced in the very next verse of this same scripture: "And do not be conformed to this world but be transformed by the renewing of your mind, that you may prove what is that good and acceptable and perfect will of God" (Romans 12:2).

Meditative Mind-Set

Feelings of inadequacy often masquerade as arrogance. During stressful encounters, we tend to function between the extremes of being unable to speak up or being all too quick to offer an opinion. When we grow up without understanding how vital it is to develop a spiritual mind-set, our judgmental natures prevent us from evaluating situations objectively.

The aftermath of an argument is a good example of how a fear-bound reality prevents us from being authentic. Most people stew in judgment by replaying what transpired over and over in their mind.

Try the following meditation to break this habit. Assume a comfortable sitting position. Take several slow, deep cleansing breaths to center your emotions. Close your eyes and visualize yourself as a free spirit floating out of your body. Imagine yourself hovering weightlessly and effortlessly, without any emotional or physical baggage. Envision the illuminating light of God's Spirit energizing your spirit.

The more opportunities you take to get in touch with your divinity, the less anxious you'll tend to feel. This exercise will facilitate your transition from faulty feelings to faith. Over time, you'll sense you're safe to release your critical nature. Your false need to personalize offenses will be replaced with a soothing stillness.

Try to maintain this tranquil state daily for at least ten minutes, starting with two-minute increments at a time. It will be difficult at first, because you're used to dwelling on life draining thoughts. Just keep returning your attention to your imagery when you become distracted. If you're unable to imagine yourself as a free-floating spirit, you can quietly focus on your breathing.

The point of this exercise is to achieve a balanced state through stillness. People who learned to believe their value is tied to how they perform will initially feel guilty or uncomfortable meditating.

My ongoing transition from fear to love includes reflecting on my true identity. I close my eyes and visualize the love within me energizing my mind, body, and spirit to confidently face each new day. "Learn to live from your true Center in Me," notes Sarah Young in *Jesus Calling: Enjoying Peace in His Presence*. "I reside in the deepest depths of your being, in eternal union with your spirit."[5]

I was determined to stop allowing my stuck child to dictate my behavior. I started paying more attention to my rising anger. I learned to quietly experience my uncomfortable feelings without automatically becoming irritated. As my erratic responses gradually subsided through my love-grounded focus, I was able to exercise more self-control. When we calmly accept what we can't change, our learned need to overreact and underreact eventually dissipates.

As the authors of *How God Changes Your Brain* explain, "By training yourself to observe your thoughts, you are learning to subdue the emotional reactivity that normally governs the neural activity of the brain."[6] Simply stated, we can retrain our brain to consciously respond as genuine adults instead of unconsciously reacting as scared children.

Spiritual truths aren't generally accessed through unstable emotions. Wisdom is intuitively discerned through a heartfelt desire to live on a higher level of consciousness that is life changing. When we concentrate on intrinsic qualities like self-respect and humility, we're assured love really does rule—even when we can't trust anyone but God. If we commit to silently being, the Holy Spirit cues us to what we need to be doing.

Anxiety gradually fades into the background when eliminating the imaginary conflict in your mind between love and fear becomes the focal point of your existence. I personally relinquish self-will every morning. I know all too well if I don't make a daily choice to "walk by faith, not by sight" (2 Corinthians 5:7), my ego will all too quickly energize my childhood victim mentality.

Love Summary

Love isn't blind; it's our contradictory core beliefs that blind us to love. Thinking you can be transparent without healing your split personality is like trying to walk in light and darkness at the same time. Your temporal orientation must be attuned to your eternal spiritual reality for love to flourish.

When we're out of balance mentally, physically, or spiritually, our overall health suffers. A fear-based reality generates unnecessary conflicts at every level of human interaction. Oppositional viewpoints take center stage in mundane matters, as well as in life and death situations.

The sad truth is most people can't even carry on a friendly conversation without finding something to complain about. If you think I'm exaggerating, I challenge you to try the following experiment the next time you converse with a friend: mark a piece of paper with a plus and minus column. Every time a positive or negative comment is made by either of you, place a check mark under the appropriate heading. My guess is you'll be amazed at how few entries you record on the plus side.

Even happy occasions can turn unpleasant without warning if we don't make a conscious effort to counter fear with love. My niece, Stephanie, hosted a slumber party for her nine-year-old daughter. As the evening wore on, a few of the participants began bickering. My niece intervened when it became apparent tensions were escalating. Her initial impulse was to threaten to send the offenders home if they continued to be disruptive.

Instead, Stephanie gave each child a turn to state her opinion quietly about what had transpired. She then instructed the girls to write down their names on slips of paper. After collecting the signatures, my niece had them make random selections. They were asked to say one nice thing about the person they had chosen face to face.

Even though a couple of the girls only halfheartedly participated—with comments like, "I like your hair, shoes," etc.—the exercise was a success. They giggled as they complied with Stephanie's request to hug each other before resuming their party. There were no further incidents. Days later, some of the mothers commented to Stephanie that her assertive approach had made a favorable impression on their children.

John 16:33 states, "In the world you will have tribulation; but be of good cheer, I have overcome the world." If your attention is only on the perceptions of your five senses, your anxiety mirrors the false power fear has over you. If you develop your sixth sense, your calm attitude demonstrates your inner confidence that love triumphs.

Your true identity is starting to come into sharper focus. Now it's time to discover how crucial an eternity perspective is to peace of mind.

Chapter 5

Walking in Wholeness

First keep peace within yourself, then you can also bring peace to others.

—Thomas à Kempis

Self-deception prevents us from recognizing our oneness with God's Spirit. False separation anxiety creates imbalances from the very beginning of our lives. Little children must be trained to temper their exuberance with respectful behaviors to experience the never ending, natural high of a heavenly existence. Perception is reality. When we learn to perceive fear-based outcomes through non-assertive conditioning, we don't develop spiritual discernment. We feel compelled to seek superficial fixes to alleviate the torment of failing to identify with our divine nature.

A person who grows up with a mixed-message belief system can communicate a call for unity that moves people to tears, follow it with a stinging denouncement of the person who just cut him off in traffic, and feel completely justified. An individual who strives to be spiritual would immediately recognize he had just contradicted himself and feel contrite. Simply stated, love is the only response of those who wholeheartedly identify with their peaceful spirit.

A nonassertive child who doesn't feel wholly loved isn't empowered to achieve his full potential. It doesn't matter if he is popular among his classmates, excels athletically, and ends up being a Rhodes Scholar. If his parents were judgmental, he will feel he can never quite measure up. His divisive love and fear reality is revealed in the disparity between his outstanding achievements and his inner turmoil. Subconsciously, he lives in dread of the day he falters and his perceived inadequacies are exposed for all the world to see. Just like his role models, he denies his wholeness through fear-driven behaviors.

Discovering the quiet strength of your inner power equips you to rise above response patterns that undermine your stability. You stop basing your value on arbitrary performance standards that keep fueling your anxiety.

When self-esteem works together with faith, our transformed mind isn't ruled by childhood insecurities. We function on higher levels of consciousness to replicate heaven on earth in thought, word, and deed.

Manifesting Abundance

We know money can't buy happiness because that would mean all wealthy people would be well adjusted. Having this knowledge doesn't stop people from associating money with solving their problems. When we don't understand the importance of a holistic approach to life, unrealistic expectations promote endless disappointments.

A poverty mentality stems from lack of awareness that we regularly deny the ever present reality of love. One of the most familiar examples is professing to value people over possessions in romantic relationships. As soon as the bloom of what passes for love is off the rose, our compulsive need for ego gratification all too quickly resurfaces. Our attention is automatically drawn to alternate, external sources of comfort.

Even if we're financially secure, a self-will orientation implants the thought of dissatisfaction in our minds. Without an eternity orientation, our primary focus is on catering to flesh-driven appetites that can never be satiated.

If more people realized they have a spiritual identity problem, they wouldn't keep blaming their circumstances for their lack of fulfillment. Spouses leave through death or divorce; children grow up and can't always be counted on; friends and relatives can prove to be untrustworthy; and everything else, likewise, provides only transitory solace.

If I had been taught I'm responsible for my happiness because love, peace, joy, etc., originate from within me, my actions would confirm my wholeness mind-set. Instinctively heeding the Holy Spirit's promptings would feel natural. Assertive conduct would be the norm. I'd be able to trust my feelings 100 percent of the time. Faith in my oneness with God would prevent me from being caught off guard when situations don't turn out the way I anticipate. Simply stated, becoming inner-directed frees me from my false bondage of anxiety.

Without spiritual insight, we just go through the motions of life. Self-deception prevents us from recognizing that our false belief in fear causes us to re-enact our childhood victim mentalities. Feeling detached from our true purpose to love never affects us alone. Its ripple effect results in man's inhumanity to man. This dynamic evolves in the following manner: misidentification with self promotes the illusion that I'm a separate entity. If I believe I'm distinct from my Source, I'm automatically left with feelings of powerlessness. Turning to the Creator only happens during times of desperation, if it occurs at all.

Even if I've also been taught God loves me, repeated references about being born sinful override this truth in my mind. On a subconscious level, my temperament and conditioning have convinced me I'm unworthy of love. This faulty ideation results in behavioral extremes that range from family members displaying aggression toward each other to nations embroiled in full-scale wars.

Problems that don't really exist in the present are revealed through our actions if our mind is stuck in the past. An imaginary rift between love-centered (adult) and fear-bound (child) choices characterizes humanity's delusional mental battle.

A healed mind that functions with wholeness of purpose intuitively senses humanity's spiritual perfection. Conduct that doesn't serve the common good is largely eliminated.

Just as the person who is addicted to drugs craves his physical fix, you'll remain dependent on superficial remedies to relieve turmoil that wouldn't exist if you reacted knowing *only love is real.* Spiritual recovery is a good way to think of your need to stop depending on external religious or worldly answers for counterfeit self-esteem.

Divine Nature Denied

Feelings of inadequacy leave you with the same two thoughts: 1) No matter what you accomplish, it's never good enough. 2) No matter how blessed you are, you're still dissatisfied.

Tom is a practicing Christian who has a supportive wife and a typical, egocentric teen-aged daughter. During our first session, Tom talked about how much he had done for his ungrateful daughter, how he sacrificed so she could attend the best schools, and how undeserving he is of her defiant attitude. He briefly acknowledged that his aggressive temperament clashes with his daughter's controlling nature.

Tom was too caught up in externals. Even though a person may be attentive to his children and encourage scholastic achievement, alternating good deeds with intimidating tactics undermines a child's confidence. Despite everything Tom did to provide for his daughter, he didn't know how to model the one thing she needs the most: self-acceptance. It never occurred to him that his daughter felt he was rejecting her, instead of her willful conduct. Even though Tom had every right to be angry, his hostile approach was doing more harm than good.

Disrespecting others through harsh language is a sure sign of lack of self-worth.

Tom understandably balked at the prospect of modifying his lifelong response patterns. Like most parents, he was more interested in motivating his child to change her behavior.

Just as we don't develop deep-seated resentments overnight, there are no shortcuts to healing self-deception. The most effective way to alter rebellious behavior is to consistently model assertive response patterns. When we don't identify with our mind, bodies, and spirit as children, we can't help but grow up feeling victimized instead of validated. Simply stated, a victim mentality of self-hate is the most pervasive addiction of all.

Having a crucifixion complex isn't exclusive to any particular socioeconomic group. Those who are wealthy and acquire possessions to the point of conspicuous consumption still have a victim mind-set. Even though recognizing God's will is humanity's will ultimately dispels false powerlessness, people from all walks of life are simply unwilling to give up their addiction to short-term fixes.

A resurrection mentality is based on God's plan for prosperity, not on intellectual or social status, what anyone else does or says, or on what has been gained or lost. This attitude frequently translates into material wealth but it isn't dependent on financial security. During times of lack, resurrection thinkers don't panic. Their peace of mind isn't unduly affected by adverse circumstances.

Even when he was impoverished and imprisoned, the Apostle Paul's faith never wavered. Living according to an eternity perspective empowered him to see past his critics' barbs to the truth. In Philippians 1:27, Paul instructs his brethren to "stand fast in one spirit, with one mind." The reason it's so difficult to comprehend this mind-spirit connection we all share is because a flesh-driven orientation fixates on fear-bound judgments.

In her best-selling book, *A Return to Love*, author Marianne Williamson describes the failure to recognize our oneness: "The human storyline, where bodies talk and move and suffer and die, forms a veil of unreality in front of God's creation. It hides 'the face of Christ.' My brother might lie, but he is not that lie. My brothers might fight, but they remain joined in love."[7]

Restoring wholeness only seems difficult to those who can't conceive of an identity beyond their physical bodies. Recognizing the necessity of an eternity perspective changes how you view yourself. Accepting this perspective is fundamental to inner peace. You may have noticed I've pluralized body and denote heart and soul in singular form throughout this book. This is to remind you the human race is comprised of a multitude of bodies, but just one spirit and mind that is centered in God's Spirit and Mind of infinite love.

A fear-based reality results in placing far too much emphasis on physical appearance. Some of the ways people call attention to their bodies alone include perfume, makeup, padding, clothing, jewelry, manicures, pedicures, permanents, dyes, wax jobs, suntans, body piercings, tattoos, plastic surgery, Botox injections, diets, and weight-reduction surgeries. If you contrast this partial list with the time the average person spends nourishing his heart and soul with uplifting thoughts, meditation, and prayer, this should give you a good idea why love is the exception rather than the rule.

A key ingredient to experiencing peace of mind is balance. If you're exclusively inner-directed or outer-directed, you run the risk of becoming obsessive. People who feel uneasy unless they are always doing something are a good example. It's no coincidence that we're referred to as human *beings*. The more time we take to be still, the less anxious we'll feel during stressful occasions. "Be still and know that I am God" (Psalms 46:10).

Being true to yourself releases you from the false hope that external goals alone will fulfill you. Transparent adults understand abundant living is a state of mind that pertains to valuing the eternal fruit of the Spirit more than the decaying fruits of earthly labors.

Conscious Living

When we heal from the inside out, we're no longer ruled by our childhood misconceptions. We experience a heightened state of consciousness. We become attentive to the present. We don't automatically hesitate to express our true feelings out of fear of being judged.

Conditioned pessimism weighs heavily on those who never discover their spirit-to-Spirit connection. Since the average person in America has far more than his basic needs met, there would be no justification for complaints if they weren't derived from a nonassertive temperament and learned behavior. There are, of course, legitimate expressions of disagreement, including instances where a person's rights have been violated. However, for the most part, people gripe out of sheer force of habit.

A former friend I used to meet weekly for lunch would invariably start out our conversations with the following theme, "You won't believe the week I just had." She would then recite her litany of perceived injustices. These grievances would variously include her latest financial crisis, particulars about inconsiderate family members, and details of her boss's demands and her spouse's shortcomings.

The more inner-directed I became, the more my conscience bothered me. I wasn't being honest by reinforcing her fear-driven outlook. All the years I had known her, she had never improved her own attitude. When I began challenging her assumptions, she was taken aback. She initially tried even harder to convince me how bad her life was. I steadfastly refused to buy into her dismal version of reality. She especially didn't like me reminding her about how blessed she really was. Not surprisingly, we drifted apart. I was relieved. Those endless dramas had left me feeling unsettled.

Because negative energy patterns pass for normal, most people will interpret your lack of support as a personal affront. In reality, the more people learn to validate only assertive behaviors, the less money they will need to spend on healthcare, which would give us all one less thing to complain about!

We emotionally regress to our childhoods every time we assign blame or feel guilty. In contrast, Jesus suffered through being nailed to a cross without claiming to be victimized.

A person who has a resurrected mind transitions from becoming offended by self-serving conduct to a faith perspective of acceptance. Those who truly seek enlightenment know there is nothing to forgive. Spiritual recovery empowers us to transcend our perceived crucifixion mentality. We learn to place our trust in our collective oneness with God instead of in those who don't know how to love.

Truth or Consequences

People tend to view eternity as a future time when everything will be perfect. Few realize that they deny their timeless nature every day through nonassertive conduct. No matter how great one's life appears to be from a worldly perspective, true contentment won't occur without a wholeness mind-set. The underlying belief that life on earth is all there is and the false need for temporary fixes is one and the same fear-rooted pathology.

If we don't sincerely believe we're united with God, *I* automatically becomes the center of the universe. We deceive ourselves that fulfillment lies in personal interests: expecting our partners to make us feel loved, securing a great job, having enough money to do whatever we want, etc.

Even if these outcomes do occur, an egotistical viewpoint represents a bottomless pit. Wishing or trying to achieve happiness according to impulsive cravings contradicts our true identity. We miss out on the daily blessings that flow from quietly trusting life to unfold as it's meant to for our spiritual growth.

Resisting God's will by criticizing, blaming, staying depressed, etc., guarantees we'll keep reaping a harvest of misery from the seeds of discontentment we're sowing. Every time we indulge in fear-minded thoughts or behaviors, we're trading our legacy of peace for anxiety that isn't real from a love-centered standpoint.

One of the most common ways we compound our self-imposed stress is by making unnecessary purchases. Let's say I buy a car. Initially, I take great pleasure in driving it, as well as in the positive feedback I receive from others. As soon as the newness wears off, my need to stave off my false feelings of emptiness resurfaces. My nearly complete lack of spiritual awareness forces me to find a replacement feel good fix as soon as possible. (Note: Delayed gratification is particularly unacceptable to those with aggressive temperaments, who have the most difficulty with self-control).

What the car really represents is a futile attempt to fill an inner void (that doesn't exist) with a fleeting external comfort. Self-will is governed by the following subconscious thought process: *I suffered through enough pain in my childhood to last a lifetime. Now that I'm an adult, I'm going to live on my own terms.*

The problem with this reasoning is fear-driven behaviors become deep-seated long before we realize, if we ever do, that we've been duped. If we don't restore our mind to its infancy state of innocence, we'll continue to plot our own courses that generate conflicts. From the way we conduct our personal lives to wars that divide nations, examples of faulty thought patterns are everywhere.

Spiritual recovery involves making decisions that are in the best interests of everyone in your family and sphere of influence. Actions that denote manipulation through cajoling, pouting, pleading, self-denial, guilt, or issuing threats are self-centered.

We can't rely on our feelings to tell us the truth if our belief system is based on giving in or getting "my way." As adults, we can only risk being honest for brief periods at a time. Our childhood personas force us to run for cover behind the false protection of aggressive and passive defenses that keep us feeling victimized. Love only surfaces occasionally through assertive conduct.

We can't help but feel defeated if we believe reality consists solely of the conflict-ridden physical realm. Without inner healing, we keep sabotaging our happiness with unrealistic expectations and denial. Seeking control and approval becomes more important than demonstrating love and respect.

Keys to the Kingdom

When you discover your true power lies within, you stop allowing your trials to steal your peace of mind. Spiritual adults know that humbly submitting to the blast furnace of life is the only way to produce refinement of character.

Filtering out the nonassertive impurities produces a domino effect of well-being: Learning to love yourself paves the way to heal the damage of lifelong misconceptions; which leads to being receptive to sensing the Spirit of truth through your conscience; which frees you to respond without the fear of rejection. Simply stated, your childish insistence that life goes your way is replaced with childlike acceptance to trust God's way.

What we mistakenly refer to as our present day misery is actually our temperaments and childhood training overshadowing our real life with self-deception. One example of history repeating itself would be witnessing your father come home from work in a bad mood that translated into the whole family suffering. As an adult, you unconsciously mimic this behavior after being criticized by your supervisor.

A person who identifies with his divine nature is centered in the present. What transpires at work doesn't affect his entire day. He is attuned to the needs of his family when he arrives home.

Making a conscious commitment to stop being governed by untrustworthy feelings transforms our attitudes over time. We experience the ultimate freedom of extending love and forgiveness, despite how others behave and whatever hardships occur.

Before recognizing the necessity of a holistic lifestyle, I never really understood the significance of James 1:2: "Count it all joy when you fall into various trials." This scripture doesn't mean you should be in a joyous mood under trying circumstances. We either allow life's challenges to weaken us or they inspire us to discover our true power within. The sooner we dispel our false attachments to self, the greater the likelihood exists that we'll experience the joy of humanity's transcendent spirit-to-Spirit bond.

When we aren't inner-directed, we find endless reasons to feel victimized: I can't stand my job. My marriage isn't fulfilling. My kids don't appreciate me. My friend betrayed me. My car needs new tires I can't afford.

Developing a wholeness mind-set empowers us to dismiss the false notion that we can only be satisfied if events conform to our personal desires. When we strive to be genuine, we become attentive to everyday blessings we learned to take for granted.

Try to imagine all you would accomplish if you really believed you're complete. Contrary to popular belief, you weren't just foolishly daydreaming. When you stop depending on your unpredictable circumstances for happiness, your perspective starts to shift from frightened child to enlightened adult. Learning to identify with love empowers you to process offenses without triggering painful memories. You respond to adversity with quiet strength that attests to the kingdom of God within you.

Needless Suffering

If, as the Apostle Paul stated in 1 Timothy 6:10, "the love of money is a root of all kinds of evil," then fear, born of self-deception, is the root of every evil. Consider the crippling domino effects of a belief system based on good and evil: mixed-messages stunt our emotional growth by causing us to feel powerless. This state of mind forces us to employ the same response patterns as adults that we used to survive our childhood; which results in losing insight of the spiritual perfection we all share as beloved children of our Creator; which produces judgmental behaviors that focus on life's miseries instead of its majesty; which compels us to develop a crucifixion mentality of never feeling satisfied, regardless of whether we're in a relationship or alone; which prevents us from discovering our true purpose: to love.

Spiritual recovery releases you from the entanglement of negative energy patterns. You accept life's ebbs and flows in much the same way you now wholeheartedly accept yourself and others, as God does—the good, the bad, and the ugly.

A nonjudgmental approach not only frees us to act in the best interests of everyone (without being controlling or controlled), it results in a dual benefit: a decrease in our pain levels during the bad times and a corresponding increase in happiness during the good times. This is the win-win situation that results from a holistic lifestyle.

There are two types of suffering: worldly and righteous. Worldly misery occurs whenever we reap the consequences of our fear-based choices. Most people who fall into this category are deep in denial. They have convinced themselves they are innocent victims who can't seem to get a break.

Righteous afflictions occur through no fault of our own. Common examples include crime victims, life threatening illnesses, chronic physical and mental disabilities, and the death of loved ones.

Even though worldly suffering is self-inflicted, and undue hardships seem unfair, the answer for both dilemmas is the same. We must learn to seek divine comfort to keep from being immobilized by our pain.

Failure to endure trials with humility and grace can produce staggering consequences over time. We don't get to "pass go" as adults and collect our rightful inheritance of abundance. Instead, we go directly to jails of our own design, where we end up feeling impoverished. We sit out our real life being monopolized by fear, as described by Dr. Hubert Benoit in *The Supreme Doctrine*:

> I am comparable with a man in a room, where the door is wide open whereas the window is protected by bars; since my birth I have been fascinated by the outside world and have been clutching the bars of the window; and my keenness for the images outside makes my two hands violently contract. In a sense I am not free since this contraction prevents me from going out of the room. But in reality nothing else shuts me in but this ignorance which makes me take the imaginative vision of life for life itself; nothing shuts me in but the crispation of my own hands. I am free; I always have been; I will realize it as soon as I "let go."[8]

The man in this illustration is a metaphor for the mind. The room represents the body. When you view your mind as an instrument to serve your flesh-driven impulses, you subconsciously rekindle your childhood pain. The turmoil that is depicted in this story reveals a soul that longs to escape the confines of the body's five senses.

Even though your misidentification with self has convinced you otherwise, you've always had a choice between abundance and poverty. You'll continue to fear "going out of the room" until you train your mind to see beyond your limited physical viewpoint. The "imaginative vision of life" you long for in the world is fleeting, at best. Your real life is in the never ending spiritual realm.

We can't be authentic if we don't understand that love originates from within us. Learning to sense our timeless essence empowers us to mentally transcend the limitations of our time-bound bodies. We grow beyond superficial concerns.

If you're having trouble understanding this concept, think about all the people who have reported out of body experiences. The incomparable sense of joy and peace they report feeling all too briefly ultimately can become a more regular occurrence if we collectively function in accordance with our mind, bodies, and spirit.

When we let go of our conditioned fears through spiritual recovery, we're no longer imprisoned by contradictory thought patterns. We don't feel constrained to keep blindly following the shallow directives of our bodies, which began dying from the moment of birth. We instinctively know we have the Mind of God.

Recognizing the illusory nature of self enables us to be more accepting of situations beyond our control. Believing that love defines who we are frees us to counter the passing strife of the world with an eternity perspective of tranquil thoughts and assertive actions.

A closer examination of the subtle ways self-deception undermines humanity's wholeness will increase your awareness of your divinity. These areas of separation thinking include: comparisons, judgmental behavior, forgiveness, and trust and respect.

Comparisons

Competition can be a healthy form of comparison. Being humbly motivated to excel in intellectual and athletic endeavors promotes unity. The problem arises when the focus shifts to egocentric motives.

A flesh-driven outlook limits us to what we perceive through our five senses. Little or no emphasis is placed on heartfelt qualities like honesty and reliability. Relationships get reduced to choosing someone with the right career and right physical attributes. When self is in charge, differing perceptions about being shortchanged fuel jealousy.

The end result of superficial posturing is viewing yourself and everyone else as either inferior or superior. The middle-ground position of people being equal, but possessing different abilities, isn't an option from a worldly perspective.

Inferiority and superiority judgments both stem from feelings of powerlessness. On a subconscious level, false separation anxiety compels those who identify with control to prove how much better they are than others. Without a spiritual frame of reference, they simply don't understand there is nothing to prove.

On a mental and physical level, the cost of basing our happiness on external factors leads to a variety of unhealthy outcomes. Anxiety, guilt, resentment, depression, and various somatic ailments are just some of the most familiar consequences of being ruled by fear. When we fixate on our separateness through unfavorable comparisons, we unconsciously choose a false existence that promotes dissension.

Depending on the degree of turmoil that results from feeling "less than," relatively benign conduct can ensue. Indulging in fad diets and copying someone else's look are two such examples. In the extreme category are anorexia, bulimia, and obsessive cosmetic surgeries. The subconscious thought process involves trying to gain some semblance of control through weight loss and attempting to resist the aging process. In its deadliest form, false feelings of separation lead to murder and suicide.

While doctors represent an invaluable resource for treating physical and emotional symptoms, in most cases, lasting cures would occur by learning to access one's true power. Instead of heart attacks, strokes, mental illness, etc., being inevitable, there would be a dramatic reversal of all diseases if holistic thinking was practiced on a global scale.

In my case, two well-meaning friends suggested I resume drug therapy for my recurring depression. Becoming Spirit-minded eliminated the need for this intervention. The bottom line is, as soon as the goal of oneness is replaced by one-upmanship, the power of true communication is lost.

Judgmental Behaviors

If adults honestly documented each time unfavorable comments were made, most of us would soon run out of paper. As with all separation thinking, being judgmental is rooted in fear.

People who lack spiritual discernment routinely judge others. In its most extreme expression, healthcare clinics where abortions are performed have been bombed and physicians murdered—all in the name of supporting life.

Those who point out the Bible mandates exposing wrongdoing are more likely to rely on verbal condemnation. A person who identifies with his divine nature isn't inclined to proffer opinions on matters of self-deception.

Galatians 6:1 recommends a benign approach: "Brethren, if a man is overtaken in any trespass, you who are spiritual restore such a one in a spirit of gentleness, considering yourself lest you also be tempted." The point is, even when scripture is cited as justification for claiming abortion, homosexuality, etc., is wrong, the Bible also condemns lying, which we're all guilty of doing.

Unless you're a judge or have walked in another person's shoes, it's a good general rule of thumb to keep criticism to a bare minimum.

Judgmental behaviors can be traced to deep-seated feelings of unworthiness. I'm only able to see in someone else that which I subconsciously believe holds true for me. The real reason I fault your performance is because my temperament and learned behavior taught me to feel less than adequate. I automatically seize every opportunity I can to point out you're wrong so I can feel better about my performance.

Children who grow up God-conscious instead of self-conscious deal compassionately with problems as adults. Fear-based actions don't upset those who live by faith. They refrain from judgment. Their focus is on attaining higher levels of consciousness that reflect humanity's oneness.

An eternity perspective enables us to rely on our sixth sense regarding self-serving actions. We extend the same mercy we receive as physical manifestations of God's unconditional love. This is the honest judgment referred to in John 7:24: "Do not judge according to appearance, but judge with righteous judgment."

If you're serious about being true to yourself, it's crucial to remember feelings follow beliefs. Core beliefs produce feelings that become entrenched in humanity's soul from infancy. Therefore, the logical approach to stop allowing fear-rooted emotional reactions to dictate your behaviors is to alter your viewpoint. If you don't like the way you've been conditioned to feel, learning to interpret troubling events with insight beats judging by sight, hands down!

Capitalizing on your inner power equips you to weather life's storms with dignity. When you're not caught up in the chaos that defines a dual belief system, your thoughts become more empathic. You regularly discern spiritual truths. Your feelings start to line up with your emerging assertive attitude.

The best part is your subconscious identification with God's will and self-will is broken. Your split personality is restored to wholeness. You're finally free to extend love, even though you regularly encounter oppositional attitudes that falsely indicate fear rules.

The most important point to remember is this revelation can be understood only from the vantage point of love. The minute you revert to conflicting love and fear thoughts, you retreat to familiar judgments of yourself and others. In fact, even after you start to behave as an eternal spirit in a fleeting physical body, you'll have to be diligent daily until your love-based outlook becomes second nature.

If I have self-respect, my spiritual mind-set is revealed by the way I treat others and am treated in return. And even when I am mistreated, I remain unshaken. I don't personalize fear-driven actions that don't define humanity. "All for one and one for all," is a much stronger position than the exhaustive *I* posturing that is necessary to ensure the ego's survival.

This universal truth now works for me instead of against me. I judged my father's self-hate reactions and likewise became judgmental. The angry behavior I could barely tolerate had become an intolerable part of my own personality until I resolved my own lack of self-value.

Forgiveness

When I was in my thirties, I watched a talk show that featured a woman who forgave the person who had murdered her young son. I was struck by her serene countenance as she spoke. I was convinced she had to be heavily medicated in order to mask the rage she had to be feeling inside.

When I was in my forties and counseled crime victims, one of my clients had suffered a similar tragic loss. Angela was understandably distraught, but she had one thing in common with the woman on television: a willingness to forgive. She wanted the assailant held accountable, but she wasn't consumed with the bitterness one would typically expect. She understood holding a grudge would only add to her anguish.

Similarly, my own inner awakening led me to the realization that the woman's calm demeanor from that long ago television show wasn't a reflection of a drug-induced state. Her serenity emanated from within. Her choice to forgive her child's killer was a clear indication her peace of mind was even more powerful than every parent's worst nightmare. These stories attest that being spiritually centered ultimately leads to an overall assertive response pattern, regardless of external factors.

In the case of verbal abuse, a wholeness mind-set enables you to stop wasting time defending yourself against another's accusations. Truth is love. Love is all that matters. Love doesn't attack fear-based behaviors that aren't real. You'll have to look no further than to Jesus's demeanor prior to his crucifixion for confirmation of this fact. Simply stated, a love-based position needs no defense.

The real winner in any disagreement is the person who says the least. Transparent adults have insight to see past character flaws. They view everyone as spiritually righteous.

The act of forgiving neither denies the validity of your pain nor absolves your victimizer(s) of responsibility. It represents your understanding that spiritual adults don't stay stuck in self-pity. Nelson Mandela never would have become president of South Africa if he hadn't humbled himself to forgive his countrymen for imprisoning him for twenty-seven years.

Letting go of resentments requires perseverance. After a lifetime of justifying a fear-bound mind-set, an exclusive love-centered belief system seems impossible to achieve. It requires faith to change the way we think and respond when it still feels unnatural. With patience, our emotions eventually catch up with our true identity.

The good news is your sense of well-being dramatically improves when you're not consumed by the false battle between self-will and God's will. By choosing to focus on humanity's innate wholeness you'll discover the abundant life really does manifest from the inside out.

Becoming inner-directed prevents us from being significantly affected by another's disrespect. Having confidence to finally accept our validation comes from God frees us from giving false power to attitudes that aren't real from an eternity standpoint.

Nonassertive behaviors are interpreted as being out of touch with reality. As a judgmental person, I used to consider a man who beat his wife to be reprehensible. Being grounded in love, I now characterize this husband as fear-controlled, while still expecting him to suffer the consequences of his actions. The main difference is I still love him in the sense that he is an integral part of the whole, instead of hating him because I view him as a separate entity who is less worthy of forgiveness than I am.

It must be stressed that forgiving someone doesn't mean you should tolerate ongoing verbal or physical aggression. People who misidentify with self are unconsciously addicted to re-creating their chaotic childhoods. Healthy behavior in these cases involves forgiveness in the context of physical separation from the offending party.

This interpretation of the way forgiveness should be handled isn't intended to judge anyone who isn't currently able to forgive or who chooses to remain in a disrespectful relationship. Whatever the reasons happen to be, it's important to understand you're never responsible for another adult's decision to mistreat you. Learning to feel unworthy is what got us into trouble in the first place.

I mention this because I'm well aware of the adverse results of a fear-based reality. Most people fail to make the connection between their high blood pressure, heart problems, emotional distress, etc., and the behavioral patterns they internalized during childhood.

The most important point to remember is aggressive behavior from a relative, partner, friend, etc., is never your real problem. Your failure to actualize the love within you is the reason you keep attracting people who remind you of your turbulent past.

Trust and Respect

Spiritual recovery requires loving one another. Feelings of this nature don't necessarily imply trust or respect, but they do require forgiveness. Identifying with humanity's wholeness gives us insight to focus on the offender's spiritual perfection.

However, trust and respect are absolutely vital in a covenant marriage. Conflicts arise whenever we agree in principle only. If your temperament isn't assertive and you learned to be disrespectful and mistrustful as a child, you may claim to value these attributes without actually behaving in a trustworthy and respectful manner. The examples that follow demonstrate how variations of this theme play out in relationships in general.

Sarah and Roger were at odds with each other from the outset of their marriage. Sarah's temperament and learned behavior taught her to regard trust and respect as indispensable. Roger had learned to view mistrust and disrespect as normal. Growing up, he responded in kind to his verbally aggressive mother. Consequently, he swore at Sarah when he lost his temper. Roger's childhood insecurities were also revealed by his refusal to open a joint checking account and by making costly purchases without Sarah's knowledge.

Trust and respect are communicated by a person's actions consistently backing up his words, not by mere language alone. Those who are self-centered and self-sacrificing unconsciously view their need for control and approval as more important than showing respect for others and for themselves. They are spiritually blind to the fact that their oppositional attitudes are responsible for their discontentment.

Pat reported tolerating aggressive behavior from her husband and child throughout her twenty-five year marriage. Pat decided it was time to start standing up for herself. Her husband responded by accusing her of being menopausal. Her sixteen-year old son, Glenn, denied being disrespectful—in an aggressive tone of voice. I have no doubt Glenn didn't understand how he contradicted himself. He grew up observing his father relate to his wife with behaviors that alternated between scant acts of kindness and fits of rage. This love-fear pattern taught Glenn it was acceptable to treat his mother rudely.

Relationships that are based on conditional love are characterized by an aggressive response pattern that primarily manifests when the dominant partner fails to get his or her way. The ensuing conflicts alternate with damage control, at which time the offending party usually makes amends to restore balance. These repeated attempts to achieve harmony are always short-lived. A mixed-message communication style isn't conducive to stable relationships. If I was raised in a chaotic environment, I'll be highly resistant to emulating my divine nature. Based on my temperament and learned behavior, I'll automatically dismiss consistent assertive conduct as unrealistic.

In marriages, fear-rooted beliefs that masquerade as love without trust and respect translate into little more than a license to procreate and an unending battle of jockeying for position, rather than two people (and their children) uniting as one entity.

A word of caution must be added: making a stand for wholeness will be met with strong opposition from aggressors. As soon as you begin to react rationally, your controlling partner will feel compelled to do everything he can do to get you to revert to the fear-bound patterns you've both perceived as normal since childhood. If you falter and become defensive, he'll use your faulty response against you as proof that you're the problem.

This illogical conclusion is based on two very potent half-truths: 1) Your partner sincerely believes he is the real victim, because he's out of touch with reality. 2) Your complicity in settling for disrespect throughout your relationship has reinforced his belief that he's right. After all, you're the one who is trying to change the way things have always "worked" in the past. In extreme cases, an unbalanced partner can feel so threatened by an assertive stance that one's life may be at risk.

If you sincerely desire to break free from the addictive cycle of abuse alternating with fleeting displays of affection, healing your feelings of inadequacy is crucial. If you merely leave without learning to identify with love, you'll be likely to keep attracting abusive partners. Acquiring self-esteem transforms your attitude from powerless to empowered.

My fervent hope is that this text will be the starting point to effect a shift from being ruled by fear to faith. The more we can communicate with wholeness of purpose—instead of being torn apart by individual power struggles—the sooner we'll be able to restore heaven on earth.

It's time to reveal the formula for completeness that is essential to peace of mind.

CHAPTER 6

Your Choice: 10 Percent Power or 90 Percent Power

It is only with the heart that one can see rightly;
what is essential is invisible to the eye.
—Antoine de Saint-Exupery

The spirit is interchangeably referred to as the heart or conscience. The soul consists of the mind, will, and emotions. It's the repository of sensory perceptions, knowledge, core beliefs, and stored memories ranging from prenatal to the recent past.

The mind operates simultaneously on conscious and subconscious levels. Conscious behaviors include choices that are made of one's free will. Involuntary actions consist of conditioned response patterns that evolve from genetic makeup and environmental factors. Unconscious programming is a product of mental capacities, temperaments, and the input received from parental influences and society at large.

Overall decisions are based on lower or higher levels of consciousness. People who identify with self-will function on the lower levels of the consciousness spectrum. Their subconscious identification with fear generates feelings of powerlessness. They attempt to mitigate their inner turmoil by seeking external control and approval. Individuals who follow God's will live on the higher levels of consciousness. Their identification with love strengthens them to emulate their divinity in thought, word, and deed. Their outward confidence mirrors their peace of mind.

Growing up believing in love and fear creates an automatic identity crisis. The ongoing internal stress of trying to process incongruent ideations forces us to seek relief in superficial remedies. Since the original problem is the way we were taught to think, searching outside ourselves never provides lasting relief. "Change your mind, change your life" isn't just a catchy slogan. It's vital to ensure a quality life.

By nature, a mixed-message belief system isn't conducive to cultivating eternal character values. Egocentric pursuits automatically take precedence over behaviors that promote everyone's best interests. We don't identify with the love, peace, faithfulness, self-control, etc., of God's Spirit, because most of the information we internalized isn't based on the whole(ness) truth.

I can be a police officer and vow to uphold the law. But if my core beliefs aren't exclusively love-centered, my false attachment to self could cause me to justify taking payoffs. This is just one of countless examples that illustrates the pressing need to transform self-serving impulses into behaviors that serve the common good. Without transitioning from love and fear to love, our actions generally contradict our words.

Personal perceptions include both true and false ideas that conflict with others' fear-driven opinions. Attitudes are dependent on external events. Love is conditional. If I'm self-deceived, it feels completely natural for me to judge whatever doesn't conform to *my* temperament and learned behavior.

Spiritual truths are constant. A Spirit-led person isn't governed by how others act or unduly affected by fluctuating circumstances. Love is expressed respectfully. If I have faith in my true character, I don't feel the need to judge faults that originate from self-deception. *A Course in Miracles* contrasts a spiritual mind-set with a flesh-driven mentality: "In the realm of knowledge, no thoughts exist apart from God, because God and His Creation share one

Will. The world of perception, however, is made by the belief in opposites and separate wills, in perpetual conflict with each other and with God."[9]

A dual belief system doesn't include the essential knowledge that one's spirit existed before physical birth occurred. As temporal beings, we start out with birth dates and, ultimately, times of death. In a spiritual sense, we are timeless.

Humanity's spirit was joined with God's Spirit before the formlessness of heaven manifested in physical form as the earth. "The earth was without form, and void; and darkness was on the face of the deep. And the Spirit of God was hovering over the face of the waters" (Genesis 1:2).

When Adam was fashioned out of dust, Genesis 2:7 states he wasn't physically alive until God's Spirit "breathed into his nostrils the breath of life." This scripture tells us our flesh is only real as long as the Holy Spirit and our spirit inhabit our bodies. Our divine nature represents an infinite reality.

If we view Adam's creation strictly from a physical standpoint, God and man suddenly appeared to be distinct from each other at that point in time. Judging by sight, Adam's flesh was visible, while their spiritual union was unseen. Living by faith dictates that the formation of a transitory body doesn't make its indwelling spirit's undying connection to the Spirit of truth any less real.

Your eternal status of oneness with God isn't altered when you suffer from delusional thought patterns. When I experienced my psychotic break in my early twenties, my fear-controlled actions didn't define who I am. My mind had to be restored through inpatient treatment that included drug therapy.

In a similar way, if you were raised to believe in a love and fear reality that doesn't exist in the context of eternity now and forever, you're unconsciously ruled by fear-rooted perceptions. Being out of touch with reality may severely diminish the quality of your physical existence, but it doesn't alter your eternal oneness with God. The spiritual solution is to restore your mind to wholeheartedly express love. Simply stated, whatever is eternal has always been and forever will be.

An oppositional belief system makes it very difficult to comprehend the profound impact fear-bound teachings have had on the human race. Without spiritual recovery, we can't relate to eternal truths on a meaningful level. In spite of seemingly fervent claims to trust in God, many people remain afraid of being cast into hell.

A fear-based mentality can persist from the cradle to the grave if we aren't vigilant. It doesn't matter how many salvation messages are proclaimed from the pulpit or watched on television. We automatically internalize the learned guilt that emanates from our childhood conditioning to feel unworthy.

We, in turn, render judgments based on inaccurate feelings that deny our completion. And this vicious cycle of contradictory communication will never end until we collectively commit to eradicate our crippling thought patterns.

Spiritual perfection represents the reality that God's will and humanity's will is identical. Mixed-messages about God's unmerited favor reinforce the delusional schism in our mind. Unresolved insecurities cause us to tune out the favor part.

Untapped Legacy of Love

From a psychological perspective, 90 percent of behaviors are habitual. Temperament and learned behaviors either predispose us to engage in love-centered or fear-based conduct 90 percent of the time. It can be assumed that Adam and Eve rejoiced in their oneness with God. Therefore, their original knowledge of love was 100 percent.

Self-deception changed the first couple's orientation from mind, body, and spirit to mind and body. When Adam and Eve were God-conscious, they experienced a heightened sense of joy that emanated from their pure Oneness. As soon as they were deceived into becoming self-conscious, they immediately lost touch with paradise. A delusional love-fear division in their mind created false separation anxiety that *still persists*. Simply stated, humanity's addiction to short-term fixes becomes meaningless when spiritual discernment frees us to recognize heaven on earth.

The first couple's split personalities confused them into denying their divine nature. In the blink of an eye, they transitioned from the highest level of consciousness to regressing to a childish mind-set. If even Adam and Eve were depicted as having been led astray after having firsthand knowledge of both spiritual and physical perfection, then it's no wonder that a false belief in fear has continued to wreak havoc to this very day. Simply stated, self-deception causes us to lose (in)sight of the ever-present reality of love.

Contentment can't be consistent when our thoughts are contaminated by fear. Christians are inundated from childhood with messages about being born sinful, gory details of Christ's crucifixion, and explicit depictions of hell. It's inconsistent to believe a God of infinite mercy condemns those who unconsciously remain in bondage to their childhood victim mentality.

If I've been subjected to fear-rooted messages my whole life, the angst my mind has subconsciously generated over the course of my lifetime may indeed feel hellish. If I don't learn to identify with love before I physically die, I'll have cheated myself out of mentally experiencing heaven on earth through peace of mind. Like most people, I'll discover the truth when my righteous spirit exits the shell of what had been my failing flesh. I'll finally be free from my conditioned torment to experience unending joy for all eternity!

The burning (no pun intended) question becomes how one reverts from deceptive personal perceptions to consistently respond in agreement with God's Mind. The answer is by spiritual recovery: learning to live intuitively, according to one's supernatural legacy, as opposed to destructively, according to one's unbridled egotistical inclinations.

Without a holistic perspective, you automatically deny your spiritual perfection through fear-driven behaviors you've grown accustomed to since birth. Misidentification with self deceives you into believing you know the truth. Your anxiety betrays your mistaken identity of fear.

When you learn to view yourself as a three-part being, you stop attributing false power to circumstances beyond your control. Your centered vantage point seeks direction from the Spirit of truth. Inner peace attests to your everlasting identity of love.

Fulfillment is a function of one's viewpoint. If we try to adhere to God's will and worldly values, anxiety characterizes most of our response patterns. This dichotomy produces conflict-filled relationships, material fixations, financial worries, and health problems.

If we're spiritually attuned, peace of mind is reflected in our dependence on God (regardless of our circumstances), healthy relationships based on self-respect, a nonattachment lifestyle, and forgiveness without judgment.

Sports superstars, pop icons, and movie stars who died from drug overdoses or suicide provide abundant evidence that identifying with love is far more important than multimillion-dollar salaries and fleeting earthly accomplishments. People who are inner-directed understand their value isn't based on status symbols or diminished when their performances falter. Humanity's true worth has always been founded on our eternity connection to our Creator.

The following power thoughts will facilitate spiritual recovery. 1) Think of your spirit as the unseen, profound part of you that is inseparable from the Holy Spirit. It's perfect, immune to illness, and is timeless. 2) Think of your body as the visible, fleeting part of you that is fallible, subject to disease, and deterioration over time. 3) Think of your mind as either functioning under duress to satisfy your insatiable flesh-driven urges or operating at peak performance with your physical being and peaceful spirit.

When we consider these three thoughts at face value, it seems like a holistic approach to life should be a no-brainer. The problem is when we're raised to be judgmental by role models who unknowingly played God, we don't even realize we're out of touch with reality. When childhood is synonymous with painful emotions, we develop deceptive coping methods long before we reach adulthood.

This is why honing our sixth sense is so vital to making the transition from fear to faith. External solutions will never cure a universal spiritual identity problem. The more we learn to depend on our inner power, the less likely we'll be to feel overwhelmed by difficult circumstances.

Our Creator's original design for humanity to thrive on wholeness thoughts has never changed. Being led by the Spirit frees us from the endless torment of a love and fear belief system. When we commit to becoming transparent, we arrive at the inescapable conclusion that *only love is real.*

Recognizing the urgency to be true to yourself unlocks the unlimited potential of your mind to function according to its highest purpose. You finally transcend the poverty mentality of the limited self.

Fact or Fear?

I used to think those who put a positive spin on trying situations were living in denial. Before I grasped the necessity of living by faith, I had no idea I was the one who was out of touch with reality.

Love is forever. Feelings are changeable. Children are highly suggestible. If I grow up believing I'm spiritually one with God, that message is very reassuring. But if I also learn I can be sent to hell, then these opposing teachings tell me I must be separate from God and everyone else. Otherwise, from a collective standpoint, if I go to hell, we all go, including God.

Since I know this explanation can't possibly be true, I'm forced to view God and humanity as separate physical entities instead of from an inclusive spiritual perspective of wholeness. A mind-body orientation automatically leads me to seek comfort in the physical realm. Even though I can never seem to find true peace in the world, it still seems safer than trusting in a God of love and fear.

A mixed-message belief system prevents us from cultivating a true eternity perspective. Self-deceived parents and religious leaders can't be expected to teach only love that they themselves never learned is humanity's essence. When childhood feelings of inadequacy aren't resolved, fear is unconsciously perceived to be more powerful than love.

The cumulative effect of not being able to identify with humanity's spirit-to-Spirit union resulted in our mind closing itself off with a "wall" of dishonest aggressive, passive-aggressive, and passive response patterns. Instead of protecting us, this defense system only provides temporary relief from false feelings of unworthiness.

We were created to reflect God's grace through the assertive behavior of self-respect. The mind's barrier of fear-rooted behaviors almost succeeds in blocking out our true purpose. However, since most people aren't raised exclusively with negative messages, there are those times when love-based actions are able to break through our aggressive and passive defenses. A general example of this assertive stance is whenever you just know in your heart the right course of action to take. These times are commonly referred to as listening to your conscience; that instinctive, compassionate response that sometimes gets past even the most hardened mind-set.

Having insight to relate to others on a heart level is commonly referred to as women's intuition. This interpretation tends to ignore the vital role temperament and learned behavior play in determining one's ability to love. Males and females alike who grew up believing in the false power of nonassertive language are ruled by egocentric impulses. Women seek counseling more readily than men, but this doesn't necessarily mean they are more receptive to change.

A case in point is Martha. She has an aggressive temperament. She expressed the desire to grow spiritually. Subconsciously, she also wanted to maintain the status quo. She admitted her root problem was her unhealthy self-concept. Martha acknowledged feeling calmer when she responded assertively. But her false attachment to self was more important than her desire to be authentic. She was unwilling to surrender her addiction to superficial remedies.

Aggressors usually only become receptive to spiritual truths after they lose everything of value. Bob was a prime example. His longstanding heroin addiction rendered him as far from truthful as a person can be. When he surrendered to God's will in 1994, his spiritual recovery required his commitment to get real. Every time Bob's victim mentality surfaced in resentment against his first wife or the legal system, NA members would hold him accountable. He was reminded that his untrustworthy judgments had led him down the path to destruction. Bob humbled himself by praying every morning for strength to stay clean and abiding by daily direction from his sponsor.

Bob's transition from fear to love made it possible for him to sense the still small voice; particularly when he was called on to give his lead at NA meetings or offer encouragement to the men he sponsored. He was amazed that he was able to provide heartfelt counsel after a lifetime of following self-will.

Breaking Strongholds

The ability to be spiritually centered depends on whether we sincerely believe God's will is humanity's will. If we choose wholeness thinking in only one area, this action is comparable to breaching, without dismantling, the "fortress" surrounding our deluded mind. Our deep-rooted insecurities prevent us from experiencing victory in every aspect of our lives.

Just as I was able to offer spiritual guidance to the clients I counseled, so did Bob with the recovering men he advised. The glaring contradiction came into play when we were able to get in touch with our true nature in the area of counseling, while still clinging to fear-driven behaviors when it came to our marital relationship. False feelings of powerlessness nearly ended our marriage when we were still newlyweds. Simply stated, the contradictory nature of a love and fear reality allows us to help others—while privately still languishing in misery ourselves.

These examples illustrate the subtle, yet highly addictive nature of self-deception. During times of conflict, we fail to recognize the central role past resentments play in undermining our stability. As time goes on, it becomes all too easy to justify angry behaviors and self-pity that first took hold during childhood.

I grew up thinking going to church and saying I believed in God made me a Christian. I equated living by faith more with those who chose religious vocations. The truth is I was unknowingly hooked on proving I was right to mask my failure mentality. I had no idea back then that my thought patterns kept me from identifying with the peace of the Holy Spirit.

The emotional fixes in my marriage occurred after I gave my husband the cold shoulder treatment until he apologized. But as with all temporary fixes, the false sense of power I felt over convincing Bob to see things my way was merely the calm before the next storm. You can't be true to yourself as long as you place greater value on control than on love.

Without healing our adult/child split personalities, we act out our false feelings of separation from our Creator through our family (familiar) relationships. A self-will focus keeps us stuck in personal perceptions of right and wrong. The faces may change from generation to generation, but the endless dramas remain the same.

If enough people were motivated by love to stop the untold damage caused by fear-minded behaviors, it's no exaggeration to say experiencing heaven on earth would be the norm. Relying on external solutions to provide the completion that is humanity's birthright will never end until we eliminate our false belief in fear. We've been conditioned that seeing is believing. But we also know appearances can be deceiving.

People who appear to be ruled by pride are really overcompensating for their painful feelings of worthlessness. Uncovering the truth requires insight to look past one's pretense of arrogance to the scared child cowering within.

Faulty core beliefs convince us that our childhood repertoire of aggressive and passive defenses is necessary for our earthly survival. Nothing could be further from the truth. The emotional wall of nonassertive behaviors we hide behind prevents us from discovering we've always been whole.

Fear-bound parenting makes it very difficult to surrender our false need for control and approval as adults. It takes courage to trust in a God we can't see after being raised by role models who never grew up emotionally.

Peace of mind depends on recognizing the eventual despair of clinging to egotistical behaviors. Every time we personalize mistreatment, we deny our oneness. We unconsciously regress to the emptiness of childhood when we didn't feel loved. Self-serving posturing is the end result.

Linda identifies with control. She readily states she appreciates her husband's many loving qualities. But her temperament and learned behavior cause her to contradict herself. She is intolerant of her spouse's shortcomings and regularly blames him for problems without assuming any responsibility.

After facing a health crisis, Linda said she was ready to change. She tried to effect spiritual recovery without transforming her attitude. Linda called on God for help to stop becoming angered by unexpected events. But she didn't seriously work on resolving her underlying inferiority complex. As a result, her attitude remained oppositional. She kept slipping back into her lifelong habit of faultfinding.

Learning to love who you are is essential to being true to yourself. You lose your subconscious need to project your resentment from being devalued as a child onto others or turning your fear-bound feelings inward onto yourself.

New Age or Old Truths?

The New Age philosophy was heralded as an appealing alternative for those who perceived Christianity as unable to deliver on the promise of the abundant life. Since the early 1970s, this movement's greatest growth has been in the United States. Less than half-filled churches across America attest to the ongoing decline of followers of organized religion.

> Through rationalism (an overemphasis of reason), Christianity and the Western world have ceased to know how to deal with their inner lives— commonly called the heart, spirit, subconscious, or unconscious. Because this whole area of our lives has been cut off and ignored, not only by Western culture but also by the church, people have not been able to deal successfully with the forces within them and have been left to seek out various escapes, such as drinking, drugs, sensual

fulfillment, and suicide. Others become neurotic
and psychotic, and still others go to the occult
and Eastern religions to satisfy the inner desires
of the spirit that are not being met by rational
Christianity.[10]

Anxiety and depression are two common seemingly
formidable "forces" created by our mind in response to a false
belief in fear. Countering this negative energy by focusing on the
inherent love of our spirit-to-Spirit bond isn't being articulated
in our churches, homes, and schools.

Religious leaders who don't stress wholeness themes are more
likely to mistake self-deception for arrogance. Likewise, most
parents don't realize their children's disrespect is linked to the
way they feel about themselves and haven't pressed for classes on
self-esteem being added to schools' national curriculums.

New Age proponents advance the notion that humanity
ultimately achieves perfection over the course of successive
lifetimes through reincarnation. A Hitler type is described as
someone who hadn't evolved to his highest awareness. While
it's painfully obvious Hitler didn't emulate his divine nature,
this explanation doesn't address the underlying cause of his
depravity. Fear-controlled thought patterns are the reality of those
who function within the parameters of their genetic or learned
schizophrenia. His extreme mental instability notwithstanding,
Hitler projected his self-hatred onto millions of innocent victims.

On a scale ranging from feeling completely inadequate to
attaining worldly standards of perfection, considering oneself a
failure would result from living life from the extreme left fear
position. One whose life veers too far in the right fear position
toward perfection would demonstrate a false sense of confidence.
Believing my faults don't diminish my value represents the middle
ground love position that fortifies me to honor my spiritual
perfection.

Perfectionists are fear-minded. They try to deal with their insecurities by becoming overly concerned with appearances. A person who suffers from this malady has no idea he has a perfect spirit, because he has never felt complete. He subconsciously believes that doing everything perfectly will alleviate the gnawing feeling from childhood that he could never get it right. The opposite occurs. His anxiety intensifies over time, because his flesh-driven focus prevents him from recognizing the problem is in the way he learned to think. No matter how hard he tries to prove how capable he is, his fear-rooted mentality still operates with the same obsessive thoughts from his past. Compulsive adherence to impractical performance standards sets him up to experience ongoing frustration. When circumstances don't turn out exactly as he plans, he automatically blames himself or others.

As a recovering perfectionist, I can personally attest that inner healing dispels your distorted perceptions of yourself. A holistic approach to life leads you to insights that affirm you really do have the Mind of God. You're no longer controlled by misconceptions that prevent you achieving your highest potential.

Earthly Wholeness Clarified

If we take a closer look at God's plan for humanity to feel complete, we can see how quickly a mixed-message belief system subverts our peace of mind. When we grow up believing in love and fear, we experience varying degrees of anxiety that all have the same debilitating outcome: feelings of unworthiness from denying wholeness of love.

Individual agendas become our top priority. We blame everything and everyone but ourselves for our lack of fulfillment. We live a spiritually impoverished life that is characterized by superficial judgments.

The manner in which your personality was originally split between love and fear can be best illustrated by revisiting your infancy. Your temperament was genetically predetermined. Your learned behavior was governed by a whole host of environmental factors. The way you were held, how often you were held, and the tones of voices you heard in the womb and as a baby are just a few of the initial influences that shaped your existing response patterns.

Imagine, if you will, what your life would be like had you been taught that God designed you to be the embodiment of His perfect peace. Starting with nonverbal and verbal prenatal cues, you have always sensed *only love is real*. Your holistic reality was cultivated by parents who were also raised to believe in their immeasurable value. As they tenderly nurtured you, your security was firmly established from the very beginning of your life.

You never witnessed hostile confrontations between your parents. You weren't regularly subjected to judgmental behaviors that caused you to doubt your timeless identity of love. *Complain* is a word that is practically foreign to you. As role models of praise, your parents' bolstered your confidence with words of encouragement and genuine displays of affection. When correction was needed, you were firmly, yet calmly redirected. During those times when you persisted in getting your way, the consequences were neither ignored nor harsh. You never internalized the fear-minded belief that your mistakes define you. On the contrary, you were advised that refusing to let your setbacks defeat you makes your successes that much sweeter.

You were taught at an early age that God's way is love, you are love because you are one with God, and love is all that matters. In short, you grew up responding in agreement with your divinity. You also learned prayer wasn't only to be used in times of desperation. You were trained to pray for God's guidance each morning and to express your gratitude to God throughout the day, regardless of how events unfolded. You were assured you carry the strength of the Holy Spirit within your spirit to overcome whatever adversities you encounter.

You discovered by example the importance of matching words like integrity, respect, and loyalty to your conduct. Being inner-directed by love, your mind had no need to build a formidable aggressive and passive defense system. You don't overreact or underreact. You were taught responding any other way than assertively prevents you from being authentic. Knowing you're completely cherished insulates you from personalizing misguided behaviors.

You were taught to become a trustworthy adult by submitting to your parents' boundaries for suitable conduct. You ultimately learned to appreciate the necessity of exchanging your childish need for instant gratification for the long-term gain of patiently acquiring the spiritual maturity to achieve your highest good.

As an adult, you have always understood that seeking out one special person to fulfill you would contradict your wholeness. You were valued from infancy to feel complete, regardless of who is or isn't in your life. As a result, your happiness doesn't depend on whether you're single or married, only on your awareness to always remain open to love. You instinctively know that responding in everyone's best interests is the only way to remain centered.

You were never made to feel guilty because your occupation deviated from your parents' expectations. They trusted you to fulfill your true purpose, regardless of the career path you chose. Feeling secure as a treasured child of God reminds you what is truly important: extending compassion to those who haven't learned to identify with love.

Since you've always been attuned to humanity's spiritual perfection, you forgo judging temporary imperfections. Your insight convinces you nothing is more imperative than remembering God's will is your will. You steadfastly refuse to be deceived by the ever changing world system you live in but have no part of, apart from communicating the never ending reality of love.

Transforming Childhood Trauma

If this description sounds too good to be true, it's only because fear-based beliefs have convinced you otherwise. As a first-grader attending a Christian school, I remember one of the first questions asked was, "Where is God?" The answer is, "Everywhere." This means there isn't any place where God's Presence isn't felt. He is as much a part of you as your vital organs. If you believe this on a subconscious level, you function on a higher level of consciousness. You wisely know the Mind and Spirit of God represent the reality of love in everyone.

A mind that has broken free from its false bondage of fear understands the importance of assertive behavior. With every newly fortified beat, your heart extends forgiveness to free everyone else who learned to view aggressive and passive actions as acceptable conduct. In the event a lifetime of angry communication has rendered your loved one's defenses impenetrable, you distance yourself, while continuing to pray for his spiritual recovery.

Restoring your mind to wholeness thoughts insulates you from unreliable feelings dictating your moods. You recognize the pressing need to exchange your blinding personal perceptions for enlightened thoughts about your everlasting identity of love. Your eternity perspective empowers you to depend on the peace of the Holy Spirit during trying times.

If, on the other hand, you only learned to relate to spiritual truths on a superficial level, or not at all, fear is ingrained in your personality. You may feel the same way I did in the first grade, as well as throughout most of my adult life. You want to believe God loves you unconditionally because such thoughts make you feel safe and powerful at the same time. But if, like me, you were also taught that this very same God could send you to a fiery hell in the blink of an eye, then that's a whole new ball game.

Instead of viewing yourself as a vital part of a benevolent Creator, your internalized beliefs grotesquely distort the ever present reality of love. Your oppositional mind-set dismisses the redemption message. God is subconsciously viewed solely in terrifying Physical form, apart from you, whose bloodied crucified Flesh you've seen depicted countless times. This same Jesus, who suffered and died because of your sins, is soon returning to make you suffer for all eternity. Simply stated, a mind ruled by a loving God + a condemning God = a belief system founded on a fear-based God.

If we contrast this dismal portrayal with an infinity mind-set, there's no contest. We gradually transition from childhood fears to faith that frees us to openly express our strength of character from within. We consistently express love without judgment through true communion of heart and soul.

A fear-driven outlook tends to manifest in extreme ways: displaying conformity to religious legalism in a desperate attempt to stave off the wrath of a punishing Creator, or engaging in worldly excesses designed to anesthetize us from thoughts of being dealt with by God at all.

In his best-selling book, *10 Secrets for Success and Inner Peace*, Dr. Wayne Dyer describes the torment of mistaken identity: "Every time you experience fear, self-rejection, anxiety, guilt, or hate, you're denying your divinity and succumbing to the influences of that insidious ego mind that has convinced you of your disconnection to God."[11]

The disheartening love-fear association that most of us have been subjected to since birth can be likened to listening to soothing music and a heavy metal band at the same time. The dissonance drowns out the tranquility of the mellow music.

Spiritual recovery equips you to trust God in a world overrun by fear-bound perceptions. Learning to love authentically releases you from the failure mentality you internalized during your childhood.

Arrogance or Ignorance?

There is only one requirement for lasting fulfillment: recognize the oneness of God's will and humanity's will. Self-will represents a subconscious carryover from our fear-rooted childhoods that prevent us from being genuine.

Adam and Eve have been endlessly vilified for forfeiting paradise. If we judge according to appearances, it seems inconceivable that the first couple would have disobeyed God. They were perfect and so were their surroundings. A closer look reveals their actions had more to do with ignorance than arrogance. Most people don't understand that pride is a cover-up for feelings of inferiority that first took root during childhood. Adam and Eve had been formed as full-fledged adults. They weren't in the Garden of Eden long enough to develop deep-seated feelings of any kind.

One can't fully appreciate the meaning of abundance without experiencing the contrasting feeling of deprivation. This is why people who grew up disadvantaged are more accepting of life's hardships and more grateful for the extras they do receive than those who learn to take their blessings for granted.

Adam and Eve only knew heaven on earth. Since they had nothing to compare their idyllic existence to, it's logical to assume they had no idea they would unleash hell on earth. Their unintended legacy to humanity was immaturity. This completely irrational short-term gain, long-term pain approach to life has been repeated throughout the ages, in spite of causing untold misery. The reason is both simple and tragic: a mind that forms a fear-love neural connection is subconsciously programmed to keep re-creating this pain-pleasure cycle that characterizes addictive behaviors.

Ephesians 4:18 describes the consequences of a spiritually unenlightened mind: "having their understanding darkened, being alienated from the life of God, because of the ignorance that is in them, because of the blindness of their heart." Self-deception enslaved the first couple to fear-bound emotions for the duration of their physical lives. If even their former state of absolute perfection wasn't enough to motivate them to move beyond their misconceptions, then it's completely understandable why most people today remain blind to the love that defines them.

If you doubt the logic of these statements, all you have to do is consider the number of adults you know, or read and hear about, who behave childishly on a regular basis without realizing it. The truth is adults who don't consistently pursue a spiritual path either act irritated or pout like children when they don't get their way.

Without insight to live by faith, fear-based beliefs poison our thoughts. Contradictory feelings govern our actions. Every time we give false power to unexpected events by overreacting or underreacting, our elevated anxiety levels deny our oneness with God.

When we're too afraid of change to listen to reason, it simply doesn't occur to us to seek divine comfort within. Expecting fulfillment to come from our circumstances convinces us of two falsehoods: 1) Feeling stressed is normal. 2) Depending on superficial remedies is as good as it gets.

Before I began meditating to stay centered, my mind would be flooded with fear-driven thoughts before I even got out of bed. Today, I concentrate on a modified version of the serenity prayer: "Thank You for courage to transition from fear to love, serenity to accept what I can't change, and wisdom to understand Your will is my will."

Believing in love and fear is like being served an extravagant seven course meal, but choosing to only nibble on the appetizer. We can't even begin to fathom manifesting the kingdom of God from within us as long as we're subconsciously governed by untrustworthy emotions. Our fears keep inevitably surfacing through nonassertive conduct.

When we restore our mind to wholeness thoughts, our insecurities ultimately vanish, because true love always conquers false fear. God is pure love. He indwells us. Fear-bound behaviors won't have any power to continue triggering anxiety response patterns if we discipline ourselves to change our reactions from judgmental to spiritual.

The following example illustrates how easily a false connection to fear is instilled at infancy: Envision yourself as a two-year-old who has gotten much less attention since your infant brother arrived. Your mother is holding your brother while she reads you a bedtime story. Unknown to you, your mother had a bad day at work and is feeling on edge.

The baby starts to cry, and your mother stops reading. As she attends to him, your jealousy prompts you to hit your little brother. Without thinking, she slaps your hand and screams at you. Now, not only is your brother picking up on your mother's hostility by wailing even louder, you cry out in emotional pain as well. Your mother continues to overreact out of exasperation. You're too little to comprehend your mother's aggression has nothing to do with the love she feels for you. This seemingly incidental episode can fester in your subconscious.

Similar incidents that play out as you grow can cause you to mistakenly believe you're responsible for your mother's lack of self-control or that she cares more about your little brother. Also, depending on your temperament, your mother may unconsciously reinforce the idea in your mind that physical aggression is an acceptable response to misbehavior.

If you multiply this scenario by the staggering number of times the average person is subjected to disrespect during his formative years, you can begin to appreciate the addictive nature of fear-minded response patterns. Developing an eternity perspective releases us from the incessant demands of our stuck inner children. We finally recognize "my way" solutions can only temporarily compensate for the helplessness we felt during our formative years.

Spiritual recovery provides heartfelt assurance that we don't have to be dependent on anyone or anything outside ourselves to feel complete.

Old Habits Die Hard

Self-deception prevents us from realizing that we repeat many of the negative energy patterns that adversely affected the quality of our parents' lives. When peace of mind is our goal, we finally break the vicious cycle of depressed and anxious response patterns.

Rick confused repression and passive-aggressive behavior with detachment. There was virtually nothing this gifted man couldn't fix. Rick perceived that his wife took advantage of his skills by always assigning him household projects to complete. He believed he was detaching from his anger by not telling his wife how he really felt and by procrastinating. In reality, Rick's behavior was passive and passive-aggressive.

Trying to deny our resentment by acting as though everything is fine or by indirectly communicating our hostility through avoidance behavior leads to stuck feelings that can eventually erupt in rage and physical and mental illnesses.

Inner healing empowers you to be genuine. You don't consider it a personal affront when others don't live up to your standards, because you're no longer ruled by the unquenchable dictates of your ego. You develop faith to trust that every experience is a learning device designed to increase your spiritual wisdom.

Amy once began a session by announcing she hated her partner. She then launched into her laundry list of his aggressive episodes. I interrupted to inquire how long she intended to rail against his childish behavior with her own inner child. Amy sheepishly admitted she was finished regressing.

I used this opportunity to remind Amy not to be too hard on herself. Even though she was sincere about embracing a holistic approach to life, she was still vulnerable to being controlled by her emotions. The intensity of her reaction indicated she hadn't yet forgiven her father for the verbal abuse he had subjected her to during her childhood.

When we aren't raised to respond assertively, we're easily triggered by reminders of our painful upbringing. It requires perseverance to exchange judgment for forgiveness. Here is a good rule of thumb to remind yourself that you're losing (in)sight of your divine nature: when your irritation over how your family member performs overrides your compassion for his own illusory battle with his stuck child.

Before becoming Spirit-led, it never occurred to me how detrimental it was to rehash disagreements with my husband to garner sympathy from my friends. This widespread practice only adds fuel to a fire that was first kindled during childhood. That was when most of us were subjected to the toxic effects of fear-engulfed conditioning that appeared to incinerate our ability to love.

Most quarrels are merely smokescreens that hide the raging infernos in our soul. As explained in chapter 2, the petty problems that appeared to spark the heated debates during our first year of marriage had very little to do with the issue at hand. Deep down, our incendiary childhood personas ignited the flare-ups that were fanned by the flames of our false belief in fear.

The egocentric "I'm right, you're wrong" attitude keeps resurfacing until we heal our unresolved hurts. We subconsciously associate rejection of our opinions with the personal rejection we felt as children.

The only honest way to give and receive love is without fear-based perceptions clouding our judgments. An eternity perspective frees us to emulate our divinity. Simply stated, developing spiritual discernment empowers us to resolve disputes without self-serving agendas.

Finding relief from a conflict-filled life can be clarified by examining the top ten reasons to stop identifying with fear-rooted ideas:

- ✓ 10. Giving in to gain approval or your attachment to being right ends up causing you to feel as defeated as you did during your childhood.
- ✓ 9. Due to reason #10, you hasten your mental and physical decline.
- ✓ 8. Following self-will forces you to settle for a life of fleeting pleasure through ego gratification.
- ✓ 7. Aggressive and passive communication prevents peace of mind from becoming your reality.
- ✓ 6. Focusing on faultfinding denies your spiritual perfection.
- ✓ 5. Due to reason #6, you don't identify with love.
- ✓ 4. Even if your standard of living improves dramatically, your underlying feelings of powerlessness keep you bound to fear-minded conduct.
- ✓ 3. Learning to love yourself is far more important than any relationship or anything money can buy.
- ✓ 2. Your failure to actualize your wholeness in thought, word, and deed prevents you from fulfilling your true purpose.

And, the #1 reason for learning to respond knowing *only love is real* is:

- ✓ 1. You have been deceived from birth into substituting a false existence for your real life of heaven on earth.

Dismissing the urgent need for spiritual recovery is like saying you prefer to be defined by chaotic relationships. When you commit to honoring your mind, body, and spirit, the kingdom of God within you is demonstrated through your consistent, loving actions.

Maximizing Your True Power

Congenital cognitive deficits notwithstanding, we're born with the ability to demonstrate true love. When we discover God's will is humanity's will, our peaceful, perfect spirit is theoretically free to function in unison with the Holy Spirit 100 percent of the time.

A false belief in fear prevents the vast majority from coming even close to discovering the kingdom of God within themselves. Based on temperament and learned behavior, most people either communicate honestly 90 percent or 10 percent of the time. At first glance, it seems inconceivable to function with a 90 percent love deficit. But the reality that there are always wars, crime, poverty, disease, divorce, and tumultuous relationships confirm fear-driven conduct overwhelmingly prevails.

A person's ability to experience peace of mind is either weakened by judgmental input or is fortified by God-centered communication. If you weren't born with an assertive temperament and weren't raised by assertive parents, your ability to love drastically dwindled from 100 percent at birth to 10 percent long before you ever reached adulthood. This lopsided imbalance represents misidentification with self. Even though your insecurities have convinced you otherwise, you're whole. The catch is you have to identify with the love that has always been inside you to develop an abundance mentality.

When we don't understand that our problems have a universal spiritual solution, we can't be true to ourselves. An egotistical perspective blindsides us from seeing that the potential for entrapment to self-deception begins at birth. From helpful developmental items to a plethora of toys that stimulate one's five senses, infants are trained to associate external objects with pleasure. It's absolutely essential to start communicating intrinsic values in word and deed at the toddler stage. Otherwise, self-seeking goals automatically become entrenched as the pathway to fulfillment. Becoming addicted to short-term gratification patterns starts out so subtlely that most people never stop to consider the eventual destruction that can ensue from seemingly harmless desires. When flesh-driven pursuits become our master when we're young, lack of insight can ensnare us until we physically die.

Without a holistic viewpoint to stop fighting the imaginary conflict in our mind between love and fear, we get caught up in false judgments. We keep complicating minor, as well as major, problems that wouldn't exist if we had become attuned to our perfect spirit-to-Spirit bond as children.

Dan is an engaging single man in his twenties. He lamented that he attracts women who aren't interested in nice guys. They are into materialism and drama. I started to explain the 90/10 theory. Dan interrupted by stating his version of this theory. He said he would be more than willing to give 90 percent and only receive 10 percent in return. Dan had no idea his statement betrayed his lack of self-esteem. If we don't learn to value who we are so we can require respectful treatment, we go through life settling for far less than we deserve.

As adults, like Dan, we become emotionally stunted giving and receiving the minimal 10 percent of love. It's a sad commentary on the false power of fear that there are precious few people in the world who transcend their egocentric impulses 100 percent of the time.

Unfortunately, even the prospect of lasting peace of mind isn't sufficient motivation to change the status quo. When we grow up defining self-will as our comfort zones, rigorous honesty is required to admit our personal perceptions have led us astray. As long as we're subconsciously ruled by our childhood insecurities, a fulfilling life will seem impossible to achieve. Most people will only accept a contradictory compromise: pledging allegiance to God's will, while continuing to play God.

Peggy has multiple health problems. She sees no problem in gossiping about her coworkers and discussing God in the same conversation. She dismisses her relentless judgments by rationalizing that everyone reverts to self-serving actions. What Peggy doesn't comprehend is people who seek to function on higher levels of consciousness strive to eliminate response patterns that don't reflect their true identity of love.

Realistically speaking, the average person who sincerely desires to transform from fear to love can achieve a 90 per cent success rate. When contrasted with the natural inclination to stay stuck in negative energy patterns 90 per cent of the time, the benefits of this dramatic reversal are enormous. Once this goal is accomplished, collectively actualizing heaven on earth will be well within our grasp.

A sample power prayer follows:

> I'm grateful I have Your Mind, God, to counter false fear with true love. I freely embrace humanity's oneness to manifest heaven on earth from within me. As I tune out the blinding dramas that prevent me from being honest, I'm quickened to exchange judgment for forgiveness. Whenever I'm tempted to focus on all the wrongdoing in the fleeting physical realm, thank you for insight to remember an eternity mind-set is the proven pathway to peace.

Love/Fear Dichotomy

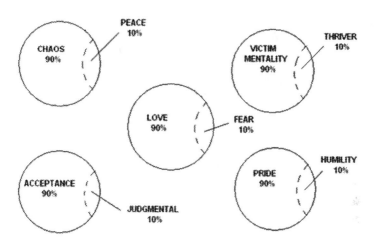

Figure 2

The above circles illustrate various representations of the love-fear schism that determine whether one's overall reactions are peaceful or anxiety-ridden. The middle and lower left circles depict general restoration to wholeness on earth. The remaining circles portray the daily choices we unconsciously make when we're out of touch with reality.

Behavior controlled by self-will dictates, *I'm going to live on my own terms*. Generational misconceptions not only pave the way for conflicts to multiply; they can significantly shorten our life spans.

Living your real life of love replaces your despair with determination to discover your divine destiny. Let's begin in earnest to eradicate fear once and for all.

CHAPTER 7

Seeing the Light through Insight

Hell is truth seen too late.
—Tryon Edwards

In the 1970s, comedian Flip Wilson's alter ego, Geraldine, coined the expression, "The devil made me do it." When we aren't raised to believe we already have all the power we need to succeed, false feelings of powerlessness cause us to gravitate to fear-driven conclusions.

When I was a little girl attending church, 1 Corinthians 6:19 struck me as a source of wonderment and puzzlement at the same time: "Or do you not know that your body is the temple of the Holy Spirit who is in you, whom you have from God, and you are not your own?" As I matured without comprehending the whole(ness) truth these words conveyed, my confusion grew; not surprisingly, in direct proportion to allowing everything but inner peace to dictate my actions. Criticizing people, places, and things that didn't suit me made it all too convenient to believe my anxiety and depression were normal.

As I became older, I started questioning why I wasn't more content, given my more than adequate standard of living. Since gaining support for my complaints had never elevated my mood for very long, I was eventually forced to admit my attitude was my real problem.

In hindsight, I had always sensed the answer was inside me. That is why I was so taken with that seemingly mysterious Corinthians scripture from my childhood. But, as always, timing is everything. I had to slowly mature spiritually before the truth could finally emerge: the lifelong battle I had waged in my head between love and fear-minded outcomes was just a figment of my imagination.

When I became serious about relinquishing my false attachment to self, I was reminded of a caterpillar's metamorphosis. After much struggling to shed its confining cocoon, it soars as the beautiful butterfly it was always intended to be. Simply stated, transcending self-defeating beliefs to become the love-centered person God created you to be is the only way to reestablish paradise on earth.

At first, it felt inconceivable that I had always had the power to free myself from my fear-bound thoughts. Even worse was conceding that I had allowed my childhood victim mentality to undermine the quality of my life until I was well beyond middle-age. As difficult as that conclusion was to admit, I knew in my heart it was true. If I was sincere about healing my lifelong depression, I had to acknowledge only one of the following choices made sense: 1) I could continue to maximize my stress level by attributing my attitude to external events. 2) I could maximize my peace of mind by depending on God's Presence to sustain me, regardless of what transpired.

Sanity prevailed. I decided healing my learned schizophrenia was much more important than clinging to a love and fear belief system that had yielded me far more pain than pleasure. My recovery journey began with several false starts before I could no longer deny the utmost necessity of resolving my lifelong feelings of inadequacy.

Becoming grounded in love occurs on a soul level. Otherwise, we continue to behave the way we did as children: responding according to the fear-rooted connection embedded in our mind between perceived adverse circumstances and feeling that our anger, depression, guilt, self-pity, etc., is justified.

As my thinking became more rational, I ultimately was able to unravel the meaning of that Bible verse I had contemplated so long ago. I was finally ready to pay close attention to the stirrings in my soul that had first sensitized me to my inner power. The Spirit of truth had been waiting ever so patiently for me to get with the program so healthy response patterns could finally take root.

I recognized the importance of meditating to quiet my anxious thoughts and being thankful for everyday blessings I had always taken for granted. As if on cue, I "miraculously" began discerning answers to lifelong dilemmas I wasn't able to figure out on my own.

For example, I had never recognized the glaring discrepancy between considering myself to be spiritual and focusing on wrongdoing. Being judgmental had always felt natural. And that was exactly the problem. I had learned to react based on feelings that denied my wholeness. I lacked understanding that consistent, assertive communication is the only way to have a real impact on those who identify with fear.

My former need to be right because I didn't feel right inside made it nearly impossible to believe—horror of horrors!—that I was to blame for my negativity. The truth is we're incapable of objectively evaluating disagreements if we have a personal stake in the outcome; especially if we haven't worked through our temperament and learned behavior issues.

If I had been taught *only love is real,* I would have been empowered to respond with God's Mind. But since my mind was split between concepts that are real and unreal, this delusional dynamic compels me to attempt to accommodate both realities. The end result is my underlying anxiety normally contradicts what I say.

A love-based reality can only emerge if we concede we can't have it both ways and still remain rational long-term. Our real choices are either conscious or subconscious: God's will or self-deception. Simply stated, if I grow up truly believing I'm like God, I'll naturally respond in love. The only way I'll behave unlike Him is if I've learned to believe what is impossible: love coexists with fear in eternity now and forever.

Without spiritual discernment to understand God and humanity represent oneness of love, the normal outcome is to remain self-deceived until we physically die. Like programmed robots, we automatically overreact and underreact to fear-driven stimuli. We're conditioned to think in terms of our differences. I may even agree you and I are equals. But subconsciously, my stuck child either believes I'm better than or less than you. Instead of concentrating on serving the best interests of the whole, my attention is naturally diverted to self-serving goals. If I say white, you say black. If you say no, I feel the need to convince you to say yes. Non-stop dissension arises from seemingly innocuous oppositional attitudes that emanate from a false belief in fear.

I'm only able to righteously judge your behavior if fear-controlled thoughts aren't influencing my responses. If I resolve my childhood trauma through spiritual recovery, I'll be far less likely to criticize how others act. My verbal reactions match my inner peace because I'm now equipped to reply honestly through assertive behavior.

Cultivating a holistic reality gradually eliminates my false need to personalize offensive conduct. I view your aggression as a clear sign you haven't moved beyond your painful past. I relate to you with God's grace. My steadfast, firm, yet compassionate approach increases the probability that you'll discover the ultimate truth: humanity was created to express God's will on earth as it is in heaven.

Humility is an essential course correction. I had to be willing to conquer my addiction to dwell on the downside of life. Discovering the love I had inside me all along never would have become my reality if I hadn't humbled myself to stop faulting everyone's behavior but my own. I'm now generally able to exercise self-control instead of feeling I have every right (wrong!) to judge others.

When we identify with love, the false power of our illusory ego to destroy humanity through fear-based ideations is finally broken. Exchanging the relentless demands of our inner children for the still small voice transforms insecurities into testimonies of a resilient spirit.

The Holy Spirit is the very Heart of God that is attached to humanity's heart. This electrifying statement has no real meaning for those who are mentally disconnected from their true power Source. Misidentification with self convinces us our survival is based on external control and approval, because that's the only way an egotistical mentality can survive.

When a child doesn't feel valued, he quickly learns to say or do whatever will get his needs met. Dishonest communication acts as a buffer that is intended to shield him from further rejection. He may tell his parents what he thinks they want to hear, resort to intimidation tactics, or repress how he really feels. The deceptive reality of fear-bound response patterns he accepts as real causes him to believe conditional love is normal.

Clashing viewpoints continue to undermine his stability during adulthood. The coping abilities of his "opponents" (family members, friends, coworkers, etc.) are built on the same foundation of mistrust that he internalized as he matured: relying on worldly goals or external spirituality for fulfillment.

As long as you continue to believe in both love and fear-based messages, you aren't likely to recover from your childhood victim mentality. You'll remain unaware that self represents a delusional construct your mind created in response to the dissonance of believing you must choose daily between opposing forces. Spiritual recovery heals your split personality to focus wholly on love. The gratifying end result is being true to yourself. The confident demeanor you display to the world will finally match the love, peace, faithfulness, kindness, etc. you were never empowered to access. Simply stated, you'll eliminate your inner torment that you've always felt forced to deny with a smiling public façade.

The crucial point to remember is you'll remain out of touch with reality until you transition from judging by sight to forgiving by faith. Peace of mind prevails only when you make a conscious choice to gracefully accept situations you were never meant to change, and refrain from paying undue attention to errors in judgment. As you gradually become more sensitive to spiritual promptings, you won't feel forced to react the same way you did during your childhood.

This is the true meaning of wholeness inferred in the Corinthians message that I first heard as a child. Believing you can be separated from your Source is like saying it's possible to live without your heart. As Paul stated in Romans 8:38–39, "For I am persuaded that neither death nor life ... nor any created thing, shall be able to separate us from the love of God."

Relinquishing your false attachment to self is only difficult short-term. Detaching from nonassertive thoughts and behaviors improves your health in the long run. You won't be continually shaken by conduct that isn't real from a love-centered standpoint.

Living by faith lies in deciding how important emotional stability is to you. Only you can decide whether responding based on how you feel is more important than identifying with your whole mind, body, and spirit.

Mistaken Identity Revisited

A closer examination of Adam and Eve's behavior reveals why inner healing is so vital to a centered life. How did the first couple go wrong when they had God Himself as their instructor?

The answer is their childlike naiveté ensnared them in self-deception. Physically, they appeared to be adults, but their actions betrayed their maturity level. The die was cast for humanity to choose superficial values over enduring virtues. We're unable to grow up emotionally mature if our role models didn't comprehend that love originates from within.

When Adam and Eve's spirit functioned in accord with the Spirit of truth, they weren't self-conscious about their physical appearance: "And they were both naked, the man and his wife, and were not ashamed" (Genesis 2:25). In modern day societies, the opposite attitude is true. People are generally so embarrassed by and obsessed with their physical imperfections that they can't even begin to relate to their spiritual perfection.

As soon as the first couple's faith was tested, hell on earth predictably broke loose. Adam and Eve had only experienced the sheer delight of feeling mentally, physically, and spiritually complete. Their transition to a short-sighted flesh-driven orientation threw them totally off balance. The first couple's bliss was instantly exchanged for despair. Imagine what it would be like to be reveling in the fullness of God's love with your partner and then, all at once, experience the illusion of absolute isolation.

Adam and Eve had only known the good life. Their rude awakening to the knowledge of good and evil instantaneously ushered in the false belief in fear. The first couple abruptly transitioned from God-centered to self-centered. Anxiety replaced reason. They felt like they had no other recourse than to take refuge in their surroundings.

Adam and Eve's nudity no longer felt natural from their guilt-ridden viewpoint. Genesis 3:7 describes this transformation to self-consciousness: "Then the eyes of both of them were opened and they knew they were naked, and they sewed fig leaves together and made themselves coverings." Translation: They lost their spiritual discernment to focus on love from the inside out. When the first couple identified with their spiritual perfection, clothing was irrelevant. Their primary interest was basking in the ecstasy of their spirit-to-Spirit union. Their urgency to clothe themselves had nothing to do with their undressed state. This action represented humanity's first experience with the highly addictive nature of self-deception: they tried to solve a spiritual identity problem with a worldly fix. Clothing symbolized Adam and Eve's attempt to "cover up" the shame they felt inside. They were now blind to love, just as most people today live in spiritual darkness by counting on external solutions that don't have the power to heal their inner turmoil.

Losing (in)sight of love prevented the first couple from remembering God's will was their will. Identifying solely with their transient physical beings gave birth to feelings of powerlessness. Since they no longer sensed their unconditional bond, Adam and Eve now feared God. Self-condemnation and projection was the end result. They employed these rationales by first trying to hide from their Creator, then by leveling blame.

The first couple unconsciously traded God's wisdom for untrustworthy personal perceptions. This is the critical point where people mistake spiritual blindness for actual separation from God. Exercising self-will doesn't mean my eternal status suddenly ceases to exist. It means I'm unable to sense the love within me. False separation anxiety is what fuels my belief that I'm apart from God. Simply stated, a mind that isn't trained to wholeheartedly love is out of touch with reality.

Adam and Eve's fear-minded belief that God had rejected them, not just their behavior, is what made their idyllic existence seem to evaporate before their eyes. Feelings of unworthiness are simply incompatible with experiencing mental, physical, and spiritual heaven on earth. Then and now, without spiritual insight to discern *only love is real,* we're not able to consistently think rationally. Simply stated, if we don't function according to the whole(ness) truth, self-deception prevents us from recognizing paradise has never been lost.

If we don't make it our top priority to recognize God's will is humanity's will, we won't function on higher levels of consciousness during our physical lifetimes. Without reawakening to God-consciousness, we aren't empowered to experience the pure joy inherent in oneness of love. Instead, our egocentric mind-set leaves us feeling empty, because superficial fixes always lose their original appeal. The most opulent lifestyles and the demise of one's body don't have any significance in eternity. The worst part of never experiencing true peace of mind is the same today as it was for Adam and Eve—failure to live our real life of love due to a false belief in fear.

Restoring Wholeness

Adam and Eve partaking of the tree of the knowledge of good and evil is a metaphor for emotional instability. We can't function according to our true purpose to love if we alternate between truth and fiction. We learn to contradict our eternal identity every time we complain (express fear-bound feelings) about our circumstances (judge by sight).

Humanity's departure from the ever present reality of love can be likened to the proverbial opening of Pandora's box. Once self-hate—born of self-deception—was unleashed in the world, it could no longer be contained. Most people either try to ignore the debilitating effects or remain too afraid to change the status quo. Evidence of this mutated cancer becomes more virulent with each passing generation.

Misidentifying with self has steadily evolved into ever increasing feelings of isolation throughout the ages. Some of the most familiar devastating global consequences include: rampant mental illnesses, abject poverty, mass murders, sexual aberrations, terroristic acts, and never ending wars.

Our physical realm is ever changing. When we subconsciously believe life on earth is our sole reality, our false belief in fear compels us to operate on lower energy levels. We automatically feel limited in how much we can accomplish. A mind that is delusional exalts self to compensate for its perceived powerlessness. This is why egotistical behaviors ultimately fail. They aren't real.

Our spiritual reality never changes. When we develop an eternity viewpoint, we function on higher energy levels, because we recognize our potential is unlimited. A mind restored to wholeness of love is infinitely energized to serve everyone's best interests.

A reality based on good and evil significantly impairs one's ability to grow up feeling complete. To a little child, whose mind is a blank slate, parents represent God. Mothers and fathers have the power of life and death over their children.

I'm not referring to tragic cases of abuse that result in a child's physical death. I'm speaking of the psychic death that occurs during fear-controlled parenting. These heartbreaking acts can be as subtle as parents communicating through words and body language that their child doesn't measure up to their standards, or as profoundly horrific as children being subjected to incest or forced into pornography.

Both extremes produce self-rejection that is either consciously or unconsciously projected onto God; hence the pressing need to renew one's mind to function as a timeless spirit who thrives in unison with the Holy Spirit in a temporary body. The longer we count on people, places, and things for fulfillment, the less likely we'll be to act honestly and attract trustworthy relationships.

The pain that results from psychic scarring during childhood can be even worse than physical abuse. The ramifications of feeling undeserving of love are so varied and complex that even mental health professionals have trouble identifying the markers in their own lives.

Angry communication is always a telltale sign. When a person doesn't have a clear understanding of his immeasurable value, an innocent comment or even a simple sigh can have the same negative impact as a sarcastic comment or a withering look.

If you're not inner-directed, you lack discernment to call upon the Spirit of truth to interpret events from a love-grounded perspective. Your pain from the past is triggered and your defenses flare up, causing you to condemn yourself or lash out at others. And even in cases where there's more than enough evidence of an underlying problem, such as drug addiction or promiscuity, self-hatred isn't usually acknowledged as the culprit. A person who doesn't adhere to society's standards for acceptable behavior is more likely to be branded as defiant.

The logical way to reverse the untold damage of mixed-messages is to believe, act, and teach *only love is real*. People are fond of saying, "if it ain't broke, don't fix it," so the opposite corollary should also hold true. It's painfully obvious that a love and fear belief system has intensified humanity's despair, so when are we going to fix it?

An uplifting power prayer to heal your deceived mind is a good start:

> Dear God, I humbly admit I've been misguided
> by my false belief in fear to fail to comprehend the
> true meaning of Your unconditional love. Thank
> You for awakening me from the nightmare of my
> judgmental attitude and for resolve and redirection
> to recognize that my heart beats in rhythm with
> Your Heart and humanity's heart, joined as One.

A spiritual perspective equips you to exchange your unpredictable feelings for faith in God's promises. Your subconscious compulsion to re-enact your childhood fears is forever broken. The blinding illusion of experiencing the wrath of God instantly dissolves in the dazzling light of His everlasting love.

The Power of Visualization

Guided imagery is a proven form of meditation that promotes a tranquil state. It's effective because our mind doesn't make a distinction between imaginary stimuli and real-life experiences.

If I'm feeling stressed about making a speech, I can picture myself beforehand speaking with confidence. Through relaxation techniques and concentration, I can decrease my anxiety level to achieve a successful outcome.

The visualization I'm proposing is contained in the *Garden of Eden* audio file that can be downloaded from my website (see listing at the end of this book). It will help you change your internalized script by taking you back to the biblical depiction of heaven on earth, before fear-rooted behaviors gained a stranglehold on humanity. And unlike the elevated stress you might feel about public speaking, this scenario isn't intimidating. You're not even cast in the starring role; Eve is. Your supporting role, however, is critical to reversing the destructive consequences of self-deception.

To prepare for your part, you'll need to find a quiet spot where you can be comfortably seated. Close your eyes, and take several slow, deep breaths to anchor yourself in the present. Focus on releasing the tension from every individual part of your body, from your feet, legs, and hips up to your neck and head. When you feel completely relaxed, with your eyes closed, the CD will prompt you to begin:

> Envision yourself enveloped in a sea of clouds. You feel weightless as the filmy mist slowly transports you back, back in time. As the clouds begin to lift, you find yourself casually attired, standing in the middle of the Garden of Eden.
>
> You gaze in awe at the splendor of your surroundings. As far as your eyes can focus

from every angle, you see lush vegetation, a spectacular array of flowers in every imaginable hue, a perfectly manicured variety of trees and vines containing sun-ripened fruits, a waterfall cascading down a majestic purple mountain, shimmering pools of sparkling blue water, and a rainbow so vivid you can clearly see each vibrant color.

As you inhale to imprint this wondrous scene in your soul and spirit, you notice the aromatic scent of lilacs. After a moment, you "drink" in the distinctive fragrance of milky white gardenias. You sample the delectable sweetness of two mouth-watering fruits, then quench your thirst from a refreshing crystal clear stream.

You feel the warmth of the sun on your skin and the coolness from the trees on your face as their leaves sway gently in the breeze. You impulsively remove your shoes to feel the velvet like carpet of emerald green grass beneath your bare feet. You briefly close your eyes to revel in delight as you sink your toes into the moist ground.

Most of all, you experience a sensation so profound not even the grandeur of the Garden can match it. This incomparable feeling from deep inside you is a purifying wellspring of overflowing love coursing throughout every fiber of your being. Your mind is illuminated with wisdom to know the unmistakable joy you're experiencing is the pure love of God's Heart pulsating in precise rhythm with your heart.

Your senses are heightened. As you listen intently to the sounds of the waterfall and to the melodic tunes of birds chirping in the trees, you suddenly hear laughter from a distance. Even before Adam and Eve come into view, you feel your innate connection to them.

You see the first couple in the clearing just ahead. Like two carefree children, they are strolling hand in hand, playfully swinging their arms. Adam reaches up with his free hand to gently remove a stray wisp of hair from Eve's forehead, then tenderly kisses her. Your heart races as you feel their love welling up inside you.

Adam and Eve sense your presence. They turn in your direction and eagerly run toward you. Your unabashed exuberant embraces evidence the instant chemistry the three of you radiate.

Your welcoming smiles conceal no hint of embarrassment at the stark contrast between their nudity and the clothing you're wearing. You instinctively know their undressed state is a physical reflection of their spiritual perfection, which enables them to be totally honest. It doesn't even occur to them to question the difference in your appearance, nor does it occur to you to look upon their flawless naked bodies with lust. The three of you are completely attuned to the oneness you share that goes much deeper than sexual attraction alone.

Your attention is momentarily riveted on our Creator's radiance of pure love that envelops the three of you in blissful awareness of your heart-to-Heart unity. From the tips of your toes to the shimmering glow on your faces, you've never felt so alive, yet so peaceful. This eternal love affirming bond enables you to immediately accept each other, without judgment, as being complete just as you are. The three of you walk off, arm in arm, into the sunset.

It is now morning. You are waking up. You feel totally energized. The next thing you know, your inborn connection to Eve involves you in her internal struggle: "You will not surely die. For God knows that in the day you eat of it your eyes will be opened and you will be like God, knowing good and evil."

You recoil as you recognize the all too familiar passage from Genesis 3:5 that signaled the birth of self-deception. Without a moment's hesitation, you enter the scene as Eve is about to lose (in)sight of paradise.

You calmly explain the half-truths Eve hasn't considered. Yes, it's technically correct to believe she won't die because a soul and spirit never dies. You enlighten Eve with the cold, hard facts of denying the ever present reality of love: toiling each day without satisfying results, giving and receiving little or no respect, seemingly endless suffering, and experiencing the anguish of physical death.

And yes, her eyes will be opened—to chaos fueled by false separation anxiety. You inform Eve that she won't be empowered to sense she still carries the peace of God's Spirit within her spirit. She will be tricked into seeking relief for her perceived feelings of emptiness outside herself.

And finally, the biggest lie of all: "You will be like God, knowing good and evil." You clarify that she and Adam are *already* like God because they are spiritually One. Believing evil is real is what will deceive them into thinking they are unlike their Creator, because God is pure love.

You hasten to tell Eve the worst part of misidentifying with fear will be feeling like she is trapped in an endless nightmare of mistrust, never awakening to the perfect love she and Adam now know and enjoy.

You go on to describe how guilt and blame will only be the immediate effects of their delusional reality. You impress upon Eve how this one seemingly harmless egocentric act will spiral out of control into her future son murdering his brother.

You pause to let the meaning of your words sink in. You conclude by saying the only hope for her and Adam to continue experiencing heaven on earth mentally, physically, and spiritually is to trust God's will is their will—by continuing to only define themselves as good—not evil.

The sincerity of your words appears to resonate with Eve. She thanks you profusely. Eve assures you she and Adam have no intention of being immortalized as the fall guys for humanity's fear-rooted beliefs!

Before you leave, you recognize Eve will need positive reinforcement to prevent her childlike curiosity from ruining her tranquility. You instruct Eve that she and Adam will need to keep two truths in mind to stay in touch with reality: *only love is real*, and *believing in fear causes paradise to seem to disappear before your very eyes.*

You slowly open your eyes to find yourself back in the present. You feel renewed. You pause for a few moments to consider the magnitude of what you've just accomplished. Your courage in making a stand for love will change the course of history.

You firmly resolve from now on to counter false evidence of fear with love-centered thoughts and actions. The best part is the longer you forego self-will, the more familiar experiencing heaven on earth through inner peace will become.

Which one of your senses were you most attuned to during this imagery? The breathtaking sights? The dazzling array of smells and sounds? The tantalizing tastes? The sensual touches? Or could it be the underdeveloped sixth sense you never honed because you weren't taught to believe in yourself as being eternally complete? If you singled out the ultimate connection you envisioned as the "three" of you wholeheartedly felt your spirit's connection to the Holy Spirit, you've been paying attention.

It can't be stated too strongly how imperative it is to stop identifying with fear through nonassertive response patterns. For example, if I paid you five compliments and insulted you once, what would you be most likely to remember? If you weren't raised with a holistic mind-set, you would undoubtedly dwell on the insult.

Petty everyday occurrences that have no lasting significance continue to wreak havoc, while we rarely savor the love that flows from within us, yearning to be extended. This is the false power a dual belief system has over most people.

What better antidote to use against self-deception to create hell on earth than to internalize a meditation that empowers you to reclaim paradise by revisiting God's original vision of love for all eternity?

Road to Resurrection

Now that the groundwork has been laid to support your need for spiritual recovery, you're in the homestretch, right? Wrong! A few perfunctory prayers, some meditation now and then, and a positive glance in the mirror when you're in the mood just won't cut it.

I know from personal experience you have to be steadfast until responding in love becomes second nature. I had read and heard from several sources that bad habits could be eradicated within twenty-one days, so that was the amount of time I had originally spent reciting my affirmations.

Self-will patterns of childhood cause us to gravitate toward the natural appeal of fast fixes. But it doesn't make sense that decades of fear-driven thinking can be quickly eliminated. A telltale sign my ego had regained control was when I started to feel more anxious than calm. I had to humble myself and resume my mirror exercises until peace of mind became familiar, despite the daily challenges I faced.

Self-help books are another example. Most people who read this genre fail to take the corrective actions that are advised for one simple reason: the book itself represents just another in a lifelong series of attempts to seek external solutions to a universal spiritual identity problem. Anything involving a serious daily commitment is either scoffed at or dismissed with the ever familiar "I don't have the time" excuse. I know this all too well because that used to be my line. It just isn't reasonable to expect to live our real life of love when we're embedded in the past through judgmental behaviors.

Humanity's oppositional nature has been variously described throughout this book as: childish inner self, adult/child split, childish persona, stuck child, inner child, and adult/child persona. These references emphasize the false power fear has to keep us stuck in the past. While it's certainly disturbing that children suffer from humanity's collective denial of reality, the only thing that is worse is perpetuating the pain by failing to become loving adults. It really doesn't matter how humanity's perceived struggle between true love and false fear is depicted. It's more important to discover that an eternity mind-set enables us to largely detach from generational misconceptions that preclude peace.

It may be helpful for you to envision your mental stability being governed by a "switch" that regulates the flow of energy in your brain. Your adult mind represents the "on" higher energy love position that lights up the present. Your inner child, ego, devil, etc., indicates the "off" lower energy fear position that is darkened by the past.

Whether your mind is enlightened or darkened is based on your ability to discern truth from deception. Every time a faulty response is chosen, you're disconnecting from your main power Source. During your childhood, you kept receiving mixed signals. The light was on for brief periods but more often than not, it was off. Growing up feeling insecure and viewing conflicts as normal is the end result.

If your goal is to be at peace based on faith that a loving God is in control, it's vital to understand the contradiction between claiming to follow God's will and consistent faultfinding. Nonassertive response patterns categorically deny humanity's wholeness.

Child in Charge

We resist changing our beliefs at all costs. All along, you've assumed only you as an adult has been in charge of your life. This is exactly what the childish persona of your personality needs you to think to ensure "it" controls how you act. This delusion manifests whenever subconscious immature behaviors override your adult desire to act reasonably.

Undesirable conduct originates from fear-bound temperaments and perceived cumulative hurts. Self-will represents humanity's refusal to grow up in response to the incongruity of being taught to believe in both love and fear. The resulting learned schizophrenia leads to the sincere pursuit of love on a conscious adult level that is unconsciously destabilized by a childish need for control and approval.

God is pure love. Fear blinds us to our eternal identity. We can't be attuned to our spiritual perfection if we grew up believing it's acceptable to be judgmental. Instead of learning self-respect to respond compassionately, we're conditioned to overreact and underreact.

A child naturally expects his demands to be met if parents don't maintain assertive boundaries. Likewise, parents who never acquired self-esteem unconsciously expect their children to make them happy. Since it's impossible to please anyone who doesn't comprehend that love originates from within, an underlying sense of mistrust characterizes the majority of parent-child interactions well into adulthood.

Even if parents are physically present, a child who lacks self-confidence feels alone. When we aren't raised to define ourselves according to our divine nature, we don't feel safe directly communicating our needs. We learned from the way our parents acted around each other and toward us to be guarded with our emotions out of fear of rejection. We discovered we were more likely to get what we wanted by passively suppressing our feelings or aggressively or passive-aggressively disrespecting our role models.

A contradictory belief system leaves us with no other choice than to rely on conditional (fear-rooted) love. Discord automatically ensues from dishonest communication patterns when the necessity of a permanent spiritual solution isn't recognized.

Had we grown up with assertive language and actions that facilitated confidence in our everlasting identity of love (as illustrated by the balanced life scenario described in chapter 6), we would all feel secure in our oneness. There would have been no need for our mind to have created an adult/child split for self-preservation purposes.

We may physically look like adults, but self-serving patterns of childhood are all too often reflected in our conduct. Even though the adult/child persona represents a bogus reality, we learned to behave as though he or she exists whenever we allow ourselves to be ruled by angry response patterns. This relates to the information presented at the end of chapter 1: If you respond contrary to the way you know is right, as though some unseen force is controlling you from within, this lie, in effect, becomes your reality.

The true test of maturity is how frequently you exhibit your childhood insecurities. One quick way to know your childish inner self is running the show is if you tend to make disparaging comments about yourself or others. If your parents never learned to be Spirit-minded, they internalized the same judgmental behaviors they passed on to you.

Fear-driven teachings cause incalculable damage. Even if we receive love-centered instruction as well, mixed-messages intensify our anxiety levels. When underlying feelings of unworthiness addict us to superficial remedies, being taught spiritual wisdom doesn't readily penetrate our defense mechanisms. Simply stated, if our core beliefs are flawed, the ability to differentiate fact from fiction is severely compromised. The expression "garbage in, garbage out" comes to mind.

A belief system founded on love and fear makes it very difficult to comprehend humanity's heart beats as one with our Creator's Heart. Religious ideologies that state it's possible to be separated from God can blindside us from capitalizing on our unbreakable spirit-to-Spirit union. False feelings of abandonment force us to seek the wholeness we already possess through people who become poor substitute "gods." If we don't honestly believe we're complete, we search in vain for someone or something to temporarily quell our unrelenting emotional pain. Our inevitable failure to find lasting fulfillment outside ourselves causes us to express our frustrations inappropriately. Following self-will signals loud and clear that we haven't emotionally moved beyond childhood.

One version of a fear-rooted monologue goes something like this:

> I really can't trust anyone. I trusted my parents, and look where that got me. What if I tell my partner I'm not as sure of myself as I seem, and my needs still aren't met? Or even worse, what if I'm rejected all over again? I can't risk being that vulnerable. I have to look out for number one. It's better just to play it safe, and keep my guard up.

This internalized script guarantees our false belief in fear remains intact. Delusional thinking convinces us things will be different now that we're adults who are "in control" of our lives.

Any happiness we discover with others without healing our conflicting thought patterns is transitory and self-perpetuating at the same time. It's temporary because it doesn't come from within, and recurring because a false attachment to self mistakenly convinces us we will be able to find fulfillment through people, places, and things: *I felt good about myself when I fell in love* (truth: counterfeit self-esteem). *All I have to do is find a way to recapture that feeling permanently* (truth: earthly contentment won't last if we misidentify with fear).

If you're serious about being true to yourself, it's vital to keep in mind that oppositional messages are highly resistant to change. The cycle of domestic violence is a perfect illustration. If I grew up witnessing both love and fear-based language from my parents,

I'll be inclined to rationalize my harsh treatment of my mate as normal behavior, while still claiming to love him.

The irreconcilable love-fear factor also applies to those on the receiving end of abuse. If your partner verbally or physically mistreated you all the time, you wouldn't stand for it. But since the aggression always alternates with an all too brief honeymoon period before tensions re-escalate, these pain-pleasure cycles reinforce the notion that going through the bad times is worth it to get to the "love" feelings that self-deception convinces you this time will be permanent.

This distorted dynamic sabotages your happiness on two levels: 1) On a conscious level, you believe your partner will make you feel loved. In reality, your partner's antagonistic behavior confirms your subconscious belief that you don't deserve to be loved. 2) When your relationship ends, your lack of faith in your wholeness compels you to illogically keep searching for happiness through unreliable external sources.

Cutting self-will down to size begins with acknowledging the truth. It might be easier to change the way you think if you view your life as choosing between the crucifixion mentality of self-will or the resurrection mind-set of God's will.

If you respond to me with consistently angry behaviors, my reactions will be fear-based or love-centered.

Crucifixion Mentality

1. I passively suffer in silence because I've never recognized my true value.
2. I respond in kind to you and then complain to others so I can feel vindicated, because judgmental behavior temporarily eases my inner torment.

Resurrection Mind-Set

1. I respond assertively because I understand your conduct stems from your misidentification with self.
2. I physically distance myself from you, while praying that you discover the whole(ness) truth about yourself.

Gail never received her inheritance because she allowed her brother to sell their family home to pay off his gambling debts. Although he subsequently lost two more homes, Gail's brother talked her into letting him move into her rental property. Less than a year later, he informed her he didn't have the rent money. Gail was distraught. She couldn't afford to pay two mortgages. She had to decide whether to evict her brother or wait until she was forced to declare bankruptcy and ruin her excellent credit rating. Throughout her life, Gail has overcompensated for the love she never received from her parents. Her poor self-image keeps her stuck in fear-driven actions. She gains approval through self-denial, then seeks consolation from friends. They reinforce her erroneous belief that she is her self-centered brother's victim. Misplaced trust prevents Gail from establishing assertive boundaries that reflect God's will.

Sacrificial behaviors that are self-serving are never satisfying long-term. As Gail's case demonstrates, her savior complex didn't have the power to rescue her brother. It represented her childhood conditioning to feel good about herself through counterfeit self-esteem.

We're highly reluctant to alter our behavior if our belief in fear-minded outcomes has convinced us conflicted lives, interspersed with brief periods of happiness, is all we have a right to expect. Most people who are out of touch with reality never stop blaming their circumstances for their lack of contentment. It's unusual to be genuinely receptive to incorporating spiritual truths before middle age.

I've only counseled one such remarkable individual. Gary was only seventeen-years old when we first met. I was skeptical he would return. His mother was the one who set up the initial appointment. I was never so glad to be wrong. Gary turned out to be a shining example that transformation from victim to victor can occur at any age.

Gary was a high school dropout who had a quick temper. He had never known his father and was living in a housing development with his mother. He had been mugged and was feeling dejected. His inferiority complex was obvious. He could have easily followed the crowd in his drug-infested neighborhood.

I counseled Gary on and off for a two-year period. I wasn't sure he would be able to relate to the concept of relying on his inner power. In hindsight, even I was talking the talk far more than I was walking the walk at that time.

Gary gradually gained confidence to break free from his poverty mentality. He got his GED and took to heart the importance of softening his aggressive demeanor. Little by little, learning to be true to himself became more important than giving false power to events beyond his control. Now thirty, Gary still keeps in touch. He had no trouble securing a good job. He owns a home, where he lives with his devoted wife and daughter.

Generally speaking, we're a "stiff-necked people" (Exodus 32:9) who all too quickly become addicted to ego gratification without a firm foundation of love. We have to be practically unable to function before we'll even consider humbling ourselves to admit our need for spiritual recovery.

I learned the hard way that developing confidence in my true identity makes much more sense than giving false power to my fears. I can personally attest to the benefits of reducing self-will from a roar to a mere whimper.

Freedom of Surrender

A lifetime of alternating between compulsively seeking approval and acting self-righteously can lead to hopelessness. Learning to identify with love restores sanity to a mind tormented by lifelong misconceptions.

You'll recognize the futility of nonassertive behaviors if you take the time to connect with your inner power. When your mind, body, and spirit function in harmony, discerning self-deception is almost effortless. The outcome is reaping the benefits of regular insights that mitigate the stress of challenging situations.

If we don't discover God's will is humanity's will, variations of the same basic conflicts recur, despite our best efforts to find fulfillment through our circumstances. The following personal examples detail how this fear-addicted dynamic operates.

As my mother's memory loss became more pronounced, she took comfort in my accessibility. I had a monitor in her bedroom and one in the basement office of our home. I had just begun a counseling session when I heard my mother start to cry. I quickly unplugged the monitor and excused myself from my client.

My mother sobbed that someone had taken her wedding rings. I was taken aback. The intensity of her reaction was completely uncharacteristic. My mother had never instigated any of the dramas that played out during my childhood. In fact, she had made this very same claim years ago without any overt display of emotion.

At that time, my attachment to being right was much more important than demonstrating the fruit of the Spirit through gentleness and self-control. I kept insisting she had misplaced them. Until she found her rings two years later, mom would periodically broach the subject. These unproductive discussions always ended the same way. I became defensive, and we were both left with unresolved anger.

Now, all these years later, my mother's lifetime of bottled up emotions were being released in a torrent of despair. This time around, I consoled her until she calmed down. She was agreeable to waiting until after my client left before we discussed it further. If I wasn't inner-directed, my history of anxiety would have triggered me to become annoyed by her inopportune timing.

After the session, I found my mother in the living room, still visibly shaken. I prayed with her before returning to her bedroom. I dismissed daunting thoughts about the difficulty of finding a needle in a haystack. I prayed God would lead me to the rings. My attention was immediately drawn to a box on her cedar chest. As I got closer, I was surprised to discover the rings in plain view right next to the box.

I knelt down and thanked God before placing the rings in my mother's grateful hands. My former egocentric need to prove her wrong was replaced by my heartfelt desire for her peace of mind. When I simply told my mother our prayers had been answered, she was ecstatic. A humble approach finally broke the cycle of repeating the same lesson with the same fear-driven result.

My second example involves this book. My understanding of computers is limited to accessing the Internet and using the word processor. Bob graduated with a degree in computer science. In the beginning, his support and technical help was invaluable. But as months turned into years, he put me off until I became irritated. When we discussed the matter later, Bob conceded my requests were reasonable. His response only made sense in hindsight. I had to remember how his childhood feelings of powerlessness manifested during the first year of our marriage. When I consistently responded assertively, Bob toned down his reactions. He largely relinquished his aggressive communication style because it was no longer effective. And yet, years later, I fell into the trap of becoming aggravated by his passive-aggressive stance.

When we feel unworthy of love, acts of self-sabotage factor heavily into our relationships. If I hadn't realized Bob's need for control was being acted out indirectly, he would have kept repeating this more subtle approach. He was unconsciously eliciting the criticism from me that he had learned to believe he deserved. Likewise, my own regression to self-will caused me to lose perspective. By overreacting, I was no longer relating to our present situation. I was judging Bob's conduct just as I had judged my father's general lack of consideration for my mother's feelings.

The legacy of fear from being raised by a mother who suffered from schizophrenia, coupled with his aggressive temperament, made Bob vulnerable to mistrusting women. Since I ultimately responded to his procrastination inappropriately, I was compounding the problem by reminding Bob of his mom's instability.

My annoyed response was also wrong because I tried to control Bob through guilt. I, alone, was responsible for not honestly communicating my frustration in an adult manner. Even though he shouldn't have responded passive-aggressively, this disagreement was a classic case of two wrongs don't make a right.

This is a good example of the 10 percent temperament response that isn't usually entirely eliminated during one's earthly lifetime. On the plus side, an eternity orientation gives us the advantage of quickly regaining a love-grounded outlook. Simply stated, spiritual recovery frees us to accept full responsibility for fear-minded response patterns that aren't real.

Despite the countless ways we try to justify self-centered behaviors, every time we fail to respond assertively, we reinforce (rather than extinguish) unwanted conduct. Unless we transform our learned schizophrenia, no win power struggles govern the way misunderstandings play out.

Both of these accounts underscore the truth of the biblical admonition that it's the "little foxes that spoil the vines" (Song of Solomon 2:15). Unresolved childhood trauma initially manifests as seemingly trivial problems. Eventually, however, each minor misunderstanding gradually weaves a pattern of ever escalating false communication that rips at the very heart of relationships.

Professing our faith through works or claiming to have detached from control and approval—while continuing to overreact or underreact—is inconsistent with love, whether or not we choose to admit it. Considering how most people regard nonassertive conduct as acceptable is a sad testament to the false power of fear that leaves us stranded as emotional prisoners in our own personal hell on earth.

Before I recognized the necessity of identifying with love, I used to regularly feel sorry for myself. I remember thinking how unfair it was that, in spite of waiting until middle age to marry, I still ended up with someone like my father. The truth is I married exactly who I was supposed to so I could learn to move beyond my childhood fears.

Generational conflicts are inevitable when we allow ourselves to be ruled by opposing realities. True soul mates connect honestly on a deep spiritual level, as well as physically and emotionally.

Just so there's no misunderstanding, Bob isn't a factor in my love-based identity. He filed for divorce after nine years of marriage. The good news is we discovered we were better suited as friends. I didn't regress into clinical depression, because I know my happiness doesn't depend on who is or isn't in my life. Peace of mind is a function of how well one is able to maintain balance through self-love working in tandem with God's love, regardless of external factors.

When we don't identify with humanity's wholeness, we stay stuck in personal agendas that keep us mired in resentments. I can now see clearly that entering into marriage as an older bride gave me a false sense of confidence.

As with all unions that are based on conditional love, self-will was only temporarily suspended. Feelings of closeness and expressions of caring were soon eclipsed by faulty personal opinions. Starry-eyed vows of "I do" dissolved into accusations about what we each did or didn't do.

Before I humbled myself to become Spirit-led, I blamed Bob for our divorce. He was agreeable to marital counseling, but my ego got in the way. Since I had already been through counseling, I deflected attention from myself by trying to convince Bob it made more sense for him to deal with his unresolved childhood issues.

The truth is Bob wasn't responsible for my unhappiness. I didn't have spiritual discernment at that time to recognize being married to someone like my father was an essential part of my healing process. I lacked awareness that my nonassertive response patterns were a red flag that I hadn't forgiven my father. My subconscious conditioning to personalize wrongdoing had kept me stuck imitating my dad's aggression whenever I became upset with Bob.

As a child, I had been deeply affected by my father's verbal abuse of my mother. Subconscious denial of my wholeness prevented me from consistently relating to Bob on a spiritual level of love. My childish persona didn't have the ability to see past my dad's or Bob's hostile facades to the anxiety-filled stuck children that dictated their behaviors. I was still trapped in self-righteous anger myself.

I now understand that both my father and Bob did the best they could from their fear-bound perspectives. I still remember an amazing sacrifice my dad had made for me when I was in college. I had planned a trip to Europe but had misplaced my birth certificate. I didn't allow enough time to have a duplicate sent to me to obtain my passport. Without being asked, my father took off from work to drive the two hour, one-way trip to retrieve the form so I wouldn't miss this opportunity.

Unfortunately, even my fond memories of my dad couldn't mitigate the damage I suffered from his failure mentality. The primary reason for emotional instability can't be stressed too often or strongly enough: being raised with love and fear-rooted messages normally precludes peace of mind.

Like the vast majority, my father died with his victim mentality intact because he never learned *only love is real.* And it took me nearly a lifetime to discover my divine nature. If I hadn't disciplined myself to heal my split personality, I would still be acting out my feelings of inadequacy through my false need for control.

Self-esteem is essential to treating others with respect. Without inner healing, we magnify insignificant offenses that prevent us from ascending to spiritual levels of consciousness. Simply stated, our false belief in fear forces us to maintain our split personalities and wonder why our relationships aren't working.

No matter how dejected you feel or how hopeless your circumstances seem, your attitude can turn around dramatically if you stop deceiving yourself about your true identity. Your very worst behaviors can only adversely affect the quality of your life until your physical death. You're eternally defined by unconditional love, because your spirit is united with God's Spirit. Simply stated, changing your viewpoint from flesh-driven to Spirit-minded empowers you to experience the joy of your timeless identity *now.*

Today, I stay grounded by not worrying or fuming over situations I don't have the power to change in my own strength. I'm confident in my holistic identity, regardless of whether I'm viewed as a failure or a success from a worldly perspective.

For those who are interested in trading a lifetime of contention for contentment, the keys to unlocking your false captivity of fear are about to be handed to you.

CHAPTER 8

Getting Real

It takes courage to endure the sharp pains of self-discovery rather than choose to take the dull pain of unconsciousness that would last the rest of our lives.
—Marianne Williamson

As difficult as eliminating fear-minded communication is short-term, it's also the noblest and most far-reaching act you could ever perform. When you discern the wisdom that has been inside you all along, there is no limit to the good you can accomplish.

Transforming an anxiety-riddled love and fear belief system into one that exemplifies love and peace can be achieved through three simple, yet highly effective, steps:

1. Facilitate renewal of your mind through mirror exercises, recorded affirmations, and assertive conduct that denotes self-respect.
2. Cultivate a personal relationship with God through prayer, meditation, and an attitude of gratitude.
3. Concentrate on confessing and correcting your own faults, while refraining from judgmental behavior.

During one of her motivational speeches, best-selling author and publisher Louise Hay addressed the destructive impact fear-driven energy can have over the course of one's lifetime:

One idle thought does not mean very much, but thoughts that we think over and over are like drops of water; and at first there's just a few. But after a while, you create a puddle, and then a pond, and then a lake and then an ocean; and by our thinking, if it is negative, we can drown in a sea of negativity. Or, if it is positive, we can float on the ocean of life.[12]

Is your focus on the evil in the world that is a by-product of fear, or do you see past short-term appearances to the infinite good in everyone? Your answer to this question reveals whether or not you're attentive to your true power in the present. The longer you concentrate on becoming more reflective than reactive, the sooner love will triumph.

This is not meant to discourage you if you've waited until your mid-life crisis (or even later) to change how you think. As explained, I was complacent about my negative energy patterns until my mid-forties. And even then, I assumed it was possible to maintain assertive behavior without self-esteem. As a result, I wasn't able to be transparent when the going really got tough in my fifties.

On the upside, without my ordeals, I never would have realized that I was responsible for my lack of peace. Once I understood that my feelings of inferiority kept me in bondage to anxiety and depression, I was determined to do whatever it took to change how I viewed life. Handling stressful situations with an ease I've never known is the fruit I now reap from the seeds of love I've sown.

Need for Affirmations

Denial of humanity's wholeness is so pervasive that the vast majority aren't even aware they have a divine nature. One's spirit represents the "missing" link that precludes inner peace. We can't feel complete if we only associate our mind with our bodies.

Until I concentrated on becoming inner-directed, I had no other recourse than to identify with my failure mentality. Like metal to a magnet, I was drawn to re-enact my past through volatile partners and underemployment.

The most important conversations we have involve self-talk. When we're born with nonassertive temperaments and are raised by fear-controlled role models, we form distorted perceptions of ourselves. As we become adults, our childhood victim mentalities determine the majority of our responses. We subconsciously attract the fear-based outcomes we mistakenly learned to believe we deserve.

A universal self-hate pattern is habitual faultfinding. This tendency is especially difficult to uproot. Self-deception is so insidious that most people physically die without ever comprehending the irrational nature of their behavior.

A talk show featured a man who had alienated his now ex-wife and their four grown children. Although there was overwhelming evidence of his verbal and physical abuse, he kept contradicting his family's claims, and insisted he loved them. Both the highly credentialed host and a renowned expert called this man on his outrageous conduct. Shortly thereafter, he blurted out to his youngest son, "Don't make me the scapegoat for your inadequacies!" Even after his attention was immediately drawn to the harmful impact of these words, he remained oblivious. "Death and life are in the power of the tongue" (Proverbs 18:21).

One of the surest ways to eradicate judgmental attitudes is with statements that affirm our supernatural identity. Repeating affirmations in front of a mirror facilitates the healing process. You speak the truth to yourself that your parents weren't able to convey, because they never learned love originates from within.

At first, you'll recite on a superficial level. When I was stuck in self-consciousness, I automatically zeroed in on my imperfections when I looked in the mirror each morning. I knew I was succeeding in transitioning to God-consciousness when

I finished my affirmations one day and began spontaneously talking to God while gazing at my disheveled reflection!

I initially couldn't fathom the idea that I have a perfect spirit; even in the context of being united with the Holy Spirit. My worldly orientation compelled me to relieve my feelings of inadequacy by focusing on the impossible goal of doing everything right. My limited perspective had the opposite of the desired effect to promote peace of mind.

When I started spiritual recovery, I would say, *I love and approve of myself.* Thoughts to the contrary flooded my mind, and I began to second guess whether affirmations were necessary. By the following morning, I instinctively knew my opposition was my inner child's attempt to maintain the status quo.

Whenever similar feelings surfaced, I made it a point to concentrate on the present by taking slow, deep breaths. I would look into the mirror and firmly announce *I release my need for perfectionism. I love and approve of who I am.*

I also had to amend the following affirmation: *Thank You for healing my anxiety.* This was changed to, *I am thankful that I have Your power to heal my anxiety.* It's essential to counter deep-rooted feelings of powerlessness with statements that acknowledge we possess God's healing power.

It takes time to absorb the truth about our immeasurable value. But the peace that is ultimately gained is beyond compare to anything of worldly value. My actions are no longer regularly dictated by fear-bound perceptions. I deal with adversity from a strength position of quiet faith in eventual positive outcomes. Meditation centers my emotions.

When you persevere despite resistance, your stress level ultimately decreases. As you strive to achieve higher levels of consciousness, your misidentification with self will be replaced by your revitalized mind, body, and spirit manifesting your legacy of abundance.

Back to the Present

Every time you criticize or personalize criticism, you energize the pain of your childhood. As natural as it is to complain about others or to feel diminished in the aftermath of being disrespected, both response patterns keep fueling your false belief in fear.

The next time you feel the urge to judge someone, try this technique. Imagine you have the ability to see through his physical façade to his perfect spirit. This is how I reacted when I saw a young man with multicolored spiked hair. In the past, I would have been thinking unkind thoughts. Instead, I said to myself, *His spiritual perfection is all that matters to me.*

Another reality check to combat judgmental behavior is to remind yourself that insecure people focus on faultfinding, confident people focus on being encouraging. By transforming your negative energy patterns into affirming beliefs, you'll start to view others with the same acceptance you're discovering for yourself.

Intimate relationships that consist of aggressive or passive partners need to heal their compulsion to be in control by getting their way or to gain approval by giving in. If your behaviors alternate between these extremes, you'll need to repeat both of these corrective affirmations: 1) I release my need for control by acting in everyone's best interests. 2) I release my need to sacrifice my self-respect because my needs deserve an equal voice with all others. A good morning practice is to remember to express GAS: Gratitude for all of your blessings; Acceptance of those who are fear-driven; and Surrender of self-will by demonstrating love through consistent assertive language.

Affirmation #1 above really hit home with me when I was my mother's caregiver. My selfless mom had always put her children's needs first. When she was released from a nursing home after fracturing her ankle, mom deferred to me regarding home care.

A hospital bed was set up on the first floor to accommodate her physical therapy.

Even after my mother was mobile and services were terminated, the therapist recommended she stay downstairs for safety reasons. Mom complied for a while, but as time passed, I sensed how unhappy she was. I decided respecting my mother's need for privacy overrode my fears of her falling again.

I had to periodically remind myself not to be overprotective, especially since I didn't want to remind mom of how controlled she felt when my father was alive. The bottom line is even if you believe you're right, respect for the other person's viewpoint should always be taken into consideration.

Pathway to Peace

The following series of affirmations are spoken to reinforce your spirit-to-Spirit union as you look into your mirror:

1. I know Your unconditional love defines who I am.
2. I sense my heart beats as one with Your Heart.
3. I release all fear-based feelings and behaviors.
4. I am peaceful because I am complete.
5. I demonstrate respect for humanity's wholeness.

Before repeating these statements, center your attention on the present with slow, deep breaths. Over time, this practice ensures contentment will become more familiar to you than the anxiety you've grown accustomed to experiencing.

Your overall actions reveal your whole mind functions in accord with your eternal spirit through the power of the Holy Spirit; or your divided mind functions in discord with your transitory physical being against you and God's Spirit.

As long as we exclude our vital spiritual element, peace of mind is fleeting, at best, because our primary focus is on superficial goals. When we're not inner-directed, identifying with love isn't our top priority. If we're not taught to be Spirit-minded, we feel like we have no other recourse than to depend on our circumstances for our happiness. Due to the unpredictable nature of life, this reasoning can ultimately leave us feeling empty. The crucial point to remember is we don't have to keep allowing purely flesh-driven impulses to undermine our true purpose to love. Developing a spiritual perspective corrects our lifelong mental and physical imbalances.

When we exchange our false bondage to fear-controlled behaviors for the freedom of recognizing God's will is humanity's will, our identification with opposing forces eventually dissipates. "No weapon formed against you will prosper" (Isaiah 54:17) if you have faith in your true identity. A love-based attitude ultimately prevails over difficult situations.

I had a difference of opinion with a new supervisor at work involving a new hire. During a staff meeting, I was calmly explaining my version of the disagreement. Although the supervisor had known me for less than two weeks, she interrupted me by siding with the inexperienced worker in front of the other employees, saying, "I'm getting sick of you!"

To make matters more intense, I had just lost my beloved mother. My emotions were very tender. If I had still been ruled by fear, I would have been indignant.

This trying experience was a major turning point in my spiritual recovery. Much to my surprise, I was only momentarily taken aback. I didn't even feel the embarrassment and hostility that would have been my normal initial reactions. I was instinctively cued to remain silent. After the meeting, I wrote my supervisor a courteous letter. I requested she show me the same respect in the future that I had demonstrated to her by not responding in kind.

Reacting with the power of God's Mind produced amazing results. The information I had tried to convey was unexpectedly confirmed within days. The employee was replaced the very next week. There was no further tension. I had a new supervisor within two months.

You'll be immeasurably blessed by staying true to your righteous spirit when you've been wronged. This same principle applies to repeating encouraging statements to yourself. Even though you may feel it won't make any difference, the emotional stability you will eventually gain will be well worth your efforts.

Whatever we pay attention to tends to become our reality. Dwelling on how lonely we feel, how we've been mistreated, or on our health problems keeps us unconsciously seeking opportunities to confirm our negative viewpoints. Love-grounded thoughts, spoken with conviction, release positive energy that produces lasting change from the inside out.

Assertions enhance your ability to be genuine. Reciting in front of a mirror reinforces the truth of your wholeness. Faithfully declaring the loving thoughts of God's Spirit within you refute your fears (separation anxiety) that He is apart from you.

- ❖ I know my life's purpose is to demonstrate *only love is real*.
- ❖ I am free from my childhood victim mentality of blame.
- ❖ I am mindful of my identity as an eternal spirit who lives in a temporary body.
- ❖ I rely on my sixth sense to discern spiritual truths.
- ❖ I can never be abandoned because I am an integral part of the Whole.
- ❖ I stay focused on the present with my whole heart and soul.
- ❖ As my self-esteem increases, my need to live on my own terms decreases, and my peace multiplies.
- ❖ My weaknesses are being perfected by my dependence on Your strength.

❖ My mind, body, and spirit are centered in love.

❖ I know love has always defined who I am.

❖ I trust in my inner power to triumph over every adversity.

❖ Loving who I am frees me from judging others.

❖ I take care of my body, soul, and spirit and I am blessed with good health.

❖ I am content with my present day life—for better or for worse—because my peace comes from within.

❖ I meditate on uplifting thoughts.

❖ Spiritual recovery empowers me to match my actions to my words.

❖ I forgive myself and all others.

❖ I rely on Your all-encompassing Presence to counter anxiety.

❖ I accept whatever happens as necessary for my spiritual growth.

❖ I am thankful that I have Your power to heal mentally, physically, and spiritually.

❖ I enrich my life by refraining from self-condemnation and criticizing others.

❖ I calmly uproot all fear-driven thoughts as soon as they come to mind (as many times as is necessary) and replace them with loving thoughts.

❖ I am balanced in all areas of my life.

❖ I, alone, am responsible for my state of mind.

❖ I rely on my inner wisdom to order my thoughts and word my mouth.

❖ I have confidence to be true to myself.

❖ I love myself for who I am.

❖ Only love-based thoughts and actions express who I really am.

❖ I stay attuned to the still small voice by tuning out the noise of the world.

❖ I have self-control to respond calmly to life's trials.

- ❖ I am blessed with boundless energy to face whatever challenges today may hold.
- ❖ I am treated with respect because I establish healthy boundaries that reflect self-respect.
- ❖ I have faith that love defines who I am, regardless of how I am treated.
- ❖ I have always been valued.
- ❖ My discovery of true love within ensures I will never go without.
- ❖ I live a balanced, peaceful life through nonjudgmental behavior.
- ❖ I have spiritual wisdom to understand Your will is my will.
- ❖ I give and receive love freely because I am rooted in boundless love.
- ❖ I honestly communicate my needs and feelings.
- ❖ I am a good steward of Your resources, and I am blessed with abundance.
- ❖ I have insight to be compassionate with those who identify with fear.
- ❖ I am spiritually empowered to process my negative feelings without judgment.
- ❖ I am content because I am complete in Your love.
- ❖ I know security comes from recognizing Oneness of love.
- ❖ I act in everyone's best interests.
- ❖ I take full responsibility for my mistakes.
- ❖ I dissolve fear-rooted thoughts by concentrating on my blessings.
- ❖ I exchange my compulsive need for control and approval for Your loving control and approval.
- ❖ I consistently respond assertively.
- ❖ I am worthy of the very best life has to offer and my love-based attitude reflects this reality.

- ❖ I stay attentive to my spirit-to-Spirit connection through my conscience.
- ❖ I release anger in constructive ways.
- ❖ I am always safe, secure, and divinely protected.
- ❖ I believe goodness and mercy follow me all the days of my life.
- ❖ I can falter and express negative energy and continue to be a centered, worthwhile person.
- ❖ I focus on the present to experience the true power of love.
- ❖ I am confident I am created in Your image to genuinely love.
- ❖ I function at my optimal level because I have Your power, love, and sound Mind.
- ❖ Your kingdom within me is all I need to be content; everything else is a bonus.
- ❖ I understand everything that happens is intended to strengthen me to attain my highest potential.
- ❖ I follow through with my responsibilities in a timely fashion.
- ❖ I have everything I need inside to live a fulfilling life.
- ❖ I concentrate on changing my behavior and accepting others as they are.
- ❖ My renewed mind equips me to love wholeheartedly.
- ❖ I remind myself as often as is necessary: only love is real; I am love; I am peaceful.
- ❖ Your infinite love restores me to wholeness.
- ❖ The true love I extend to all others returns to me multiplied.
- ❖ I have insight to see through false appearances to humanity's spiritual perfection.
- ❖ I counter my childhood feelings of victimization by remembering my validation comes from within.
- ❖ I am too blessed to stay depressed.

❖ I gladly trade the stress of being right for the peace of being humble.

❖ I can handle anything with You in control.

❖ I am slow to speak, quick to listen, and slow to engage in fear-minded behaviors.

❖ I am thankful for Your favor every day of my life.

❖ I release my false need to recreate the chaos from my childhood by overreacting and underreacting.

❖ I replace my complaining habit with an attitude of gratitude.

❖ I observe without judgment.

❖ I release my habit of staying stuck in the past by dwelling on how others act.

❖ I recognize there is nothing to forgive because everyone does the best they can based on their temperament and learned behavior.

It's particularly important to recall these last two affirmations when disagreements arise. Feelings of inferiority compel us to judge conduct that differs from our personal opinions. From a health standpoint, it makes more sense to learn to function on higher levels of consciousness than it does to stew about difficult situations that may never change for the better. If I had kept dwelling on my prolonged period of adversity, not only would this book never have been written, I definitely would have had to resume taking an antidepressant. Instead, I was able to manage my downcast moods by changing my self-concept.

Repeatedly affirming my true identity facilitated my transition from fear to faith. Focusing on wholeness thoughts resolved my conditioning to view others as less than or better than myself. Accepting people for who they are is far less energy draining than relying on judgments that may not be true.

To eradicate your childhood misconceptions, keep the following thoughts uppermost in mind: 1) If you aren't naturally assertive or you didn't have assertive role models, repeating positive statements help you get in touch with your divine nature. 2) It's more beneficial to verbalize your affirmations in the mirror before you begin your day.

It's also essential to avoid operating in the extremes of "all or nothing" thinking. A balanced approach always works best. When I started mirror work, I would spend at least fifteen minutes proclaiming a long list of assertions. This overcompensation caused me to avoid reciting until I realized I was being obsessive. If you miss a day or more, it's important not to give up or be self-critical. Just get back on track as soon as possible. Consistency is the key to success.

Mirror Work Demystified

Most people have difficulty repeating affirmations in front of a mirror. The excuses given by men include thinking it's unmanly or just plain silly to talk to yourself in a mirror. Many men and women alike consider the practice unnecessary or embarrassing. For some, the process feels too threatening. One of my former clients who suffered sexual abuse as a child told me she avoids mirrors as much as possible.

The real reason lies within. If we aren't raised with a spiritual orientation, our egocentric outlook only sees the need for others to change. When we grow up denying humanity's wholeness, most of our energy is naturally diverted to self-will pursuits.

It's crucial to understand exactly what your transformation entails if you're serious about being true to yourself. Your subconscious identification with fear since birth has made you highly resistant to change. Unless you have a sincere, intense desire to experience peace of mind, your victim mentality will keep you addicted to chaos. The false power of self-deception has convinced you that you're not the problem. If you've been conditioned to blame your circumstances for your misery your whole life, the prospect of altering your core beliefs naturally feels threatening.

People who lack insight avoid spending ten minutes daily in a mirror affirming love. But when it comes to flesh-driven goals, the opposite is true. Countless hours are spent exercising to get in shape and trying to stave off the aging process that has no meaning in eternity. Likewise, workaholics spend inordinate amounts of time away from families they purport to love to establish thriving careers. On a subconscious level, they need to feel important to counter latent childhood insecurities.

The universal proclivity to discount spiritual wisdom in favor of accommodating egotistical impulses is examined throughout the book of Ecclesiastes. The central theme that is used to characterize a self-will lifestyle is, "All is vanity."

Even when I sincerely believed I was on a true spiritual path ten years ago, I was still unconsciously identifying with my ego. This is how determined the average person's childish persona is to keep one stuck in the past. I kept denying the necessity of mirror work until I could no longer tolerate just going through the motions of life.

The longer one waits to transition from an earthbound viewpoint to an infinity orientation, the more difficult it becomes to identify with love. In the hope you'll be encouraged not to delay your recovery as long as I did, it's important to reiterate how our mental and physical health can end up being seriously compromised by our seemingly harmless false attachments to self.

In spite of the public image you project, how you really feel about yourself deep down inside determines the overall quality of your life. You can tell your partner you love him, but if you don't love yourself, your relationship isn't mutually satisfying. Much of your behavior reflects your lack of self-respect, expressed through angry communication styles.

If you weren't raised to believe you're whole, you sense something is missing. Anxiety only seems natural because you never learned to identify with your peaceful spirit. Your dependence on worldly goals for fulfillment forces you to seek escape from your perceived feelings of emptiness outside yourself.

It's as though you're stuck in a time warp that compels you to re-enact your fear-rooted childhood. Even though external religious and secular solutions only provide temporary relief, you've learned to settle for counterfeit love. It's all you've ever known.

Your despair has taught you to rationalize the abuse, alienation, and contradictions. If it was good enough for your parents, who are you to think you deserve to be treated any better? Concepts like "unlimited potential" and "abundant living" are pure fantasy according to your fear-based reality. Your only consolation is in knowing most people feel exactly the way you do.

After a lifetime of not comprehending God's will is humanity's will, self-deception has indeed prevented the vast majority from believing they have always had the power to manifest love and enjoy peace of mind. "A negative self-image blots out the joyous brilliance that is the true essence of their identities, which therefore goes unrecognized."[13] This insightful quotation was taken from the late Dr. David Hawkins's book, *Power vs. Force.* This pure genius was a renowned psychiatrist, prolific author, and popular lecturer. In addition to writing numerous scientific papers and being featured on inspirational videos, his television appearances included The MacNeil/Lehrer News Hour and the Today Show. His extensive biography is listed in *Who's Who in America.* Dr. Hawkins's groundbreaking research led him to develop a numerical map of consciousness that pinpoints levels of energy fields ranging from twenty to one thousand.

If you're tired of feeling like a big zero based on worldly standards of achievement, think again! Inner healing empowers you to recognize that your immeasurable value is based on your timeless identity—minus the transient earthly embellishments and entrapments you've tacked on in the false hope of feeling empowered.

The truth is you've always been defined by love. Developing your insight to see yourself through God's eyes of unconditional acceptance changes everything. As you become more and more attuned to your perfect spirit-to-Spirit unity, you're mentally transported to higher levels of consciousness devoid of fear. What does this mean in plain English? I'm glad you asked. Simply this: transforming your mind to discover the natural high of your inner power makes your self-imposed enslavement to artificial highs unnecessary.

There is no better way to see yourself as you really are than to look in a mirror. And I'm not referring to your physical appearance. Your ego tries to keep your attention on your physical imperfections to distract you from sensing your spiritual perfection. The eyes are referred to as the windows to one's soul. As you continue vocalizing love-centered thoughts while gazing at your reflection, you hone your insight to see beyond your fleeting flaws to the infinite value of your true essence.

If you doubt the impact your flesh-driven focus has had in shaping your conduct, ask yourself how many of the following fear-rooted habits you identify with:

1. not following through with something you really want to do on the basis of how it might look to others
2. telling people what they want to hear to get what you want or to gain their approval
3. spending beyond your ability to repay
4. feeling uncomfortable when you're physically alone— without Internet access, television, phone, or musical stimulation (this same malady manifests in children who complain of boredom unless they are continually

interacting with friends, playing computer games,
texting, etc.)

5. making comparisons and either feeling smug or dissatisfied

6. being unable to relax without feeling anxious or guilty,
   because not keeping busy makes you feel lazy

7. focusing on complaints, although you enjoy good physical
   health (contrasted with those who have serious health
   issues and don't gripe)

8. believing gifts or other gestures of kindness undo the
   effects of repeated antagonistic behaviors

This last habit is the most misunderstood. Aggressors have no
awareness that the emotional damage they inflict far outweighs
how extravagant or apologetic they may act in the aftermath of
rage. External fixes are no substitute for true self-respect that
promotes loving relationships.

Repeating affirming statements that you didn't receive during
your formative years ultimately expels thoughts that you just don't
measure up. Positive declarations, initially spoken with reluctance
and disbelief, gradually give way to a firm resolve to end your
addictive pain-pleasure existence. Deep-seated attitudes of self-
condemnation and resentment "miraculously" turn into heartfelt
feelings of acceptance and forgiveness.

As adults, we all have the responsibility to do what our parents
were incapable of teaching us: identify with the love within us
so we can comprehend the eventual misery of refusing to accept
responsibility for our own happiness.

The warring factions of our perceived split personalities cause
us to fixate on petty differences. When we learn to center our
attention on the longings of our righteous spirit, faith cues us to
respond with compassion.

When viewed in terms of following a fear-bound, superficial,
never satisfied, flesh-driven lifestyle or embracing a love-based,
deep, fulfilling, Spirit-led existence, the choice is obvious. The

problem is our oppositional belief system has always felt familiar. It doesn't occur to us to make the connection between our fear-minded attitudes and our inner turmoil. A good reality check is to remember that familiarity breeds contempt.

A former client described how she used mirror exercises to restore her mind to wholeness of love. Kate originally came to see me with hopes of saving her drama-filled marriage. When she finally realized there was no basis for honest communication, Kate concentrated on developing an authentic self-image.

A year after her divorce, she became involved with a man who treated her with kindness. As soon as their initial attraction waned, fear-controlled patterns began to surface. Growing up, Kate had witnessed her mother's jealousy throughout her parents' marriage. Her mother even chastised her father if she perceived he was being more attentive to the women he viewed on television.

One evening while watching a program with her new partner, he made a favorable comment about a woman on the screen. Kate was immediately triggered to personalize his reaction to mean she wasn't attractive. Instead of acting on her impulse to become defensive, Kate dealt with her rising jealousy by excusing herself to go to the bathroom. She looked into the mirror, took a couple of deep breaths to center her emotions, then firmly announced, *I have the power to choose how I feel. I'm lovable exactly as I am. I feel peaceful.* By refusing to let her childhood insecurities undermine her relationship, Kate was able to maintain self-control.

If looking into a mirror isn't convenient, you can breathe deeply, then say to yourself, *These feelings will pass if I don't allow them to dictate my conduct. Only love-based actions express who I really am.*

When you stop allowing yourself to be deceived about your true value, unstable emotions won't determine the majority of your actions. You have all the (inner) power you need to dissolve fear-rooted beliefs that seemed all too real during your childhood. The more determined you are to be authentic, the sooner unhealthy coping practices will become a thing of the past. When you concentrate on uplifting statements, even-tempered reactions will become more familiar than the smoldering resentments that ensue from a contradictory belief system.

If you sincerely desire to become all you were meant to be, there is no time like the present to discern your spiritual perfection being reflected from your mirror.

Staying the Course

Making a recording of your affirmations is another good way to reinforce a holistic reality. This method provides convenient access after disagreements, when your still raw emotions prevent you from speaking the truth to yourself.

It will be helpful to listen to your CD until affirming thoughts automatically came to mind. The object of this exercise is to saturate your heart and soul with as many loving references as you possibly can. When you think about the numerous times during the day that you involuntarily drift into unhealthy thought patterns, you'll have a good idea why training your focus on enriching thoughts is so important.

You also can include your own personal variation of the following monologue, along with your recorded affirmations:

> I've allowed my childhood pain to convince me I'm unworthy long enough. I now recognize the futility of seeking validation through external sources or by judging others. I realize the same Spirit who dwells in my heart resides in everyone else, despite behaviors that seem to suggest otherwise. Thank You for freeing me from my prison of aggressive and passive behaviors that have held me hostage to false fear. As I commit to

being open-minded to acknowledge the fullness
of Your everlasting love, I'm reassured all is well,
despite my fleeting earthly difficulties.

The most important factors for staying on track are to be realistic and to remain consistent. No one ever eradicates lifelong patterns without experiencing setbacks. When you do falter, it's essential to neutralize fear-based thoughts with truthful declarations.

If these methods fail and childhood coping tactics resurface, try to regain your composure as soon as possible by taking several deep breaths. You then can repeat whatever variation of this affirmation feels comfortable to you: "Love defines who I am. I have all the inner strength I need to overcome this trial."

It's essential to counter conditioned fear responses by returning our attention to the present as soon as possible. The closer I came to my book's final draft, the less attention I paid to self-care. I felt pressured by my impatient stuck child to set an unrealistic timetable for completion. I would obsess for hours on end at my computer, while ignoring my need for rest.

When sleep deprivation gave rise to thoughts of what a poor role model I was for my book, I snapped back to reality. I had unconsciously reverted to being controlled by my childhood anxiety. I recovered by resuming meditating and becoming more attentive to my regular sleep schedule.

The onset of a serious personal assault was so destabilizing that I couldn't even think about my normal affirmations. I kept from being overwhelmed by repeating two key phrases that came to mind: "Spirit, not self" and "faith, not feelings." Fixing my attention on my true power prevented my all too familiar anxiety and depression from compromising my health.

It really doesn't matter if you're feeling defeated by minor every day annoyances or devastating occurrences. Your misery will seem like it will never end as long as you keep deceiving yourself that you can personally handle life's unpredictable twists.

Paradise Mind-Set

The more you learn to embrace life, the reality version with all of its pleasures and pitfalls, your strengthened character will ultimately dispel the false power of fear to catch you off guard with unexpected challenges.

John 14:27 plainly states, "Peace I leave with you. My peace I give to you; not as the world gives do I give to you. Let not your heart be troubled, neither let it be afraid." If you're having difficulty believing your life was meant to be peaceful, it's because your learned anxiety response denies your legacy of peace.

Feelings of powerlessness automatically emanate from a mixed-message belief system. By identifying with the love within you, you're empowered to mentally transcend life's obstacles in three stages: 1) You instinctively heed promptings from the Spirit of truth. 2) You lose your fear-rooted need to judge. 3) You achieve a balanced mind, body, and spirit. Simply stated, an eternity perspective equips you to shift your attention from the assaults of a dying physical realm to your never ending wholeness.

Meditation is an essential component of spiritual recovery. When we grow up viewing conflicts as normal, we find every excuse we can think of to avoid being contemplative. Disciplining ourselves to be silent only seems unnatural because we weren't raised to identify with our peaceful spirit. Using words to try to control others is a disconcerting pervasive habit that all too quickly can become one's comfort zone.

Aggressive and passive-aggressive personalities are addicted to the temporary satisfaction they derive from proving their point. The worst part of relying on defensive measures to regain control is not realizing we're caught up in the pain–pleasure cycle that precludes peace of mind.

Joyce is a very articulate woman. She regularly criticizes her family and friends. She has no idea her glib tongue has worked against her. She suffers from hypertension and even ended up in the emergency room one evening when her blood pressure spiked.

I tried to point out the correlation between her tendency to overreact and her health issues. Even though she agrees with me, Joyce still doesn't grasp the necessity of moderating her attitude. She is steeped in faultfinding, because, like most people, she learned to underestimate her incomparable worth. Joyce unconsciously gets her counterfeit self-esteem fix by gaining the upper hand in disputes.

Complaining about what everyone else does wrong keeps us in bondage to a victim mentality. When we grow up subconsciously associating judgmental responses with the fleeting pleasure of being right, we don't comprehend the ultimate price we pay is undermining our health.

Meditation frees us from unknowingly playing God. We slowly but surely detach from the false power of our circumstances by becoming mindful of our true power within. By shifting our attention inward, we learn the unmistakable value of talking less and listening more.

Initially, stilling yourself for even five minutes will feel uncomfortable. A mind that is used to racing and drifting to fear-driven thoughts will resist staying attuned to the present moment. To resume your tranquil state, quietly refocus on your breathing every time you're distracted. Eventually, this practice will help you remain calm, regardless of what transpires during your day.

Keep in mind the resistance you encounter in becoming transparent will pay off immensely in the long-term—providing you persevere beyond the short-term growing pains. It's no easy task to conquer the deceptive lifelong thought that lasting fulfillment is possible through external goals alone. You have to decide whether it's more important to maintain the debilitating energy of self-will or to consistently connect with the life-affirming energy of your divine nature. Developing an eternity vantage point prevents stressful situations from continually interfering with your peace of mind. In *How God Changes Your Brain*, Dr. Andrew Newberg states,

> Activities involving meditation and intensive prayer permanently strengthen neural functioning in specific parts of the brain that are involved in lowering anxiety and depression, enhancing social awareness and empathy, and improving cognitive and intellectual functioning. The neural circuits activated by meditation buffer you from the deleterious effects of aging and stress and give you better control over your emotions. At the very least, such practices help you remain calm, serene, peaceful, and alert.[14]

Meditation doesn't have to be limited to times when you're alone. You can train yourself to disengage from fear-minded thoughts and behaviors when you're in a crowd. Silently repeating *love*, *spirit*, and *all is well* centers your attention on peaceful thoughts. "Loving God ... healing Jesus ... Spirit of truth" is a comforting Christian meditation that corresponds to humanity's mind-body-spirit connection.

Guided imagery is another effective way to transition from your leaned need for chaos to your birthright of peace. The following visualization illuminates this truth. An expanded variation of this meditation is included in the *Garden of Eden* audio file. After completing your deep breathing and relaxation exercises, picture yourself enjoying the perfect vacation. (Note:

The perfect qualifier is important because most people don't experience the ideal vacation).

> You leisurely spend the day indulging in one pleasurable activity after another. You begin by enjoying your favorite breakfast at an inviting corner café, followed by sightseeing breathtaking venues at your own pace.
>
> You are totally immersed in the beauty and serenity of your surroundings. Your radiant smile reflects your state of mind. You easily tune out the commotion of traffic and people scurrying about. You're not worried about being on time or meeting deadlines. After indulging in a dinner that was a culinary masterpiece, you cap off the evening's outstanding entertainment by luxuriating in a whirlpool under a peaceful moonlit sky. Upon returning to your hotel room, you undress and slip beneath the soft, silky sheets of your comfortable bed. You soon drift off to sleep, thinking about the absolutely marvelous day you just experienced.
>
> The next thing you know, morning arrives and your alarm clock jars you back to the reality of returning home. As you scramble to shower and pack before checkout time, you abruptly feel melancholy. Thoughts of impending pressures dampen your mood. You think your feelings of sadness relate to returning to the rat race your life has turned into. The explanation is rooted much deeper.

Did you notice any similarities between this visualization and the feelings the Garden of Eden imagery evoked in you?

Being carefree on vacation is the closest most people come to duplicating that long ago paradise experience. It's initially difficult to readjust to our normal routine after vacationing. By stretching our imagination, we can conjecture we feel similar to the way Adam and Eve did when self-deception transformed their idyllic heavenly state into hell on earth.

Each time we leave our vacation sites, our fear-bound mind-set causes us to act as though we're being exiled from paradise "lost" all over again. In reality, the Garden of Eden alone was never intended to symbolize paradise. No matter how ideal a particular place may be, there is no physical setting that can compare to the blessings that flow from a spiritual lifestyle.

Adam and Eve's bliss didn't originate from their geographic location. It came from being in touch with the only truth that has everlasting significance: oneness of love. Even if they had started out in a slum, the first couple's first-hand knowledge of their unbreakable bond with their Creator would have guaranteed their contentment forever. Unfortunately, as soon as they misidentified with self, they lost their ability to love. Their false belief in fear prevented them from mentally, physically, and spiritually perceiving paradise. The stage was set for humanity to blindly follow their lead.

The real reason we become upset or depressed is thinking exclusively in terms of flesh-driven desires causes us to unconsciously long for the physical perfection that images of Eden conjures up in our mind. When we're dominated by fear, we illogically deny the spiritual perfection we've always possessed to fantasize about an earthly goal of excellence that is impossible without true love!

In much the same way, when we envision heaven solely as a specific physical location above the clouds, we miss out on experiencing the kingdom of God within us through peace of mind now. Turmoil ensues every time we allow someone or something to overshadow our faith in God to calm life's storms.

Simply stated, identifying with our divinity through self-respect leads to the discovery that inner peace *is* paradise.

The Garden of Eden meditation will be instrumental in restoring your mind to reclaim heaven on earth. An eternity perspective fortifies you to survive the very worst of ordeals with dignity.

By returning again and again to the point in time before false fear entered the world, your seemingly unending anxiety will revert to your legacy of peace—not only when you're enjoying your vacation, but every day. The only temporary interruptions of your centered feelings will most likely occur due to multiple stressors occurring in proximity, trauma due to serious illness or injury, or the death of loved ones.

For those who are still doubting Thomases, I offer Joni Eareckson Tada as concrete proof that a fulfilling life doesn't evolve from our circumstances lining up with our expectations. Millions know Joni as the courageous Christian teenager who refused to languish in despair after a diving accident left her a quadriplegic. In the ensuing four decades, Joni became an accomplished artist, author, and host of radio and television programs, to name just a few of this extraordinary woman's remarkable accomplishments. If she had remained flesh-driven, her future would have been bleak indeed. The harsh reality of requiring total care for the duration of her physical life would have made her bitter.

Instead, Joni's life attests to the indomitable nature of humanity's spirit when our focus is on love. She recently has even had to deal with cancer. Her astounding courage inspires countless others to stay faithful in the face of adversity. This amazing story drives home the point that we can't have it both ways. We must decide daily whether we're going to be ruled by love or ruined by fear.

High Road of Humility

I had to be completely honest to heal from the inside out. My anxiety escalated every time I allowed myself to get caught up in arguments that only afforded me a fleeting sense of power if I got my way.

Wholeness can't be achieved when unresolved childhood trauma keeps surfacing through the cracks of adult façades. I thought I had forgiven my father when he died unexpectedly in 1981. But my mood didn't mellow considerably until decades later. I transformed from regularly overreacting to stressful situations to generally observing without becoming emotionally attached to the outcome. This major attitude adjustment is when I knew for certain I had truly (subconsciously) healed my fear-minded perceptions regarding my dad's aggression.

A crucial step in my spiritual awakening was to stop deflecting my need to deal with my own character defects by pointing out others' shortcomings. I admitted to my confidant whenever my own actions were fear-driven. James 5:16 confirms the need to shift our attention to self-assessment: "Confess your faults one to another, and pray one for another, that ye may be healed."

We can't be peaceful and judgmental at the same time. Everyone has to decide which state of mind is more important. Self-deception prevents us from conceding when our own attitudes make a bad situation worse. When we learn to respond in everyone's best interests, our stress levels dramatically decrease over time.

Our daily actions either increase our feelings of separation or oneness. If we don't believe we're all in this together on a heartfelt level, fear-addicted thought patterns cause us to feel estranged from one another.

I may impress you with my lavish lifestyle, but you won't necessarily trust me because worldly gain has no eternal value. You'll be more likely to respect me if I own up to my faults.

Establishing a common ground paves the way for honest relationships. Simply stated, people who are more concerned with being right than being loving don't move beyond their misidentification with self.

If the universal need for spiritual recovery was recognized, programs that target specific addictions, such as Alcoholics Anonymous, Narcotics Anonymous, Overeaters Anonymous, etc., would be unnecessary. Just imagine how different the world would be if people universally acted the opposite of the way they were raised and focused on what others do right. What a concept! The groundswell of positive energy would make us feel like we had died and gone to heaven.

Granted, it's no small task to replace a critical attitude with humility. After a lifetime of either trying to avoid conflicts or becoming defensive, it simply feels unnatural to respond any other way. And that's exactly the point. You have to ask yourself if you want to continue living a natural judgmental life or a supernatural peaceful existence.

When we become genuinely interested in doing our part to reclaim paradise, we wake up giving thanks to God for the strength to get through each day. At the same time, we are mindful that everything else in life—from the houses we live in to the food we eat—is a luxury that isn't guaranteed to the vast majority on our planet.

In America, where operating in survival mode isn't the status quo, it's all too easy for minor grievances to take center stage. Throughout the day, whenever you're assailed by negative thoughts, simply repeat as many times as necessary to yourself, "Spirit-led … attitude of gratitude … I am peaceful."

Healing our childhood misconceptions is essential. We can't help but feel discontented if we grew up with victim mentalities. We either suffer in silence, or we keep thinking and talking about our difficulties.

Fear-controlled issues have a life all their own. Counterfeit self-esteem is sought through our support networks. If these comforters aren't Spirit-minded, their advice doesn't ring true. They side with our subjective versions of reality due to their own unresolved fears; offer suggestions that our egos prevent us from following; or are too afraid of hurting our feelings to tell us the truth. Simply stated, when we act as though everything is exactly as it needs to be to produce spiritual maturity, we experience true peace of mind.

Circle of Love

The guided imagery exercise that follows complements your affirmations. It can be accessed in the *Garden of Eden* audio file. As you become receptive to your peaceful spirit, your stuck child loses power each day to control your thoughts. Your false allegiance to fear is no match for the love that has always defined you. You now regularly connect with your inner power.

The beginning of this message depicts a brief confrontation scene. It's designed to evoke strong emotions that are effectively countered by concentrating on God's still small voice. Adults who haven't resolved their childhood pain don't know how to be true to themselves. If you tend to become argumentative when you're angry, you may tense up during this sequence.

The best way to handle this resistance is to calmly take several slow, deep breaths to return to your centered state. It's important for you to remain open to experiencing the unpleasant feelings. Learning to feel safe to process stressful situations without overreacting or underreacting promotes serenity and self-control. You'll no longer be ruled by your unreliable emotions. As you substitute the healthy coping skills contained in this meditation, you'll outgrow the deceptive childhood response patterns that continue to plague you.

Let's begin:

You are reclining in bed. It's late evening. A nightstand lamp illuminates your room. You are ready to fall asleep.

Your tranquility is suddenly shattered by the harsh voice of your partner. He lashes out at you in rage. You momentarily freeze in response to his icy glare. As he storms out of the room, your pounding heart silently begins to muster its old defenses. Feelings of hurt and anger bombard your senses.

Instantaneously, your transformed soul recovers. You mobilize the neurons of your mind to release toxins from every part of your being with deep, calming breaths. You first focus on your feet by slowly inhaling. As you slowly exhale, you visualize any tension evaporating through your toes into thin air.

You gradually work your way upward, relaxing each muscle group with love-affirming breaths that loosen your calves ... your knees ... your thighs. As you center your breathing on your hips ... then on your back, you become more and more relaxed.

You now concentrate on soothing your stomach ... your chest. You feel the tightness melting effortlessly away. You continue releasing the tension from your arms ... your shoulders ... your neck ... and your face. Your sense of relaxation deepens. You feel warm all over.

You soon become aware of a gentle stirring deep inside. You sense the now familiar presence of the Holy Spirit. As the feeling grows stronger, a shimmering circle of light surrounds your heart.

Beginning as a tiny ripple, the Heartbeat of God slowly increases in intensity. Its sound waves breach your remaining defenses like an ocean wave washing over the shore. As your cleansed heart now beats in perfect harmony with our Creator's Heart, your innermost being is bathed in a warm, soothing sensation of complete relaxation.

You smile in instant recognition of the peace you've grown accustomed to experiencing. Your unification with the Spirit of truth is now complete. You observe with transfixed fascination as this once tiny beam has now broadened into an ever-widening circle of dazzling brilliance. This magnificent light of infinite perfect love gradually grows stronger and stronger until it can be contained no longer.

You marvel in wonderment as the Spirit's rejuvenating, gleaming force field suddenly flows from your heart, while still remaining attached to you. God's boundless energy makes its way to the surface of your skin. It streams out through your pores, covering every square inch of your body before radiating outward in all directions.

You reflect on your blissful state of mind. You are truly humbled that God's Presence can feel both omnipotent and serene at the same time. You gradually sense that the magnitude of our Creator's all-encompassing love has multiplied exponentially.

Conscious of your oneness, you are acutely aware of your vibrant connection to humanity in a magnificent unending circle of pure, radiant love. You delight in the incomparable feeling of shared ecstasy.

After a few moments, you slowly begin to awaken. As you open your eyes, you're beaming from ear to ear. Your arms are wrapped around your body in a loving embrace. You gradually become aware of your loved one sleeping soundly. He is positioned on his side, facing away from you. You turn to him with the same feeling of love you felt when you first awoke. You encircle his body with your free arm. You soon drift off into the deepest, most peaceful sleep you've ever experienced.

You awaken in the morning feeling refreshed and energetic. Your heightened awareness of your divine nature empowers you to fulfill your true purpose to love. You confidently express your deepest thoughts without reservation. Your security of wholeness frees you to accept yourself as deserving the very best life has to offer.

As you acclimate to the kingdom of God within you, your transformed mind becomes more and more attentive to the present. Peace has now become the norm. All but a faded memory are the fear-rooted beliefs that seemed to have dampened your spirit when you depended on the earthly realm for counterfeit love.

Inner wisdom allows you to see through the barrier of self-condemnation that triggered your partner's aggression. Even though his identification with fear prevents him from living by faith, your understanding of his true identity of love is all you need to know.

A quick disclaimer is needed to ensure we're on the same page. If taken at face value, it may be possible to conclude this meditation implies mistreatment deserves to be rewarded with a loving embrace. This interpretation would be contrary to the theme of this book.

Consistent assertive behavior is the only effective way to deal with hostility. In the event this approach is unsuccessful, it's advisable not to remain in an abusive relationship. It's possible to still love another from a safe distance, because learning to value yourself teaches that you always deserve to be treated with respect.

In the context of this meditation, both embraces are intended to reflect an overall acceptance of yourself and humanity that typifies eternal wholeness, in spite of isolated occurrences of separation behaviors that are manifested through nonassertive response patterns.

The spiritual recovery process can be likened to being locked away in solitary confinement all your life. The key to your false prison of fear has finally been handed to you. As the door swings wide open, the light that now enables you to see with clarity of vision forever vanquishes your darkness.

If you're having difficulty comprehending how solitary confinement applies to you, stop and think about how often you've felt all alone, despite sharing a home with your spouse and children or being at work or in a crowded room, etc.

These feelings of emptiness surface because no one or no thing—*nothing*—can ever truly satisfy you, apart from the love you've always carried inside you. By seeing the light that you're complete just as you are, you'll realize all the other loves in your life can't even begin to compare to the only true love you can always count on to "never leave you nor forsake you" (Hebrews 13:5).

Subconscious level healing changes everything. The false separation anxiety that resulted from believing love can coexist with fear is now gone. The imaginary barrier your mind erected that had separated the eternal realm from the worldly realm with delusional thoughts of good versus evil no longer keeps you off balance. Your freedom from self-deception affords you insight to recognize the whole(ness) truth: *only love is real because there is no distinction between heaven and earth.* You instinctively know you've never been just a separate physical entity. Simply stated, when we break free from our flesh-driven beliefs in fear-minded outcomes, it feels natural to wholeheartedly emulate our eternal spirit-to-Spirit connection in thought, word, and deed.

The idea for the "Circle of Love" title of the preceding meditation came from the final song at our wedding reception. The soloist instructed everyone to form a circle around Bob and me. As we slow danced in the center, the guests were cued to slowly narrow the circumference until we were surrounded. The lyrics were so awe inspiring that we all started spontaneously embracing each other. As the strains of the melody wound down, there wasn't a dry eye in the house. I've never been involved in anything that came close to the joyous intensity of that experience.

Like most brides on their wedding days, I had no idea back then that our love was just a façade that would soon be marred by our lack of self-esteem. Nevertheless, even our divorce can't diminish the power of this beautiful memory.

I would venture to guess this outpouring of joy on a far grander scale is the scenario that will be ultimately played out when spiritual enlightenment is collectively achieved.

The longer you identify with the love that has always defined you, the more sense it will make to simulate the earthly equivalent of humanity's everlasting reality of oneness—in whatever changing form your relationships take.

CHAPTER 9

Free at Last!

Resolve to be thyself: and know that he who finds
himself, loses his misery.

—Matthew Arnold

Being able to identify the problem is half the battle.
Lasting change won't occur until you acknowledge that
self-deception has kept you from fulfilling your divine
destiny. There is an old comic strip that illustrates this point: a
disgruntled looking Pogo surveys the landscape and proclaims to
his sidekick, "We have met the enemy, and he is us."

A sure way to derail our quest for peace of mind is to dismiss the
universal need for spiritual recovery. The meaning of wholeness
is lost when we personalize events that have no real meaning in
the grand scheme of things. Honest relationships occur when we
exchange blame for compassion.

A love and fear existence results in mind clutter that produces
erratic behaviors. I remember an occasion during my initial recovery
period when thoughts of disbelief and resentment were relentless.
As soon as I looked in the mirror to recite my affirmations, I started
to cry. The longer I gazed at my contorted expression, the more I
felt sorry for myself. My impulse was to just forget the whole thing.
It certainly didn't *feel* like the process was working, which is exactly
the problem that plagues us throughout our lives: being controlled
by fear-minded emotions that subvert genuine love.

There is no comparison between the stress that I allowed to
precipitate my nervous breakdown when I was twenty-two and

the anxiety I experienced thirty years later when I became my mother's sole caregiver. Much more extreme circumstances didn't produce the same crippling result. Becoming inner-directed equipped me to depend on my true power.

Anxiety is widely believed to be the trigger for illnesses. This is why it's so vital to learn to function on higher levels of consciousness that express God's will on earth, as it is in heaven. When I identified with flesh-driven goals, I was ruled by unreliable feelings from my childhood. When I made a firm commitment to pay attention to the spiritual aspect of my personality, my lifelong anxieties decreased. Being attentive to the still small voice empowered me to develop self-control.

A person who is mentally, physically, and spiritually centered doesn't become upset with people who don't change toxic behavioral patterns. He demonstrates *he* has changed through assertive responses that benefit everyone.

There were many times when it felt like my evolution from fear to love would never take place. But the contentment I now experience from *beginning* to comprehend my oneness with God was undeniably worth the short-term growing pains. After unconsciously languishing in a victim mentality that kept being fueled by unpredictable occurrences, I finally understand how priceless inner peace is. (Note: I emphasized the word beginning, because I haven't attained the higher joy and complete peace of mind levels of consciousness at the present time).

Inner healing is essential to a meaningful life. Believing it's possible to choose between love and fear-based behaviors can be extremely debilitating over time. Love has no opposite. It always was, is, and ever will be. Anything that appears to oppose love isn't real. Fear only seems real when our sixth sense remains undeveloped. Without insight, we're mentally stuck in time in past behaviors that have never served our best interests. Growing up self-deceived compels us to be overly concerned with what we perceive through our five senses. No matter how successful or content we appear to be, this dynamic promotes inner torment. Simply stated, love only exists in the timeless present—where peace flourishes.

Healing our oppositional attitudes reverses the continual drain on our energy levels. No matter what we say or do, if we subconsciously identify with our childhood fears, we aren't able to genuinely love. We attempt to restore our imbalance through external control and approval, personal judgments, and counterfeit self-esteem. These efforts always end up being exercises in futility, because they are predicated on self-will.

If we become attuned to the present, we're more interested in outcomes that have eternal value. Healing the imaginary division in our mind equips us to mature from the inside out as a righteous spirit who extends God's grace through our physical beings. We sense the necessity of being patient with those who are steeped in the mayhem that is perceived to rule the world. As we stop obsessing over trivial differences, the quality of our lives keeps improving. Simply stated, there is no fear-rooted self in reality now and forever, only oneness of love.

Most people don't understand how detrimental it is long-term to oppose events beyond their control. I used to be one of those people. Lack of spiritual discernment prevents us from realizing how we respond to a difficult situation is far more important than what actually transpires.

When we form false attachments to self, it seems perfectly natural to judge people who act differently than we do. A holistic orientation frees us from believing fulfillment lies in having our expectations met.

The moment you take your last breath, disagreements and possessions lose all relevance. The only legacy that matters is demonstrating your true character. The greatest tragedy of all is when people die without realizing their false belief in fear prevented them from living their real life of love.

Alfred Nobel was the inventor of dynamite. When his brother expired, the newspaper erroneously published Alfred's obituary instead. The headline read, "The merchant of death is dead." This stark characterization was Nobel's wakeup call. By the time he actually died eight years later, he had donated $9 million of his fortune to recognize extraordinary achievements. He is remembered worldwide each year when recipients are awarded the Nobel Prize.

The moral of this story is the longer we misidentify with self, the less likely we are to fulfill our true purpose. Becoming Spirit-minded heals feelings of powerlessness that we express through fear-bound judgments.

This conversion from reacting based on painful, past experiences to responding from within, based on love, is all too rare. When we grow up believing mixed-messages are normal, it doesn't occur to us that we've been processing information with a mind that is stuck between childhood and adulthood.

If you weren't taught to thrive as a peaceful spirit who occupies a temporary body, your conflicted reality bombards you with apprehension. A prevailing belief in fear is evidenced by your moods varying according to your circumstances. Simply stated, a mind designed to love is trapped in turmoil if your inner child dictates your conduct.

The subconscious thought process of a dual belief system boils down to this assessment:

> If I give up self-will, I'll never be able to cope. I'm used to blaming others for my unhappiness. Since adults aren't helpless, I won't get any more sympathy whenever I'm mistreated. Even worse, I'll have to stop depending on my standby gratification patterns to offset the anxiety and anger I've learned to live by. I have to resist change at all costs. My whole identity is at stake!

The whole(ness) truth is you've been living a fractured adult/ child identity that keeps you in bondage to your own personalized version of earthly hell. Every time you rail against your troubles, you keep missing the chance to break free from the pain from your past.

Since it's impossible for life to unfold in agreement with everyone's viewpoints, it's logical to conclude harmony can only flow from a master plan. If children were raised to accept life's trials as necessary to foster dependence on God's will, there wouldn't be so many complaining, disillusioned adults.

It's crucial to teach children the value of delayed gratification at an early age to prevent them from becoming addicted to quick fixes. If we don't develop patience when we're young, we're destined to encounter as many obstacles as it takes until we come to the realization that we can't grow up emotionally without self-control.

Becoming dependent on temporary payoffs blocks our ability to love. Our egocentric focus compels us to view ourselves as unfulfilled. Without recognizing denial of humanity's wholeness is our real problem, a vicious cycle ensues. We keep seeking outside relief from our fear-controlled mindset that reinforces our feelings of emptiness. An external perspective prevents us from identifying with the peace of the Holy Spirit through our spirit.

As difficult as relinquishing a dual belief system is in the short-term, it's better in the long run to learn to identify exclusively with love. Otherwise, contradictory behaviors can leave us feeling more hopeless (and acting more childish) with each passing year. Resisting God's will results in perceived persistent problems. Heeding God's will transforms problems into opportunities for consistent spiritual growth.

Without a doubt, humanity's failure to separate fear-minded thoughts from what constitutes reality has remained unchanged throughout the ages. Spiritual blindness only allows us to see bits and pieces of the truth. Self-deception convinces us we possess knowledge we don't actually have. We lack awareness that our subconscious beliefs continually interfere with our ability to give sound advice.

My counseling job (discussed in the introduction) is a good example. I used to emphasize to clients the necessity of demonstrating assertive conduct. While this is true, I now understand this goal can't be accomplished without changing how we think. Faulty thought patterns must first be minimized through an integrated approach that meshes self-esteem with a spiritual lifestyle.

Another example of partial truth is the way my former husband viewed his addiction as the root problem. Bob agreed with his sponsor that his decision to use was based on his overconfidence in thinking he would be able to control the outcome. The whole truth is Bob's drug abuse and arrogance were both symptomatic of his self-hatred.

When we don't resolve our delusional conflict between love and fear, we settle for success that is defined by superficial achievements. The root cause of our instability remains intact.

It was commonplace for Narcotics Anonymous and Alcoholics Anonymous members I knew to be overly impressed by those who had accrued the most clean and sober years. Defining victory on the basis of numbers can lead to a false sense of security. Quantity isn't nearly as important as one's ability to humbly demonstrate quality through love-centered relationships.

AA and NA sponsors who don't commit to spiritual recovery in all aspects of their lives end up substituting their personal beliefs for God's will. It's all too easy to succumb to egotistical feelings of self-importance when dealing with addicts who hang on a sponsor's every word, because they are desperate to salvage their lives.

Just as authentic parenting involves teaching a child to rely on the still small voice as he matures, sponsors who are committed to truth must stress to those they mentor the necessity of surrendering self-will daily. Recovery requires transitioning from the advice of a charismatic personality to becoming sensitive to direction from the Spirit of truth.

Learning to value who you are, instead of hating yourself for your fear-driven actions, empowers you to believe God's unconditional love defines you. When healing is superficial, people are forced to obtain their quick fixes through alternate destructive behaviors. Proof of this statement can be seen through the smoke-filled haze of recovery meetings, where cigarettes are the addictive substitute of choice for many members.

This observation isn't intended to imply that those who are currently involved in twelve-step programs should abandon this method of healing. However, it is logical to conclude the success rate of AA and NA would be enhanced by addressing humanity's identity crisis. Introductions at these meetings currently include the qualifying statement, "I'm an addict." In reality, everyone who doesn't identify with love is addicted to fear-minded behavioral patterns. A more generic announcement that deals with the core issue could be more beneficial: "I'm recovering from self-deception."

As repeatedly stated, being attentive to the present moment is essential to staying grounded in reality. Continuing to proclaim past failures can end up sabotaging the recovery process. Pejorative labels tend to reinforce unresolved feelings of inadequacy.

By developing an eternity vantage point, a person would discover he's no more an alcoholic than those in the general population are sinners. Vulnerability to relapse would occur only if the recovery process wasn't authentic.

In hindsight, I know of only two recovering addicts who actually followed through with all twelve steps. I'm more familiar with those who only renewed their mind in the area of their drug addiction. The discrepancies in their personal lives confirmed they were still functioning with a fear-bound mentality.

Complicated, albeit well-meaning, solutions don't usually alleviate lifelong feelings of failure. Genuine spiritual recovery heals irrational core beliefs in general. Thinking in terms of one's inner power, as opposed to higher power, reorients perceptions from external to internal. Believing that God is readily accessible instead of faraway is a seemingly simple change that can make a big difference in dispelling the false feeling that one is all alone. Simply stated, discovering the love within you equips you to function in agreement with your divinity.

Putting It All Together

One of the most familiar ways we grow up insecure is being taught we're sinners on the road to hell who are saved by God's grace. The demoralizing nature of this mixed-message leaves those who aren't assertive feeling guilty as charged instead of redeemed.

To make matters even worse, the secular world has also essentially failed to recognize how indispensable self-worth is to understanding the truth about love. The lack of harmonious relationships attests to the necessity of first altering individual attitudes to effect change on a global level.

Infants are born without pretense. Learning to believe love and fear can coexist leads to dishonest communication patterns. Thinking in terms of humanity's wholeness is a power position. Viewing the human race as separate physical entities creates subconscious perceptions of powerlessness.

A temporal viewpoint prevents us from maturing as a righteous spirit whose mission in life is to promote everlasting values. We feel estranged from one another. Without an eternity perspective, we don't exemplify love through the assertive communication of self-actualization that benefits everyone.

A love-fear reality compels us to imitate our parents' poor self-worth. We become accustomed to aggressive, passive, and passive-aggressive expressions of anger: displaying overtly controlling behaviors; repressing our feelings to gain approval; or pursuing our desires through indirect control.

As children, most of us learned to appease our parents to ensure our emotional survival. As adults, coping methods that prevent us from being transparent keep us off balance. Our self-styled reality enslaves us to arbitrary performance standards that produce judgmental behaviors. We become trapped in vicious cycles of conflicting expectations that alternate with seeking transitory relief from our pain.

Continuing to depend on superficial fixes can intensify feelings of victimization as one grows older. The longer you delay healing your childhood fallacies, the less likely you'll be to discover you've always held the key to your emotional prison of fear.

Restoring Harmony

Substituting self-rule for God's will is like saying we prefer chaos over peace. When the illusory ego is in charge, the focus on what *I* want and how offended *I* feel creates relationships that function at cross purposes.

When we become inner-directed, we function with the power of God's Mind. Our reference point becomes our righteous spirit-to-Spirit connection. Honing our sixth sense convinces us intangible traits like love, humility, and forgiveness are far more important than singling out differences.

God-consciousness equips us to maintain balance between our transitory physical and eternal spiritual reality. Self-consciousness compels us to believe our lives are impermanent, because we feel insignificant deep down inside.

When we aren't raised to identify with our inner power, our unhappiness stems from being unable to find fulfillment as fleeting members of the human race. Our subconscious fears deceive us into believing the clock isn't timeless, it's ticking. We depend on external remedies to offset being consumed by the thought that we have no control over how much time we have left before it's all over forever.

The irony is our judgmental natures prevent us from truly enjoying the self-centered pleasures we've become addicted to in whatever time we do have left. Our attention on fear-driven feelings translates into being physically alive but spiritually dead to the undying reality of love.

Most people fail to grasp the far-reaching implications of this statement. We can be physically healthy, involved in outreach ministries, well liked, and wealthy. But if we don't identify with oneness of love, we don't have the most important ingredient of all: peace of mind.

If Adam and Eve were portrayed as having lost their spiritual focus in a perfect world, it's easy to understand how successive generations have continued to spiral out of control. Self-deception constantly bombards us with temptations to satiate our egocentric impulses. History clearly reveals how falling into this seductive trap programs us to feel responsible for or cheated by life's unpredictable occurrences.

Without discovering that God's will has been humanity's will all along, the good we do is negated by intolerance when others fail to live up to our subjective standards. Unimportant allegations and self-pity that promote no-win disagreements become the norm. When we're sincere about developing an eternity vantage point, we align our physical reality with our spiritual identity. We no longer feel victimized by our circumstances. We're strengthened to accept the bad times as necessary so we can fully appreciate the good times.

True Maturity

A good test to know if you're on a true spiritual path is if you don't overreact or underreact to unforeseen events. If you're passive, you attempt to alleviate your perceived feelings of powerlessness by trying to placate others who can only help themselves. This coping method leads to the eventual release of pent-up emotions through rage or serious illnesses. If your temperament is aggressive or passive-aggressive, you express your unresolved fears through personal judgments that fuel your anxiety and depression.

If we don't follow the example of the Master, self-will breeds disaster. We fall prey to the insidious influence of our egocentric mind-set. Forsaking spiritual truths fortifies our imaginary crucifixion complex.

Myra related how difficult it was initially to process her irritation without judgment. She had bounded out of bed into her new puppy's droppings. Her spouse had promised to let the dog outside before he left. Ordinarily, she would have phoned to tell him how inconsiderate he was in no uncertain terms.

After fuming for a few moments, Myra regained her composure by breathing deeply and focusing on the nine qualities that constitute spiritual enlightenment. By reevaluating the situation honestly, Myra was cued by her conscience to remember it was her idea to acquire this dog as a companion for their other pet. She was also prompted to think realistically about how fortunate she is to have a dependable husband who takes the animals to the vet and tends to them when she's unavailable.

If you genuinely desire a peaceful life, personifying love should be your top priority. While intensifying fear-controlled behaviors with even more negative energy feels natural, responding with grace enables you to live supernaturally.

Most people would be amazed at how much better they would feel in the long run by altering their knee-jerk reactions to escalate daily irritants into needless battles. Through spiritual recovery, we reap untold benefits by remaining calm. Trading judgmental commentary for detaching from false emotions is the difference between night and day.

Adults are less likely to behave rationally if nonassertive behaviors were routinely expressed during their formative years. Leading neuroscientist Dr. Andrew Newberg states in his book, *How God Changes Your Brain*, "If you allow anger and fear to dominate, you will lose the neurological ability to think logically and act compassionately toward others."[15]

Our false attachments to self prevent us from being truly grateful for our blessings. A poverty mentality compels us to focus on what we don't have and what everyone else does wrong. We become enmeshed in resentments and depression without realizing we've regressed to our childhoods.

Becoming transparent requires merging the adult/child factions of our personalities. Learning to love who we are, even when we feel unappreciated or unlovable, is a critical first step in reclaiming heaven on earth by identifying with our joyous divine nature. The longer we allow fear to cause us to resist the Holy Spirit's gentle tug at our heartstrings, the more out of touch with reality we become. Simply stated, we either feel victimized because we're ruled by self-deception, or we feel energized because we're governed by the whole(ness) truth.

Transforming into a centered adult ensures constructive response patterns. Just as a healthy child matures responsibly by learning to respectfully accept correction from assertive parents, spiritual growth involves humbly following God's lead to love, regardless of how life unfolds.

Simplifying Your Life

Growing up in a world where nonassertive communication dominates can make acting self-righteously seem so normal that changing one's attitude is unthinkable. Fear of change convinces us to cling to lifelong negative energy patterns, even though we sacrifice our health in the process.

One man told me a love-based existence is unrealistic, because "life just isn't that simple." Little did he know he had just identified the crux of humanity's primary problem: identifying with the fear-rooted self is exactly what prevents us from embracing the true simplicity of love.

We can't experience harmony between our impermanent physical and infinite spiritual identity when we depend on our circumstances for security. Without a wholeness perspective, unpredictable events keep us feeling unsettled.

Either God is the center of our universe, or self is the center. The most extreme examples of people out of touch with reality are individuals who murder family members, then openly proclaim their love for their victims without missing a beat.

When we're controlled by fear, we aren't aware that we regularly contradict ourselves. Even when we admit we need professional help, what we really expect is to receive confirmation that something or someone other than ourselves is responsible for our unrest.

Inner peace requires complete honesty. The good news is fulfillment isn't a complicated process. What could be more straightforward than becoming authentic through love-grounded thoughts and actions, daily communing with God, and owning up to our mistakes?

This restructuring process alters the way the brain interprets information from anxious to peaceful. But even with scientific data that proves you can indeed teach an old brain new tricks, the familiarity of self-will still causes resistance to simple solutions. A belief system replete with chaotic conditioning naturally results in perceiving life as difficult.

You can't expect to be optimistic when you dwell on problems instead of the problem-solver and expect others to make up for the misery from your past, which only God and you have the ability to heal from within. Simply stated, most people die suffering the consequences of a misspent life rather than admit they have allowed their childhood pain to override their true purpose to love.

If we don't develop faith to believe we've always had everything we need inside to enjoy abundant living, our learned compulsion to alternate between the pain of self-deception and the fleeting pleasure of external comforts causes us to miss the whole point of life.

Taking the initiative to identify with the love within us simplifies our existence. Our attitudes finally line up with our Creator's original plan for humanity to experience heaven on earth through peace of mind.

Higher Level of Consciousness

Are you like most people who prefer to maintain their false sense of autonomy rather than endure the short-term growing pains that becoming real requires? Or are you among the determined few who are no longer willing to have history repeat itself by continuing to suffer with the anguish they felt as children?

Breaking free from entrenched denial involves learning to really pay attention to who you are spiritually, in addition to what you accomplish in the earthly realm. Think about all the people you know who routinely protest the dark clouds in their lives without being grateful for the silver linings. Inner peace will continue to seem impossible until you realize that fulfilling your life's purpose is far more important than focusing on individual agendas that don't produce lasting satisfaction.

Regina is a dear friend of mine. Her husband's name is Jim. Like most couples, they had often found themselves at odds with each other. Regina is very family oriented. Jim didn't feel the need to consult his wife before making costly purchases. On the upside, Jim was a tireless worker. He spent most of his free time remodeling their modest home so they could move to a better neighborhood.

Shortly after they relocated, Jim was diagnosed with cancer. He eventually had to quit his job. Although they have faced one setback after another during the last four years, their relationship has evolved into personifying love. They have become each other's top priority. Regina misses work to accompany her husband to his chemotherapy appointments. Jim's gruff nature has mellowed considerably. Their courage and strength is an inspiration to everyone who knows them. They take turns buoying each other's spirits.

During one low point, Jim discussed how badly he felt about not being able to make love. Regina gently corrected him. "You make love to me every day." She then explained how her tension instantly dissolves when he greets her with a smile and a steaming cup of coffee after a hard day's work; how much she treasures the admiration she sees in his eyes; the peace she feels when he strokes her hair as they relax in front of the television; and the comforting way he cradles her in his arms each night.

On another occasion, they had just left his doctor's office. His pain medication was doubled. Regina became distraught when she lost the narcotic prescription that couldn't be refilled for thirty days.

Jim was very understanding. Regina continued to berate herself for being careless. Jim calmly informed his wife that he was giving her ten minutes to get over her guilt, because two toxic people were one more than he could handle. The tension was immediately broken as they both burst into laughter.

This poignant story illustrates the priceless benefits we reap when we make it a point to live each day as if it were our last. When we merely agree without restoring our mind to wholeness thoughts, our deep-rooted belief in fear can cause us to feel like our lives have been in vain.

Contradictions abound when we deny the reality of love in everyone. Atheists tend to be more truthful regarding their relationship to God than most people. They deny the existence of a supreme being. Those who describe themselves as religious affirm a higher power's presence and may even appear outwardly faithful by performing good deeds. But a closer look reveals their overall angry communication styles betray their claims.

Even the venerable Apostle Paul fell prey to self-deception: "For what I am doing, I do not understand. For what I will to do, that I do not practice; but what I hate, that I do" (Romans 7:15). This paradox occurs because a love-fear belief system creates a corresponding discrepancy between what we say and how we act.

Almost no one sets out to hinder his or her children's chances for success by training them to confuse fact with fiction. For example, the clear-cut correlation between stealing and feelings of victimization makes it easy to teach most children to avoid this behavior. But associating aggressive and passive responses with dishonesty is a much more difficult sale if these false language styles have been tacitly endorsed since childhood.

Spiritual truths aren't usually well received in our quick-fix culture that doesn't emphasize patiently honing one's insight. We have no trouble relating to the overt damage caused by sickness or broken bones, because we see tangible evidence of these maladies.

But if we weren't raised to be mindful that our true power originates from within, we're unaware of the extensive covert harm a person suffers from repeatedly being on the receiving, as well as on the giving, end of hurtful remarks.

We can only superficially agree to a love-based approach to life if we don't have spiritual discernment. Most of our actions are dictated by the misconceptions of our childhood. The false hold of fear-bound response patterns has us so convinced we're right that we actually feel distressed when we try to oppose our self-will orientation by responding in a consistent assertive manner.

Learning to believe it's normal to overreact and underreact tricks us into subconsciously believing fear is more powerful than love. Coupled with the fact that we offset our painful feelings with pleasurable remedies, makes it doubly difficult to recognize the pressing need for self-esteem. Instead of heartfelt affection, we're conditioned to settle for shallow expressions of love.

Without inner healing, everyone who consciously or unconsciously viewed themselves as victims during childhood continues to assign blame as adults. Untrustworthy personal opinions prevent us from truly forgiving those whom we perceived mistreated us during our formative years.

Long after we have physically separated from our families by distance or death, we unconsciously act as though our offending parents are still standing in front of us. We repress our true feelings and attract people who trigger our unresolved feelings of victimization; victimize our partners, children, etc., with aggression when their conduct activates our learned defense mechanisms; or alternate our behaviors between these two extremes.

We can't function with wholeness of purpose as long as our perceptions remain skewed. Feelings of loss of control, resentment, depression, etc., are rampant. Without spiritual recovery, the ego demands that either we or others pay for the mistakes made by our role models. We lack awareness that non-assertive behavioral patterns keep us subconsciously bound to our childhood trauma.

Peace becomes our everyday reality when we collectively attain the level of consciousness to discover there is nothing to forgive. We recognize oneness has always defined humanity without equivocation. The false love-fear association that had seemed so real since childhood won't be the prevailing mindset. You'll stop being ruled by the inconsistencies that had characterized your critical parents' behaviors. The obsession to play God by trying to rescue others or by passing judgment on those who don't comply with your viewpoint will become totally unnecessary. Your futile lifelong search for the acceptance you've always had but never felt will vanish. Simply stated, you will finally be free to express yourself through joyous emotions that had been blocked by needless suffering when you identified with a mixed-message belief system.

When my mother was healthy, she was used to taking care of others' needs. She had a gentle spirit and wasn't argumentative. I was accustomed to getting my way. As her condition deteriorated, the tables were turned. Not only was my mom more dependent on me, memories of my dad's tirades were triggered when she became uncharacteristically demanding.

Discovering the love within me ultimately enabled me to stay centered during those increasingly stressful times. I had to decide daily to accept whatever transpired—no easy task for someone who grew up identifying with a compulsive need for control.

Mom's anxiety intensified when dusk drew near. She didn't recognize her familiar surroundings. She repeatedly asked to go home. I compared our codependent relationship to that of emotional Siamese twins. If I was out of her sight, mom would call out for me. If I didn't appear immediately, she would become more insistent.

As the day wore on, I felt more challenged by this drastic behavior change. It was especially difficult for me to be patient during dinnertime; especially since cooking has never been my strong suit!

Mom's bed was set up in the living room. I was in her line of sight from the kitchen, but she wanted my undivided attention. Trying to explain that I would be in to feed her as soon as possible didn't always calm her anxieties.

I had been consistently reciting my affirmations in the mirror for many months at this point, but there were still times when I would lose my composure. I would eventually shout, "Leave me alone!" Mom would then yell, "Shut up!" And I responded, "No, you shut up!"

Even though I knew my mother's demands were caused by her intensified feelings of helplessness, my conditioning to personalize her agitation caused me to lose touch with reality. I was still unintentionally reverting to my false attachment to self.

The good news is my stuck child didn't prevail during these episodes. Because I was more attuned to my divine nature at that point, I recognized my anger stemmed from being unable to alleviate the fears of the person I adored most in the world. My Spirit-led focus also enabled me to discern my hostility most likely reminded mom of the way dad had addressed her. These insights allowed me to stop unconsciously imitating my father as soon as the rant was out of my mouth. I neither felt justified due to the highly stressful nature of my circumstances, nor guilty. I simply apologized and resumed my meal preparations.

A couple months later, my determination to identify with God's will started to pay off. Same scenario. Mom wanted my full attention. I immediately sensed the rise in my anxiety level. The big difference was when I was told to "shut up," I didn't take it personally. Instead of automatically responding in kind, I actually smiled to myself. I had finally replaced the stranglehold I had allowed my father's self-hate to have over me with self-control. Simply stated, when love becomes the driving force of your existence, you slowly but surely detach from your childhood victim mentality.

Trying to change others, surrendering to depression, or continuing to think or talk about upsetting events keeps you trapped in torment that isn't real. You won't be empowered to genuinely love until you resolve your childhood insecurities. Charlotte Joko Beck described this transformative process in *Everyday Zen,* "We must observe the thought content until it is neutral enough that we can enter the direct experience of the disappointment and suffering. And that experiencing is ultimately nonverbal. When we experience the suffering directly, the melting of the false emotion [anxiety] can begin, and true compassion can emerge."[16]

Self-deception can be overcome only if we stop kidding ourselves that overreacting and underreacting can ever produce long-term benefits. Recognizing that our core beliefs are the root cause of our misery is crucial to healing our split personalities. Believing *only love is real* enables us to respond assertively to offenses that have no bearing on humanity's eternal wholeness. The false power of aggressive and passive displays is broken when we discover our true power is internal.

As long as my attention was fixed on how I was mistreated, I was subconsciously reverting to the past. By learning to view myself as complete, I healed my childhood need to become irritated. Over time, I learned to quietly experience the uncomfortable nature of feeling out of control without acting on this false emotion.

I was committed to stay the course through affirmations, prayer, and self-correction. My angry childish persona eventually lost its ability to weaken me through fear-driven behavior. As I relied more and more on my inner strength, it started to feel natural to be the neutral witness instead of the unstable reactor. I'm now content most of the time instead of automatically becoming upset by unanticipated problems.

Half the battle is recognizing the urgent need to exchange being governed by egotistical impulses for being grounded by the Spirit of truth. This short-term pain, long-term gain journey from love and fear to love must be undertaken if we sincerely desire to appreciate the totality of life. Otherwise, our conditioning to respond to the chaos of the world keeps adding to our misery with each passing year.

When eliminating our oppositional belief system becomes our top priority, we finally understand that staying focused on the present is indispensable. We *honestly* love everyone because we're no longer ruled by contradictory beliefs. I emphasized this word because I know people who claim to have forgiven their parents, whose continued aggression indicates they are still dominated by unresolved resentments.

Do you regularly become upset by how others behave? Do you get annoyed when your good deeds are repaid with disrespect? If this is the case, you may want to consider healing your family of origin relationship through forgiveness meditations, so you can function on a supernatural level.

The longer you're in bondage to chronic anger, anxiety, depression, etc., the more detached you become from the ever present reality of love. It may be helpful to remember that most people are fear-minded. When you change your frame of reference to encompass your peaceful spirit, you recognize the unmistakable value of remaining composed during trying times. Criticizing what others do wrong must be replaced by honing your insight to see humanity's spiritual righteousness if you sincerely desire to be true to yourself.

Genuine relationships are built on becoming the higher awareness that observes unhealthy behavioral patterns without reacting the way we did during our childhood ordeals. Cultivating love-based thoughts facilitates transcending our faulty temperaments and learned behaviors. We respond with the Mind of God.

You will know when you become transparent, because you'll finally start seeing the best in everyone and stop attracting people who confirm your subconscious feelings of unworthiness. You won't think of yourself as having a separate agenda from those you had considered to be the source of your pain. The best part is your hurtful past will no longer keep contaminating your current relationships.

Monica kept trying to justify her clashes with her sister, Shirley. Even though she was completing her affirmations, Monica wasn't able to maintain her emerging confidence when her sibling was present. After further inquiry, Monica admitted that aside from her brief mirror exercises, she wasn't tuning in to the Spirit of truth or engaging in honest self-appraisal. She was regressing to her stuck child mode.

When Monica and Shirley argue, they feel a false sense of power. They unconsciously use each other to symbolically tell off their domineering father. Aggressive expressions of anger only make us feel powerful in the heat of the moment, or when we recount our subjective versions of events to others.

Negative energy patterns are extremely damaging in the long run. If you know you're right beyond a shadow of a doubt, nonassertive actions are still counterproductive. Even siblings who were raised together don't process experiences in the same way due to their differing personalities and intellectual abilities.

Self-deception doesn't allow us to consider the true depth of anyone else's trauma. Without a wholeness orientation, I only remember how <u>I</u> suffered during my childhood. Inner healing empowers us to be more empathic.

Monica had convinced herself that her sister "knew better" than to be so self-centered. Not only had she discounted Shirley's legacy of fear, Monica sabotaged herself by allowing her sister to control her through anger. Simply stated, true spiritual growth can't occur without releasing the entrenched habit to find fault.

Monica had to be willing to step out of her comfort zone of "my way" to concentrate on healing her own fear-driven response patterns. She had to consider whether her learned need for control was more important than being honest.

She decided to change her attitude. No matter how her sister behaved, Monica was committed not to argue. It was difficult, but she gradually learned to endure Shirley's inner child's hostility without reacting aggressively. She also started paying attention to her sister's good qualities.

As Monica became more accustomed to observing the chaos she had come to love and hate, she broke free from her clashing communication style. Even though she falters from time to time,

Monica reports that she usually avoids taking short-lived power trips.

Contentment comes from trusting you have God's wisdom to overcome your lifelong regression to the past. You live your real life of love in the present based on two interdependent beliefs: 1) You humbly relinquish judging those who identify with fear. 2) You regard yourself and everyone else as cherished creations of our Creator—even if it's from a distance and even if others don't afford you the same courtesy.

As your mind, body, and spirit work together in harmony, you're ultimately energized to detach from painful emotions that had blocked the supernatural flow of love from within. You experience the enduring satisfaction of becoming a beacon of calmness who guides those who have lost their way back to the ever present reality of love.

Recovering Wholeness in a Fractured World

Think of spiritual recovery as a golden opportunity to do for yourself what no one else ever can: recognize the only validation you need comes from your eternity connection to God. Living by faith largely releases you from the futility of depending on anyone or anything for lasting fulfillment.

We personified turmoil as babies. Crying was the only means available to communicate our needs. The sporadic positive reinforcement of verbal and physical comforts that elicits temporary good feelings, alternating with largely negative messages, formed the basis for our delusional belief system. This codependent love-fear cycle keeps us addicted to seeking relief through external sources.

When fear-minded role models teach us to define right and wrong, self-reproach and criticism are inevitable. If the necessity of inner healing isn't recognized by the time we reach adulthood, we graduate from mainly blaming our parents, siblings, and friends to judging everyone—from our partners, spouses, children, coworkers, and bosses to the countless anonymous people who we falsely perceive to be the sources of our displeasure.

Integrating your adult/child persona to exemplify wholeness of love dispels your feelings of powerlessness. Becoming Spirit-minded empowers you to renounce fear-bound behaviors—even though this adjustment will cause you to briefly experience withdrawal symptoms of heightened anxiety until you grow accustomed to centered response patterns.

You have to be willing to let your learned need for control and approval die by not feeding your negative thought patterns with endless judgmental behaviors. This way, you can be spiritually born again as a love-grounded adult.

Subconscious level healing restores you to your infancy state of wholeness. How will you know when this miraculous conversion occurs? God's still small voice will be at the forefront of your thoughts, while the critical parent's voice will be relegated to the far recesses of your mind.

This transition from victim to victor can't take place without an assertive mind-set. When we don't outgrow our childhood fears, we fixate on weaknesses because children are naturally afraid. If we don't develop spiritual discernment as we mature, we can end up feeling desperate. Who we are is never good enough; those in our lives don't perform well enough; and we can never get enough or do enough to alleviate our perceived separation anxiety. Our false belief in the solitary I keeps confirming our feelings of emptiness.

It's also critically important to be sensitive to those who are dependent on their circumstances for fulfillment. Fear-addicted people do the best they can based on their temperaments and learned behaviors. If you agree with this statement without purging fear from your soul, you won't be able to demonstrate the empathy that characterizes a spiritual lifestyle. Your desire to extend God's love has to be greater than your conditioning to imitate your role models' self-rejection for your life to significantly improve.

An eternity vantage point enables you to recognize true love is mental, physical, and spiritual. A holistic reality ensures the choices you make will be love-centered, rather than the existing self-serving and self-sacrificing approaches that most of us grew up believing would fulfill us.

Contentment doesn't result from subconsciously trying to accommodate God's will and self-will, from external spirituality, or from pursuing a worldly agenda. Inner peace is a natural consequence of learning to love from the heart, with respect and without blame. Becoming authentic involves adhering to the following spiritual truths:

1. You stay attuned to the present moment with assertive thoughts and actions.
2. You don't judge individual flaws.
3. You assume full responsibility for your state of mind.
4. You extend forgiveness unequivocally.
5. You praise God and strive to find the bright spot on even the darkest of days.

Abiding Faith

When we're ruled by fear, we find endless ways to express our dissatisfaction with life in general—even after hearing about catastrophic losses and squalid living conditions that make our existence look like fairy-tales by comparison.

If you don't develop an eternity viewpoint, you'll keep unconsciously confirming your childhood feelings of inadequacy. Even if you're well off, denying your spiritual perfection compels you to recreate the pain from your past.

Jesus could have been born the son of royalty in a palace. He chose to be the son of a peasant girl, born in a stable to teach humanity the priceless value of humility. When we contrast the way Christ lived with how people relentlessly pursue their own desires, it's no wonder there is so much unrest in the world.

Trading our reliance on people, places, and things for the lasting love that originates within equips us to live the abundant life in thought, word, and deed. Inner healing releases us from the bondage of feeling sorry for ourselves when our personal goals don't come to fruition.

A mixed-message belief system sidetracks us from our true purpose. We lose perspective that everything happens for a reason, even inexplicable behavior. A teen-ager commits suicide after being relentlessly bullied. Her soft-spoken mother had never been an activist. Anguish motivates her to crusade against this fear-rooted practice. She perseveres. Legislation is enacted that gives hope to those who once believed no one cared.

Irrational behaviors appear to dominate when we aren't raised to be God-conscious. When a self-conscious person is disrespected, he lashes out in anger that can turn violent, acts out his inferiority complex indirectly, or feels consumed by his torment, which can tragically lead to suicide.

Our mistaken identity of fear leaves us with unpredictable emotions lying just beneath the surface of our consciousness, like a lion waiting to pounce with ferocity. Unstable response patterns will remain the (dis)order of the day until we recognize the necessity of becoming inner-directed.

Learning to view yourself as a divine, physical extension of God's grace equips you to live your real life of love. Becoming attuned to spiritual truths blocks your childhood victim mentality from defining your conduct.

Matthew 12:34 states, in part, "For out of the abundance of the heart the mouth speaks." The word *ear* is centered within the word *heart* for a reason. If you take the time to really listen with your heart, you'll "hear" the Spirit of truth guide you to calmly deal with the vicissitudes of life. Regularly meditating to become attentive to the still, small voice results in emotional stability that far surpasses any grandiose goal you could ever hope to achieve on earth.

When it comes to being true to ourselves, faith is vital. In Matthew 14:28–31, Jesus used a parable to demonstrate how quickly we can become fearful if we're governed by our feelings. In verse 28, Peter asks for power to join Jesus on the surface of the sea. No sooner had Peter began walking on water than he became terrified and started to sink. Verse 30 explains, "But when he saw that the wind was boisterous, he was afraid." Like most people, Peter allowed his circumstances to defeat him. His fear-bound thoughts led to panic. Self-deception caused him to lose touch with the Embodiment of love that was staring him right in the face!

This story tells us it makes no difference whether God is seen in the Flesh or is spiritually discerned. When we don't tap into our true power within, we automatically attribute false power to situations that trigger unresolved insecurities. No matter how many good things happen in our lives, our overall conduct is defined by our crucifixion mind-set. Simply stated, we fixate on whatever goes wrong when we don't feel right deep down inside.

Learning to identify with love strengthens us to stay centered. Even when we're faced with adversity, our resurrection mentalities equip us to take comfort in our divinity. The longer we stay grounded spiritually, the less likely we are to succumb to our childhood fears during trying times.

I was recently faced with a daunting situation that occurred on the heels of losing my beloved mother. It was fraught with complications that could have jeopardized my health, if I had allowed fear to dictate my responses.

I was initially tempted to tell my closest friends so they would commiserate with me. I prayed daily, but I wasn't wholeheartedly releasing this trial to God. As a result, I became overwrought. My anxiety didn't subside until I stopped trying to seek resolution on my own terms. The very day I relinquished control, I received the same message from two different sources that emphasized the necessity of "resting in God." Isaiah 26:3 said it best: "You will keep him in perfect peace, Whose mind is stayed on You, because he trusts in You."

Shortly thereafter, I was introduced to an amazing woman. Ruth had been challenged by a similar experience many years ago. The timing of our meeting was no coincidence. Her insights were exactly what I needed during what turned out to be the most difficult year of my entire life.

As things went from bad to worse, I received well-meaning input from those who were concerned about me. When I started to get confused, I instinctively knew I had to depend solely on my inner wisdom for direction. The peace I ultimately experienced never would have occurred if I hadn't surrendered my false need to be in control. Simply stated, God's will is humanity's will when we resolve our love versus fear mind-set.

Spending time regularly connecting with our unshakable Source of strength facilitates peace of mind. Whenever intrusive thoughts distract me from my perfect spirit-to-Spirit reality, I silently concentrate on love and faith to return my attention to the present.

Even if you have to repeat these commanding words to yourself hundreds of times a day to break free from pointless ruminations, it will be well worth your investment of time. There are more than sixty references in the New Testament alone that describe the awesome influence of love and faith working together.

For maximum results, make it a regular practice to meditate on whatever quietly contemplating the love within you brings to mind. Nothing is more important than eradicating thoughts that distract your attention from your oneness with God. Simply stated, fear-minded feelings transformed by faith = true love in action.

Amazing Grace

When we commit to develop self-respect, we overlook conduct that is reminiscent of not feeling good enough during childhood. We realize negative assessments only have the power we give them to upset us.

Inner healing equips us to focus on everyone's divine nature, regardless of the contradictions that are manifested through human nature. When we heal our false perception that we're torn between good and evil, self-deception no longer has free reign to disrupt our serenity. A mind that is restored to wholeness of love understands the offender is trapped in fear. When we falter and give in to an aggressive or passive moment, we're cued by our conscience to resume responding assertively.

Experiencing freedom from making critical or self-deprecating comments is essential. Instead of automatically overreacting or underreacting, "the peace of God, which surpasses all understanding," (Philippians 4:7) determines our actions.

The most important point to remember is our inner turmoil will never end as long as we subscribe to an oppositional belief system. If we don't align our thoughts with the Spirit of truth, underlying feelings of unworthiness that we subdue in one area will continue to surface through alternative destructive actions.

A transcendent, holistic approach to life involves understanding the governing principles of a fear-controlled reality:

1. Angry people suffer from self-deception.
2. Aside from the standards that apply to a society's legal system, the concept of right and wrong is subjectively based on temperament and learned behavior.
3. Those who fail to discover their spiritual identity of love don't grow beyond their deep-rooted insecurities.

As we learn to view ourselves as inseparable from God, the sense of failure we identified with during childhood recedes into the background. A healed mind that doesn't feed into victim dramas with judgmental comments is the gratifying result.

One client understood this truth when I inquired whether her role models' response patterns or the generous lifestyle they provided had a greater impact on her attitude. Without hesitation, she replied that her parents' abrasive behaviors had harmed her far more than the numerous material advantages she received had helped her.

No matter how much we do for others, we unconsciously reveal our lack of self-worth through nonassertive language. Adult children look for reasons to get angry. Authentic adults seek peaceful solutions.

Living according to the reality of love isn't for the faint of heart, that's for sure! Even though learning to value who I am changed how I reacted to stressful situations, there have been many times during the ongoing refining process that I've experienced more pain than gain. It wasn't easy to resist the ongoing temptation to feel sorry for myself when my circumstances kept worsening. But I was determined not to revert to the false comfort of my childhood victim mentality. I had indulged in counterfeit self-esteem fixes far too long.

If you're serious about exchanging your addiction to superficial remedies for a permanent spiritual solution, God will reveal signs and wonders that will keep you headed in the right direction. When you're feeling desolate, kindred spirits will show up to mentor you. Your attention will be drawn to messages that are exactly what you need to hear. Seemingly insurmountable circumstances will turn around. With diligence, you won't automatically become angry or tell people what they want to hear.

During one trying period when I was feeling particularly beleaguered, a Bible verse kept coming to mind: *Do not grow weary in well-doing.* The exact scripture is found in Galatians 6:9: "And let us not grow weary while doing good, for in due season we shall reap if we do not lose heart."

If we're honest, we acknowledge we spend most of our life waiting. We wait to give birth, to grow up, to drive, to finish school, to secure the right job, partner, etc.; not to mention all the waiting in endless lines and traffic. We may not always be patient, but most people learn to accept these normal delays as part of life.

In much the same way, consistently striving to be led by the Spirit produces self-control. You endure the attendant growing pains of discovering your true purpose to love with resolve and dignity. Accepting God's timetable for resolution of challenging situations may very well be one of the hardest things you ever do, but it's also the tried and true path to peace of mind. Simply stated, the short-term pain, long-term gain approach of spiritual recovery is far preferable to the exact opposite self-will alternative.

Heartfelt Healing

A person who consistently pays attention to the Holy Spirit through his sixth sense is finally free to love completely. He doesn't suffer from false separation anxiety. Fear-rooted thoughts that perpetuate imbalances don't rule his behavior.

A former client phoned to tell me he had passed a spiritual reality test with flying colors. Nathan had approached a woman in a social setting. Before he even introduced himself, she exclaimed, "Get away from me, loser!" Although Nathan conceded he felt embarrassed for a moment, he stayed true to himself. Instead of acting on his impulse to retreat, he continued to mingle with others. Confidence in his identity of love kept him from giving false power to her mistaken identity of fear.

The typical reaction when unresolved inferiority is triggered is to personalize the offense. When we only live by sight, we become defensive or repress our hurt feelings. It doesn't dawn on us to view judgmental conduct as a clear sign of the offender's lack of self-acceptance. Feeling hurt when kindness isn't reciprocated or becoming upset by others' abrasive ways prevents us from seeing through the exterior bravado to the stuck children within that governs all faulty communication.

Before I became determined to identify with love, I would frequently grow impatient with my mother's challenging behaviors. Even though it was completely illogical to become irritated by a condition she had no control over, a conflicted reality dictates we either overreact or underreact. Being my mother's caregiver for nearly a decade was invaluable in helping me practice what I preach. When I began this book, my marriage was intact and my mother's decline was in the beginning stages. She was still able to take care of most of her needs.

I started out being more enamored with the idea of becoming Spirit-minded without realizing how much diligence an honest conversion requires. I was able to articulate many of the right ideas through my writing. My thoughts flowed like nothing I had ever experienced. I eagerly counseled others about how vital their spiritual component is to their stability without realizing I still lacked heartfelt understanding.

The problem I didn't realize back then was my enthusiasm was still primarily ego-driven. It emanated from the emotional high I felt at the prospect of becoming an author and from the insights I was imparting. On a subconscious level, I had lost my focus on the Source of my inspiration through self-deception. As a result, my heady feelings took center stage.

Like the erected framework of a house newly under construction, my book was a mere shell without substance. My concepts weren't nearly as fully developed as they needed to be. The richness of God's truths didn't even start to take shape until I was really in the thick of things—outwardly on my own without any substantial means of support; and yet, with all the inner strength I needed.

My grief at my mother's passing was tempered with gratitude. I had prayed daily that she wouldn't have to spend her final years in a nursing home. My prayers were answered. I was also grateful I was able to express my undying love in a way that never would have been possible without spiritual recovery. I delivered my very best friend's eulogy.

Even though I was empowered to speak from the heart, I was even more surprised by my impromptu reaction afterward. I had just sat down when I realized the mourners were weeping. I suddenly found myself standing back up, offering comforting assurances that mom's spirit was finally free. This was completely uncharacteristic, because my conditioned response would have been to function as an emotional basket case.

My mother and I had always been very close. We never became embroiled in the adolescent battles that typically define mother-daughter relationships. I wasn't aware of the codependent nature of our interaction until mom also had to be hospitalized when I suffered my nervous breakdown in my twenties. Our undeveloped faith was no match for the fear that gripped us both back then.

Now here I was, decades later, faced with the prospect of history repeating itself. Only this time the roles were reversed. Mom was the fragile, emotional one who was out of touch with reality. The all too familiar pattern of history repeating itself when fear is perceived to be real most certainly would have been my fate yet again; especially since my circumstances were far more overwhelming than when I had just graduated from college.

Depending on my inner power was especially important during my precious mother's final bittersweet days. The last time mom was able to speak, she looked at me and kept commanding, "Pray!" She spoke with such urgency that I was overcome by emotion as I dropped to my knees.

The next thing I knew, she was staring intently ahead. Her tone changed from anxiety-ridden to heartfelt. The intensity of my own anguish melted away as my soft-spoken mother exclaimed her final words, "Praise the Lord! Praise the Lord!"

The spiritual realm I was unable to see had apparently come into sharp focus through mom's now heightened insight. Second Corinthians 4:16 illustrates this translation from flesh to spirit beautifully: "Therefore we do not lose heart. Even though our outward man is perishing, yet the inward man is being renewed day by day."

The dramatic change from fear to love on my mother's face was unmistakable that day. Even though I was devastated that our earthly connection was going to be severed, I took blessed comfort in knowing my treasured mother was transitioning from torment to tranquility.

Everything we think, say, and do either reflects our Creator's love or mimics our false identification with fear. If people put forth the same energy into healing their learned schizophrenia that they exhaustively expend to maintain their physical appearances, the world would be a peaceful place.

No matter how much effort and money is spent trying to ward off the ravages of time, physical and mental deterioration is inevitable. When we concentrate on becoming attentive to our perfect spirit-to-Spirit bond, we're no longer overly concerned about the aging process.

When you discipline yourself to shift your focus from the chaos you grew up perceiving to soothing spiritual thoughts, you discover heaven isn't some far off place. Those who long for God's kingdom to be established on earth don't understand it still exists simultaneously, because their sole focus is on what is discerned through their five senses.

Our love, peace, faithfulness, self-control, etc., within us remain largely untapped when we aren't raised to identify with our mind, bodies, and spirit. Our external orientation leaves us with no other choice than to feel incomplete. We fail to recognize the illogical nature of seeking validation outside ourselves that we already possess as physical manifestations of God's Spirit.

Before healing my split personality, identifying with my powerless self caused me to worry about minor, as well as major, matters most of the time. I knew I should be "anxious for nothing" (Philippians 4:8). I certainly wasn't deprived in any way. I had to become determined to resolve my childhood anxiety and depression. Learning to appreciate my true value paved the way for me to discern God's still small voice through my sixth sense.

A purely flesh-driven reality compels us to function on the lower levels of consciousness. We pay lip service to the revelation that God's kingdom isn't external in the traditional sense of the word. As such, the kingdom was never meant to be ruled by self-willed pretenders to the throne, who unconsciously play God through fear-controlled judgments.

Allowing the never ending reality of love to permeate our thoughts and actions is what establishes peace on earth, as it is in heaven. Training our mind to respond in agreement with humanity's oneness, despite worldly dissonance, awakens us from our nightmare of separation anxiety behaviors.

Without an eternity perspective, we don't understand that the long-term gain of spiritual enlightenment is well worth the short-term pain of changing our attitudes. When we don't subconsciously trust that God is in control, the cumulative effect of being disillusioned by circumstances beyond our control prevents us from enjoying optimal health as we age.

The sooner you discover that your true power is contained within you, the greater the likelihood exists that you won't feel besieged by the challenges of growing older. Just think how much better you would feel and act if you started countering your normal mental and physical decline by becoming attuned to your spiritual perfection.

When you respectfully realize you really do have God's Mind, you thrive at every stage of life, in eternity *now* and forever, as the aforementioned Corinthians scripture attests.

Relinquishing the false bondage of fear to discover your rightful place in paradise has been inside your heart all along empowers you to actualize your legacy of abundant living.

CHAPTER 10

Reclaiming Paradise

We are already one and we imagine we are not.
And what we have to recover is our original unity.
—Thomas Merton

A love-centered person focuses on the present. He demonstrates his inner power through his dependence on God's will, consistent assertive conduct, and nonattachment to material possessions. His peaceful attitude promotes harmony in a world that is perceived to be evil.

A fear-based individual lives in the past. He variously expresses his feelings of powerlessness through compliance to religious dogma to avoid eternal damnation, angry response patterns, and reliance on ego gratification. His inner turmoil is perpetuated by judgmental behavior.

Learning to identify with the love inside you replaces your spiritual blindness with insight. Confidence that comes from within can't be diminished by fear-driven behaviors, unforeseen occurrences, or by tragic events. You normally respond assertively, adopt an attitude of detachment, or you distance yourself from relationships that keep you languishing in your childhood response patterns.

Taking responsibility for your own happiness frees you from becoming upset when others don't conform to your expectations. You view your former oppositional attitude as a slippery slope that subconsciously led you to "prove" how bad life is in general.

Feelings of anxiety and depression that have always seemed as natural as breathing are fading into the background. Both injustices that can't be rectified and everyday problems are endured with faith that love prevails.

There is very little to be upset about when we begin to comprehend the magnitude of being one with a loving God. When our viewpoints are limited to our temporal existence, our insecurities loom large. Self-deception hinders us from admitting our mistakes.

Julia was always quick to point out everyone else's faults. I asked her two questions. 1) Were they to blame for not living up to her standards? 2) Was she responsible for attracting people who reminded her of her childhood?

Julia recoiled. She was accustomed to receiving support when she recounted details of her perceived mistreatment. Hearing that she was responsible for her anxiety went against the crucifixion role she had learned to portray.

If you sincerely want to change how you feel, it's important to know your resistance to inner healing is completely understandable. When the victim stance of leveling accusations takes root during childhood, it takes courage to transform into an assured adult who observes conflicts without becoming embroiled in the emotional fallout.

Although it's a dramatic improvement, giving up the inconsistencies of a mixed-message belief system feels threatening. If it's always seemed normal to alternate between experiencing more pain than pleasure and settling for temporary remedies, the prospect of changing how you think and act can seem like you're losing your identity. Striving to respond knowing *only love is real* can feel like you're forsaking your native tongue for a language that was barely even spoken in the Garden of Eden!

The fact that Adam and Eve were depicted as opening the floodgates for torment to enter the world isn't surprising at all.

This is the inevitable result of a reality founded on love and fear. When we lose (in)sight of our divinity through self-deception, we become addicted to the bitter fruit of chaos of the tree of the knowledge of good and evil. When we discover God's will has always been humanity's will, we reap a bountiful harvest of peace, love, joy, etc., from the tree of life.

Just like the first couple, most people cling to nonassertive behaviors, because it's the only way they know how to respond. In reality, following self-will is like saying we want to spend our lives regressing to our childhood victim mentalities—either overreacting or underreacting.

When we function in discord with a mind that is out of sync with our perfect spirit, we tend to act as complaining, unpredictable children. We become mired in single-minded resentments from the past. We deny the ever present reality of love by relying on our circumstances for happiness.

When we function in accord with our restored mind, we respond as upbeat, trustworthy adults. We're grounded in the whole(ness) truth that emanates from staying focused on the present. We humbly seek God's guidance through conduct that values love and forgiveness more than egocentric desires.

Inner healing releases you from your stuck child to express yourself without fear of rejection. You're spiritually reborn to enjoy life's pleasures and roll with the punches. The one big difference between your former and present existence is you're no longer addicted to counterfeit self-esteem. True respect for yourself and others grounds you in peace of mind that is infinitely greater than anything the world has to offer.

Transcending a poverty mind-set translates into behaviors that reflect unconditional love instead of conditioned fear. Life was never meant to be spent arguing or being sullen. From the moment we're born, the survival instinct to satisfy "me" kicks in with a shrill cry.

As adults, entrenched self-centered and self-denial behaviors keep us from seeing the big picture. We don't comprehend that our short-term gain approach to life causes long-term pain.

Neither ongoing acts of kindness nor repeatedly becoming angry have the power to convince others to surrender their childhood victim stance. Regardless of whether we grew up being criticized, abandoned, or physically or sexually brutalized, the common denominator is the same: we feel undeserving of love.

The primary theme of this text has been to emphasize that the greatest threat to our well-being is the imaginary battle we unconsciously learned to wage between love and fear. Without a holistic vantage point, we naturally perceive ourselves to be weak. If we feel insignificant, it's difficult to avoid being drawn into petty offenses.

James 3:10–11 captures the essence of this pervasive paradox: "Out of the same mouth proceed blessing and cursing. My brethren, these things ought not to be so. Does a spring send forth fresh water and bitter from the same opening?"

The truth is God's Spirit is joined with humanity's spirit in eternal oneness of love. It's your subconscious attachment to self from childhood that deceives you into believing you're merely a separate entity.

Becoming inner-directed dispels the nonexistent love versus fear rift in our soul. We're no longer compelled to allow anyone or anything outside ourselves to dictate our states of mind. We view trying circumstances as necessary opportunities to demonstrate peace really does flow from the inside out.

The following examples illustrate how failure to discover the love within us pervades every walk of life with needless, tragic consequences.

A documentary featured a story about a homeless man. He was given $100,000 to rehabilitate himself. The producer arranged for support, which included mental health and financial counseling. Since free will was an important part of the project, the man wasn't obliged to avail himself of these services. He chose to rely on his own judgment.

Key factors that accelerated his downward spiral back to poverty were his refusal to obtain employment, his expenditure of $35,000 for a new truck, and his decision to purchase a car for someone. Instead of accepting responsibility for his illogical decisions, he concluded people couldn't be trusted.

However, the man also added this outcome was inevitable because he has "never felt right inside." Even this telltale admission didn't lead the skilled interviewer or the producer to pinpoint self-hate as the reason for his misery.

Another extreme account involved two beautiful teenagers who were sexually intimate with the same young man. The object of their affection got a third woman pregnant. His total disrespect was exceeded only by the glaring lack of self-worth these ladies displayed.

Instead of concluding he didn't deserve either one of them, the two women launched all-out war against each other. Verbal threats, cyberbullying, and physical confrontations ensued. What a rush for this player's ego! Learned schizophrenia ultimately culminated in one woman being convicted of the other's murder. Two promising young lives destroyed because they had no insight they were already complete without a man.

An even more heartrending story involves a college professor who is a Harvard graduate. She was arrested for murdering several of her coworkers, presumably after she was denied tenure. A prominent psychiatrist was interviewed about the case on television. He inexplicably characterized her as having "high self-esteem."

Even though the assailant most likely believed she had been treated unfairly, she placed too much emphasis on her impressive academic credentials. Opinions based solely on one's qualifications don't ring true. The disturbed professor's irrational decision to be ruled by rage clearly reveals she felt anything but confident inside.

Regardless of your background, restoring your split personality to wholeness thoughts frees you from the ultimate victimization: feeling abandoned by God. Learning to awaken the love inside you makes all the difference. You no longer feel like a separate entity. You stop treating others as if they are God by allowing them to judge you, and stop trying to play God by judging or trying to rescue others.

The *Garden of Eden* meditation can be an effective tool for anxiety management. Mentally revisiting the tranquil setting that appeared to have vanished when self-deception ushered in fear will have an overall, calming effect. Unstable emotions lose their ability to control your moods when you stop identifying with behaviors that keep you stuck in the past.

The power of this meditation lies in its emphasis on inner healing. Restoration always originates from within. For example, broken bones heal from the inside out, not the outside in. Likewise, you must change the way you think to achieve your highest potential. Otherwise, continuing to blame your circumstances for your problems will undermine your health.

In *Scarred by Struggle, Transformed by Hope*, Joan Chittister describes the freedom of becoming authentic:

> It brings metamorphosis of soul. If we are willing to persevere through the depths of struggle we can emerge with conversion, independence, faith, courage, surrender, self-acceptance, endurance, purity of heart, and a kind of personal growth that takes us beyond pain to understanding. Enduring struggle is the price to be paid for becoming everything we are meant to be in the world. What we see is the fullness of the [real] self come to birth the only way it really can: in labor and under trial.[17]

Believing deep down that we really are all in this together, regardless of how daunting our personal trials may seem, is the only way to be fully alive. We trade the poverty mentality of egotistical behaviors for the abundant blessings we reap from functioning according to God's will.

Garden of Eden Reality Check

A false belief in fear prevents us from recognizing the devastating impact self-deception has had in preventing humanity from reclaiming heaven on earth. Adam and Eve's dissatisfaction with having access to every tree but one is a metaphor for the insatiable nature of the ego.

The tree of the knowledge of good and evil represents the untold damage that ensues from not identifying exclusively with love. An untenable love and fear belief system enslaves most people to the personal perceptions of their five senses.

When we fixate on the first couple's physical adjustment of going from riches to rags in the blink of an eye, we miss the life changing lesson we must learn so we don't keep repeating the mistakes of the past. External conditions aren't nearly as important as is one's mental state. The worst part wasn't that Adam and Eve lost touch with their tangible paradise. We can live simply and be happy if we're secure in our identity of love. The real heartbreak was that they subconsciously identified with oppositional attitudes for the remainder of their lives. The first couple never recovered their peace of mind by reconnecting with the pure joy of their innate oneness with God. Simply stated, even if you were appointed the ruler of the world, you would still end up feeling powerless deep down inside if you identify with a love and fear ideology.

Learning to trust in your inner power frees you from allowing your problems to dictate your state of mind. You don't suffer from chronic anxiety or depression, because you finally comprehend that God's love eternally permeates humanity. You intuitively understand the Garden of Eden symbolized the physical manifestation of humanity's spiritual perfection.

The synchronicity of one's mind and spirit united in perfect love with the Mind and Spirit of God isn't emphasized in mainstream theology. Those who are saved are also considered to be sinful.

When we're not taught our identity includes our peaceful spirit, our flesh-driven outlook can eventually become an unrelenting source of anguish. But unlike the fire-and-brimstone version, the inner turmoil most children experience growing up is considered normal. Self-deception starts out so subtly that we don't even realize we're becoming our own worst enemies.

Hell rears its ugly head every time love is denied through parental judgments that have little or nothing to do with universal spiritual truths. These feelings of insecurity from childhood start out as seemingly harmless, almost unnoticeable anxiety producing response patterns that preclude seeking divine comfort from within.

As an adult, childhood feelings of inferiority are repeatedly reinforced by nonassertive communication. Demonstrating heaven on earth as an everlasting spirit that's briefly housed in a physical body only rarely occurs.

We unknowingly compound our denial of the kingdom of God within us by expecting our partner, children, career, etc., to compensate for the love we never felt as children. The ensuing angst leads to an ever increasing sense of isolation. Instead of identifying with the permanent high of the timeless love inside us, our false belief in fear compels us to settle for the transient highs proffered by the time-bound realm.

Ongoing enslavement to a crucifixion mentality is reinforced by a fundamental religious message that promotes anxiety: A God of everlasting love sends people to never ending torture in hell.

This glaring inconsistency prevents most people from believing in their divinity.

A heaven and hell belief system forces most of us to deal with the threat of eternal damnation by unconsciously acting as our own judgmental gods. By deeming ourselves and others as unworthy, we beat God to the punch, so to speak, with our own individualized versions of earthly hell.

As children, this process begins as we innocently put our faith in non-assertive role models who demean or overindulge us. As adults, we continue the deception by subconsciously refusing to grow up emotionally and by failing to recognize God's will is humanity's will. We become demeaning and overindulgent caricatures of our true selves, who vacillate between being untrustworthy and relying on people who can't be trusted. Simply stated, when we aren't wholeheartedly loved during childhood, our mixed-message mindset expresses the ensuing anxiety through angry response patterns.

The worst part of believing healthy relationships can be based on both love and fear-minded actions is not realizing we're out of touch with reality. It's a sad commentary that the vast majority never reclaims heaven on earth by following God's simple command to love. Even if you're the only member of your family who transforms from misidentifying with self to being Spirit-led, the long-term physical and mental health benefits are enormous.

Spiritual recovery restores balance (wholeness) to a mind that had falsely perceived itself to be fractured between love and fear-based ideations. When we become grounded in love, worldly goals become secondary to demonstrating honesty and respect. "But seek first the kingdom of God and His righteousness, and all these things shall be added unto you" (Matthew 6:33). People who grow up identifying with fear don't realize how much their happiness depends on taking this brief scripture to heart. When personal fulfillment becomes the top priority, we set ourselves up to feel like we're still lacking—no matter how wealthy we are—because we're doing the exact opposite of what God's will requires. If children were taught to heed this advice, an abundance mind-set would feel more natural than the prevailing poverty mentality of a flesh-driven lifestyle.

The delusional war between love and fear began at infancy, when we heard harsh language, and learned to equate happiness with toys as toddlers. As we grew, so did our demand for ego gratification. As love continued to wane throughout adolescence and into adulthood, we unconsciously became trapped in the persistent scarcity thought: "If only … I'd be happy." Simply stated, if you sincerely desire to experience the fulfilling life that has always been your birthright, you must discover God's will is your will.

As Matthew 4:17 plainly states: "Repent, for the kingdom of heaven is at hand." *Repent* means to change the way we think. *At hand* denotes being readily accessible. Experiencing heaven on earth now through inner peace is a function of recognizing the urgency to develop an eternity mind-set. If we don't make every effort to identify with the love within us, self-will keeps causing us to reap the bitter fruit of hell on earth.

Tina is firmly planted in her personal hell. Her identification with fear is rock solid. Even though she agreed she was only a victim as a child, she didn't have faith to back up her words with loving actions. She kept trying to convince me that her family's self-centered conduct is responsible for her depression.

Tina wanted me to agree her anger was righteous, instead of self-righteous. The truth is her family's lack of self-value is as much of an obstacle for them as Tina's own feelings of inadequacy are for her in preventing her spiritual recovery. She is addicted to counterfeit self-esteem. She deflects attention from changing her own behavior by focusing on her family's shortcomings. If she doesn't shift her attention to discover her true power within, Tina will keep unconsciously reinforcing her childhood trauma.

Tragic Self-fulfilling Prophesy

Besides the basics of food, clothing, and shelter, true love is all anyone really needs to feel complete. Inhabitants of Third World countries are often more content than those who prosper in industrialized nations. People who aren't raised to place undue emphasis on material possessions tend to be more appreciative of God's blessings.

Self-reliance keeps us in bondage to our insecurities. Nothing the world has to offer will ever be enough to stave off the underlying childhood victimization ideation: "It's me against the world."

There is an easy way to know if you're ruled by fear. Do you dread the thought of living alone or dying alone? The real reason for feeling this way is because most people learn to live by sight instead of faith. The truth is we're never alone.

When we regard only what we perceive through our five senses as real, our contentment fluctuates with our circumstances. Without insight, we fail to discover a purposeful life is based on embracing the unseen: God, spirit, love, wholeness, etc. Dr. Hubert Benoit succinctly characterized humanity's inability to separate fact from fiction in *The Supreme Doctrine:* "The man who expects the true life from the world of manifestation, from the world which he knows, wait, for it in vain until his death."[18]

This truth unexpectedly hit home recently in a staggering way I never could have imagined. My ex-husband, Bob, attended my mother's funeral. He lingered during the gathering afterward to offer words of comfort. I was touched by his sensitivity.

I barely had time to adjust to the unfamiliar quietness of life without my mother's presence. Just three months later, I was faced with the harsh reality that Bob had relapsed. After recovering from the initial shock, I realized the composure he had displayed the day of the funeral was just a façade that masked the torment he felt inside. When I tried to get him to focus on the spiritual recovery that had set him free from drug addiction eighteen years earlier, I quickly became aware his ego was in charge.

I had intended to distance myself for the sake of my own emotional healing. But God had other plans. His son Steve's out of town graduation was a month away. I was worried about the shape Bob would be in or if he would even be able to show up for the event.

We attended together. I was relieved Bob's demeanor didn't betray his misery. Steve never suspected anything was amiss. The only thing that was obvious that day was the love and pride Bob undeniably felt for his son.

During the next several months, I went into rescue mode. Until God's higher purpose dawned on me in hindsight, I believed He was using me to counter Bob's self-hate with love. The timing was my proof. If Bob had come back into my life when I was caring for my mother, I wouldn't have been able to be there for him.

Initially, my anxiety level intensified. His perceived struggle between love and fear seemed to shift from moment to moment. He wanted to get help but was afraid of losing his great job. He would reach out to me one day, then ignore my phone calls the next. He would take his prescribed vitamins, then take narcotic pain pills. He said he wanted to live, but his actions contradicted his words.

I told Bob not to contact me anymore. I didn't want to risk suffering the pain of another death so soon after my mom's illness had finally run its course. Two days later, Bob phoned to tell me he had an appointment to enter rehab.

I was encouraged by Bob's attitude during his treatment. He had high praise for the caring staff. Bob was put on antidepressants for the first time in his life. We both hoped he would be able to stay the maximum twenty-eight days. But his insurance only covered a twenty-one day stay.

On the positive side, Bob's company granted him medical leave. A recovering addict with twenty-three years of sobriety agreed to be his sponsor. Bob moved into the basement of my home and started attending recovery meetings daily.

Almost immediately, the illusory love versus fear battle resumed full force. On the drive home from the treatment facility, Bob expressed his gratitude for having a familiar place to stay. That very same evening, he started challenging the rules he had agreed to abide by just prior to his discharge. He had memory problems at this point. When I reminded him about keeping appointments and making phone calls, Bob would alternately be appreciative and annoyed. When I told him the need for spiritual recovery was universal, he replied, "I'm sure not going to surrender to you!"

My conditioning to counterattack was replaced with calmness. My eternity orientation kept me from feeling personally attacked this time around. I sensed that this experience was as much for me to redeem myself from my own egotistical conduct during our marriage as it was for Bob to see God's love through me.

Two weeks later, Bob phoned to say he was suicidal. At the time, I was waiting with my friend at her doctor's office. I quietly explained I would be there as soon as possible. I don't honestly know if I didn't become upset because I was cued from within or because I wasn't able to take immediate action. But this particular incident definitely set the stage for the tone of my future reactions.

When I arrived home, it was clear Bob had relapsed. He was anxious to commit himself to the local hospital's behavioral unit. Despite seemingly conflicting evidence, he really didn't want his disease to win. Bob was discharged after only three days. It wasn't long before I became suspicious that he was using again. My natural impulse to be judgmental was replaced by God's grace to minister to him compassionately.

I was stunned several weeks later when Bob said he wanted to go to church. On two separate occasions, he had experienced a feeling of momentary peace and knelt down with me and prayed for another chance. But I viewed this particular request as a major turnaround. I was convinced Bob would get his miracle. A few days after the service, Bob said he still felt empty inside. I quietly explained that relying on our feelings is what got us off course when we were children.

Bob had learned the importance of not giving in to his impulses when he originally surrendered to the recovery process. In hindsight, he had suffered too much neurological damage to think rationally. Like everyone who doesn't eventually pursue a spiritual path, Bob's inner child was stuck desperately seeking external fixes. One of his greatest fears was inheriting his mother's schizophrenia. The opposite was true. He was brilliant. Not only was he a master electrician who could handle any repair job, there wasn't anything he couldn't build, including a revolving tunnel and a larger than life, fire-breathing Godzilla!

Bob never understood the ramifications of his lack of self-respect. He finally developed drug-induced schizophrenia. The last few months of his life, he was prescribed the same dosage of an antipsychotic drug that my mother had been treated with during the last stages of her dementia. If he hadn't felt paralyzed by self-loathing, he never would have returned to the hellish lifestyle he had escaped from for sixteen years. Without a wholeness power perspective, our powerless selves perceive an exacting God of vengeance.

Bob played God and judged himself guilty of being a corrupt, desolate soul, despite overwhelming evidence to the contrary. His amazing first wife, Regina, had forgiven him years ago for all the misery he had subjected her to during their turbulent marriage. She chose instead to focus on the awesome son they had produced. Likewise, his loving father forgave him for all the untrustworthy conduct that defines drug abuse. Just before he died in 2001, Bob's dad told him about the hiding place of a sizeable sum of money. Bob equally divided the proceeds between himself and his two siblings. He even continued to faithfully contribute to a trust fund his dad had established for his three beloved grandchildren.

Bob's true character was also evident when we divorced. Even though he was childlike when it came to managing money, he didn't leave me with any debt that wasn't my responsibility to assume. He also left me with substantial assets.

Bob lamented that his father had to be really disappointed in him. My protests that both his earthly father and his heavenly Father knew the truth about his identity were to no avail. His abject self-hate had convinced him his false fears were even more powerful than God's everlasting love.

My prayers were for Bob's beautiful mind to be restored to wholeness. God's will was for us to finally identify with the love that we had unconsciously denied during our marriage.

Bob had inadvertently put me in a financial bind. This situation was reminiscent of the economic hardships my father regularly generated. Even though my reaction was toned down, the anger in my voice was unmistakable. Bob apologized, but I was too caught up in self-righteous indignation to take his inner turmoil into account. He was forced to eat his leftover rigatoni cold, because I denied him access to the microwave upstairs.

By the time I returned from work the next day, my compulsion to personalize Bob's actions had subsided. Without inner healing, my lifelong poverty mentality would've continued to dictate my conduct. My childish inner-self would have avoided contact with him. As it turned out, I would have regretted missing out on what ended up being our most important night together.

My Spirit-minded attitude made all the difference. That Friday was exactly the way God had intended it to be. There was no judgment for past or present transgressions—only love. Bob had just gotten paid. He gave me $150 less than I had requested. I suspected he needed that amount for drugs, but I didn't question him. I was grateful to have gotten any money at all, considering his desperate state of mind. Even though Bob had repaid me hundreds that day, he thanked me for not taking all of his money. I asked if he was being sarcastic. He responded that he was sincerely sorry for everything he had put me through.

I was even more surprised a short time later when Bob gave me the $150 and even added an extra $100. He just had $40 left for work expenses the next day. He said he wanted me to keep the money. He didn't want to be tempted to use.

Later that evening, he finished washing his clothes. When he opened the dryer, my socks were inside. He sat down on the sofa and started pairing them. Usually, this gesture wouldn't be significant. But Bob had never washed or dried my clothes. I normally did the laundry when we were married. I had expected him to toss my socks on top of the dryer, so he could finish his own clothes for work. But on this particular night, he wasn't in a hurry at all. I watched almost transfixed as he finished pairing my socks.

This simple act of kindness was followed by several more. I tried to make amends for not allowing Bob in my kitchen the previous night. I asked whether he wanted to come upstairs for dinner. He had already eaten, but he asked if I wanted to share the cookies he had bought.

A short time later, I was having difficulty with a website. I hadn't intended to ask for help. Bob surprised me by volunteering his assistance. In the past, he had been irritated with my lack of knowledge in this area. Being adroit with every facet of computers, Bob couldn't fathom how anyone could have trouble completing basic tasks.

By nightfall, his face was flushed. He felt feverish. I told him to lie down in bed. He turned on his side. As I applied a cold compress to his forehead, I instinctively drew close and wrapped my free arm around his chest.

Almost as quickly, I realized Bob's despair had constrained him to avoid his close friends, much less intimate contact. I told him I wouldn't be offended if he preferred me to give him space.

He replied my embrace reminded him of the way we had cuddled when we were married.

The next morning, I was devastated to discover Bob's torment was over. But his ego had won a hollow victory, because it could no longer exert influence over a false shell. In spite of my feelings of anguish that his healing didn't take place on earth, I now take comfort in knowing my formerly deceived ex-husband finally understands the truth: *his time-bound misidentification with fear had no bearing on his timeless identity of love.*

I believe it was no coincidence that Bob was buried from the church he had attended just days prior to his actual transformation from flesh to spirit. Dewitt Clinton, the minister, composed a profound poem in his memory:

"Beyond the Clouds"

Although clouds may diminish sight so we see not the sun.
Unseen, it continues the course it wishes to run.

And there is a hand outstretched we often fail to see,
The Creator of all, looking down on you, even on me.

Some folks live their whole life as if under that cloud,
Divine favor unseen like it were wrapped in a shroud.

Others truly love God, but may stumble and lose sight of His face,
In their darkest hour, somehow, they cannot ask for His grace.

The lesson they would whisper to us all if they
could,
Is, "We may not have seen—but still, beside us
He stood."

"Sometimes we could not see Him through a fault
not our own,
But that does not mean He wasn't there, and we
were alone."

"It simply means our sight was not perfect, that
we were weak,
And when we could hold on no longer, He carried
home the meek."

The eternity connection between Bob's spirit and the Holy
Spirit that he found all too briefly when he pursued spiritual
recovery will never be disrupted again. His fleeting earthly hell,
though it seemed interminable, can't begin to compare to the
unending peace and joy he now realizes was meant to be his
legacy on earth, as it is in heaven.

Reconnection to Heaven on Earth

The basic principles of activating the love within you to dispel
fear have been condensed into ten reality checks:

1. I resolve to extend compassion to those who never move
   beyond their fear-rooted temperaments and learned
   behaviors.
2. I resolve to exchange my addiction to counterfeit love for
   lasting love that originates from within me.

3. I resolve to view my trials as opportunities for spiritual growth.

4. I resolve to become a full-fledged adult by accepting responsibility for my state of mind without self-condemnation or judging others.

5. I resolve to maintain a balanced mind, body, and spirit through actions that serve the best interests of the Whole.

6. I resolve to affirm my true identity through consistent assertive behaviors.

7. I resolve to maintain healthy relationships by expecting nothing less than giving and getting the respect me and others deserve.

8. I resolve not to lose (in)sight of my divine nature by thanking God for my blessings each morning and for granting me peaceful sleep each night.

9. I resolve to function on a higher level of consciousness by recognizing God's will is my will.

10. I resolve to reclaim paradise "lost" on earth each day by staying mindful that *only love is real.*

Going Deeper

A final word of caution needs to be stated about the necessity of becoming inner-directed. In the prologue, I detailed how being attentive to external expressions of spirituality, without dispelling my inferiority complex, failed to alleviate my identification with fear-rooted behaviors.

Learning to regard yourself as being wholly loved, in spite of how you grew up feeling, is the best thing you can ever do for yourself. An eternity viewpoint breaks the vicious cycle of blaming your circumstances for your inability to achieve your full potential.

Maintaining the status quo is like choosing to stay ankle deep in water along a crowded shoreline of the ocean. You feel comfortable due to the familiarity of your surroundings, but you pay a steep price: you're still controlled by fear. You're stuck in the same place as everyone else who hasn't mentally moved beyond his or her childhood pain.

Spiritual recovery beckons you to exchange your self-limiting thoughts for illuminating ones. Just remember that changing the way you think isn't a quick fix. Your misplaced focus on the ever demanding *I* will keep trying to scare you into staying shallow. You'll be tempted to maintain your false comfort zones. After all, why rock the boat when it just seems natural to keep judging what you see?

Love challenges you to muster the courage to venture deep within yourself to discover all you were meant to be. Taking the plunge to seek truth beyond the worldly realm won't feel right. You're in unseen territory. It requires faith and fortitude to keep moving forward while faulty thought patterns threaten to sink you with recurring waves of false separation anxiety.

Becoming transparent empowers you to view the storm with the same acceptance you have during the calm before and after the storm. As you ultimately rise above your false feelings of powerlessness to go with the unrestrained flow of God's all-encompassing Presence, you'll wonder why it took you so long to be true to yourself. *A Course in Miracles* offers a compelling reason to re-evaluate your unsatisfying flesh-driven lifestyle:

> The roads this world can offer seem quite great in number, but the time must come when everyone sees how alike they are. Men have died when they realized this, because they saw only the pathways offered by the world. And when they learned those roads led nowhere, they lost their hope. And yet those were the times they could have learned their greatest lessons: all must reach this point and go beyond it.[19]

The question is do you reach this point of honest self-appraisal now so you can attune your spirit to the Spirit of truth? Or do you cling to your familiar thought patterns and hold out false hope that the cure for your discontentment must still be in the self-created chaos of the earthly realm?

Love is the most powerful force there is. From Adam and Eve's seemingly harmless first misstep to every deviation from heaven that has occurred on earth ever since, all roads that entice us to stray from our divine destinies turn out to be dead ends.

The age-old question, "What is real?" will remain elusive to those who unconsciously hold themselves hostage to fear. The answer is simply: love. The most heartbreaking aspect of denial of humanity's wholeness is feeling that life has no meaning. Author Jeff Imbach summarized the scope of the problem in *The River Within:* "When we're cut off from our innermost life, we get into an endless round of failed attempts at life."[20]

The most expensive gifts we could ever bestow pale in comparison to the incalculable value of being empowered to genuinely love—without expecting anything in return. When we lose our fixation on ego gratification by paying close attention to the still small voice within, we find our true purpose. Assertive behavior that is unadulterated by fear-based judgments is the transcendent outcome.

There are no random acts. Everything that occurs represents an opportunity to grow beyond the constraints of the illusory self. I thought I was ready to submit my manuscript a few months after my beloved mom transitioned to wholeness. As if on cue to prove me wrong, Bob re-entered my life full force. I, of course, viewed his timing as inopportune. I certainly didn't want to put my work on the back burner again after all the years it took to get to this point. But no other choice makes sense when we're called to love.

I was quite shaken by Bob's departure, because it was completely unexpected. Until the very end, he appeared to be healthy. Even his affect didn't reveal the depths of his desolation.

I couldn't figure out why I hadn't sensed his torment. Ever since I was a child, I've been highly sensitive to others' emotional distress. As I had stated, I never wanted to marry because my father's hostility had impacted me so profoundly. Even though his self-hatred was mainly directed toward my mother, I had literally felt like *I* was experiencing her pain.

And yet, there was no question in my mind that Bob was going to recover. It just didn't make sense that I had missed what should have been obvious warning signs. And then it happened. The answer hit me like a thunderbolt. I suddenly found myself engulfed in waves of despair that had to have been just a small measure of the anguish Bob had felt.

Then, just as instantly, I intuitively understood the connection between Bob's tortured state of mind and humanity's suffering: Failure to follow God's will has nothing to do with arrogance and everything to do with conditioned unworthiness that originates from self-deception. From this vantage point, unconditional love makes perfect sense.

Without insight, deep-seated feelings of inadequacy deceive us into justifying our disrespectful response patterns. We unconsciously judge others' egotistical behaviors to cover up for our own unresolved failure mentalities. People who have confidence in their oneness with God's Spirit respond compassionately.

Generational misconceptions prevent us from being able to evolve to love on an edifying, spiritual level. A flesh-driven reality binds us to the superficial judgments of our five senses. We automatically associate self-centered conduct with defiance. Honing our sixth sense frees us to recognize *everyone* who engages in fear-based conduct that has no relevance in eternity now and forever is self-deceived.

A holistic perspective changes everything. I immediately knew my manuscript was nowhere near complete. I had to painstakingly weave this information throughout my text for my message to ring true. In hindsight, I instinctively knew it was no coincidence that Bob showed up before I submitted my book for publication.

In *Power vs. Force,* Dr. David Hawkins revealed the gratifying result of discovering the whole(ness) truth: "In the process of examining our everyday lives, we can find that all of our fears have been based on falsehood. The displacement of the false by the true is the essence of the healing of all things visible and invisible."[21]

Whether you believe in God, Buddha, Allah, etc., the most important thing you can do is connect with your inner strength so you can begin to banish your false separation anxiety once and for all. Awakening from your nightmare of self-deception to function on higher levels of consciousness grounds you in your timeless identity of love. Your (*visible*) behavior consistently matches your (invisible) peace of mind to function in perfect mental, physical, and spiritual harmony.

Genuine spiritual recovery produces routine supernatural results that you've been conditioned to perceive as isolated miracles. Mental and physical cures will be commonplace if you muster the courage to restore your beautiful mind by dispelling your ingrained fears.

Paradise is the awesome, never ending reality that awaits us all. The only question that remains is whether you choose to recognize the love that has always been inside you *before* or *after* you physically die.

Epilogue

D o you choose love or fear? This is the only question that has everlasting significance. You can continue to navigate in the troubled waters of self-deception and feel flooded with anxiety, or you can "walk on water" by learning to identify with your peaceful spirit. Until you comprehend that a loving God's will is your will, depending on your circumstances for happiness will keep you drowning in drama.

Our emotional prisons assume multiple forms. Anxiety, abusive relationships, chemical dependence, depression, eating disorders, overspending, physical illnesses, and pornography barely scratch the surface of the countless ways we punish ourselves and others when we're out of touch with reality. These consequences represent the fruit we reap as a direct result of the seeds of false fear that are sown during childhood. Peace of mind comes by tracking from fruit to root to ultimately experience the joy of God-consciousness.

If you only try to eliminate a particular habitual behavior without addressing your underlying feelings of inadequacy, more fear-driven fruit will keep springing back up, like relentless weeds, to defile you in other areas. The challenge is to turn the tide on your split personality by embarking on a spiritual recovery voyage. Fear can either stop you dead in the water, or it can motivate you to triumphantly ride the crest of your wave.

Amazing surfer Bethany Hamilton did just that after she stunned the world by returning to the same ocean where a shark had severed her arm when she was a teenager. By refusing to surrender to a very real fear, she not only completed the grueling work it took to learn how to surf all over again; she managed to regain her status as a champion competitor. Unlike the actual threat Bethany bravely chose to face daily, our fears don't come fully equipped with a gaping maw of flesh-eating teeth! On the contrary, our demons aren't even real. They are figments of our imagination that can be conquered with a whole lot less stamina than Bethany needed to triumph over her personal adversity.

Understanding that your misidentification with self is the only thing that separates you from God's power should provide you with ample motivation to emerge victorious from the raging squalls on the sea of life. With wholeness of love at the helm, operating at top speed is a far cry from just drifting along in your own strength, being buffeted by every fearful wave, until you inevitably capsize. Whether or not you choose to grasp onto the life preserver of love so you can weather your storms with dignity is entirely up to you. Cost factors into every decision that is made, from mundane matters of daily living to actualizing your legacy of abundant living in eternity now and forever.

If the resounding voices of judgment you grew up with feel safer than exploring the uncharted depths of the still small voice within, you'll decide the cost is too great to accept my challenge. But if you're ready to admit that the temporary payoffs you receive for maintaining the status quo are no longer worth the ever deepening sense of isolation you must endure, then that's a (whole) different story. You'll ultimately realize the short-term pain of surrendering your subconscious attachment to self is a small price to pay for the long-term gain of peace of mind.

Even if you aren't convinced *only love is real*, you should still be encouraged. The mere act of reading this book has planted a seed for transformation. It can always take root and grow to full maturity when the timing is right.

I leave you with two of my favorite passages. The first one, titled "Wisdom," is by an unknown author.

Wisdom

A person should be able to rise above his possessions, his body, his circumstances and the opinion of others. Until you are this, you are not strong and steadfast.

A person should also be able to rise above his own desires and opinions; and until you are this, you are not wise.

Great will be the unrest and pain of anyone whose mood is determined by events beyond their control and the approval of others.

To detach oneself from every outward thing and to rest securely upon your own inner strength, this is unfailing wisdom. Having this wisdom, a person will be the same whether in riches or poverty, since riches cannot add to his true strength, nor can poverty rob him of his serenity.

To refuse to be enslaved by any outward thing or happening—this is true wisdom and strength which will never fail you.

The second quotation is from the best-selling book of all time. It's as brief as the above message is long, but it beautifully sums up the four recurrent themes of this book:

For God has not given us a spirit of fear, but of power and of love and of a sound mind. (2 Timothy 1:7)

Endnotes

1   Foundation for Inner Peace, *A Course in Miracles* (New York: Penguin Books, 1975), p. 61.

2   Charlotte Joko Beck, *Everyday Zen* (New York: HarperCollins Publishers, 1989) p. 139.

3   Dr. David R. Hawkins, *Power vs. Force* (Carlsbad, CA.: Hay House, Inc., 1995), p. 316.

4   *A Course in Miracles*, p. 94.

5   Sarah Young, *Jesus Calling* (Nashville: Thomas Nelson, Inc., 2004), p. 53.

6   Dr. Andrew Newberg and Mark Robert Waldman, *How God Changes Your Brain* (New York: Ballantine Books, 2009), p. 176.

7   Marianne Williamson, *A Return to Love: Reflections on the Principles of a Course in Miracles* (New York: Harper Collins Publishers, 1992), p. 250.

8   Dr. Hubert Benoit, *The Supreme Doctrine* (Portland, OR: Sussex Academic Press, 1995), p. 169.

9   *A Course in Miracles*, p. X.

10   Mark Virkler and Patty Virkler, *Communion With God* (Orchard Park, NY: Buffalo School of the Bible, 1983), p. 11.

11   Dr. Wayne Dyer, *10 Secrets for Success and Inner Peace* (Carlsbad, CA: Hay House, Inc., 2001), p. 141.

12   Louise Hay, *Totality of Possibilities*, Hay House, Inc., Carlsbad, CA, 2005, Audio CD.

13   Hawkins, p. 106.

14   Newberg and Waldman, pp. 149–50.

15   Newberg and Waldman, p. 132.

16   Beck, p. 73.

17   Joan D. Chittister, *Scarred by Struggle, Transformed by Hope* (Grand Rapids, MI: William B. Eerdmans Publishing Co., 2003), p. 19.

18   Benoit, p. 164.

19   *A Course in Miracles*, pp. 653–54.

20   Jeff Imbach, *The River Within* (Colorado Springs: Navpress, 1998), pp. 75–76.

21   Hawkins, pp. 129–30.

About the Author

Cynthia Sholtis has utilized her psychology degree in nearly every facet of the social services field during the past 35 years. Her experiences have ranged from working with the developmentally delayed and being the director of the social service department at a geriatric facility, to counseling children and adult victims of crimes and providing spiritual counseling.

These varied interactions have taught her the most valuable lesson of all: a quality life depends on understanding one's true value.

To download Cynthia's meditation audio file or to purchase the CD, visit *www.InnerPeaceSimplified.com*.